"Who hasn't day-dreamed through a time-wasting meeting, wishing there were a better way? There is, and it isn't magic. This book laid it all out for me with amazing detail and clarity. The *why* and the *how* to structure your meetings; laced with science, psychology, human nature and real-world business needs. Meeting science and implementation techniques blend here in an interesting and (dare I say) entertaining style. Reading this book is time very well spent - was your last meeting?"

—Scott McGrath, Chief Operating Officer at OASIS-Open

"In *Where the Action Is*, J. Elise Keith shifts the work conversation from how to minimize time spent in meetings to how to make this essential business activity productive and enjoyable. In all my years facilitating group conversations, this is the first time I've found a book about meetings that provides a taxonomy of meeting types—what kind of collaborative work do we need?—and guidance for determining a purpose, structure and audience for each type. For leaders, facilitators, and consultants working in organizations where business performance depends on the collaborative engagement of knowledge workers, this book is a must-read. "

— Diana Larsen author, *Agile Retrospectives: Making Good Teams Great* and creator of the "The Agile Fluency Model: A Brief Guide to Success with Agile."

"Passion, drive and knowledge will not set you apart. The ability to lead meetings will. *Where the Action Is* explains how it's done, making this a must-have resource for anyone looking to advance their career. Ms. Keith has done the research for you. Now it's up to you to put it to work."

—Paul Axtell, President, Contextual Program Designs and author, *Meetings Matter: 8 Powerful Strategies for Remarkable Conversations*

"Despite the rapid digitization of work, meetings remain an essential part of our human collaboration. Keith's book is the first lucid guide to elevate the quality and effectiveness of every meeting in the digital age. Implementing its recommendations will recover significant value to your organization. It's time to heed her advice and make meetings work."

— Fadi Chehadé, Partner, Abry Partners and former President & CEO, ICANN

"Like businesses, communities of faith suffer when bad meetings get in the way of working effectively to achieve their mission. Indeed, some of the challenges Ms. Keith describes are exacerbated by the fact that churches and similar organizations rely heavily on volunteers—volunteers who may bring more willingness than skill to their leadership, volunteers who can easily opt out or burn out, and "volunteers" who may never volunteer in the first place if meetings seem like a waste of time. *Where the Action Is* offers many useful tools to help faith and volunteer-driven communities examine, evaluate, and improve their meetings."

— Siri Harding, , Elder, Reedville Presbyterian Church

"J. Elise Keith has given us a very practical look at why we get stuck believing meetings are a waste of time and how to create meetings that are productive, engaging work experiences. She takes the reader through each meeting stage, showing you how to plan, structure and lead productive meetings. Chock full of stories, tips, and tools, this very readable book is a superb guide to meeting effectiveness. If you lead, plan, or attend meetings, this book is for you."

— Dick and Emily Axelrod, authors, *Let's Stop Meeting Like This*

"*Where the Action Is* provides a comprehensive exploration of why meetings are where work should happen ... and how to make this a reality. Many of the recommendations will cause you to question just what you are doing in meetings right now. Most of the book's recommendations rely on a structural rather than behavioral approach to running meetings. My decades of meeting experience have taught me that structure is where the secret to great meeting resides. But meeting structure can be hard to see. This book makes structure clear and useful to anyone running meetings.
Where the Action Is includes advice for meetings in general, and for addressing specific meeting situations. Read it and keep it handy for ongoing reference."

— Richard Lent, Ph.D., author, *Leading Great Meetings:*
How to Structure Yours for Success

"If you aspire to fun, productive and efficient meetings you can either learn by trial and error, inflicting much pain on your organization along the way, or benefit from the tips on design and execution Elise Keith lays out in her excellent book *Where the Action Is*."

— Neal Bastick, CEO, MeetingSphere, Inc

WHERE THE ACTION IS

Where the Action Is

The Meetings
That Make or Break
Your Organization

J. Elise Keith

SECOND RISE | PORTLAND, OREGON

Where the Action Is is a work of nonfiction. Nonetheless, some names and personal characteristics of individuals or events have been changed in order to disguise identities. Any resulting resemblance to persons living or dead is entirely coincidental and unintentional.

Second Rise
1800 SW 1st Ave, Suite 606, Portland, OR 97201
www.secondrise.com
info@secondrise.com

Ordering Information: Special discounts are available on quantity purchases by corporations, associations, and others. For details, contact the publisher at the address above.

Printed in the United States of America
Edited by Chris Higgins
Book design by Janet Tingey
Cover and Illustrations by Katie LaRosa

ISBN 978-1-7322052-0-8 (paper)
978-1-7322052-1-5 (ebook)
Library of Congress Control Number: 2018905111

To the Lucid Meetings community for the gracious support and unrelenting schooling you've given us over the years, and to the Lucid team: Amy, Tricia, and most of all, John. You know which one.

Contents

Part 4 The 16 Types of Meetings That Work

Introduction

When you ask leaders in a high-performing organization about the key to their success, the answers are all over the place: failing fast, radical transparency, operational excellence, strong core values, a continuous improvement mindset... so many different North Stars to follow.

Then, if you ask them for an example–to tell you what that looks like in practice–they will all describe a meeting.

I don't believe that anyone sets out to become a meeting expert. Not a single child in my daughter's kindergarten class said, "Facilitator!" when asked what they wanted to be when they grew up.

My friend, the facilitator Beatrice Briggs, did her doctoral research studying Sanskrit. Author and trainer Paul Axtell was a chemical engineer. The academics began by digging into what makes a social movement successful, or how politicians start wars. As for me, I wanted to work in the theater.

None of us went in search of meetings, but that's where we found ourselves and where we discovered the real action. Perhaps that's an experience you and I share? If you've picked up this book, I'm sure you too have found yourself in more meetings than your younger self could have believed possible.

Every organization I've encountered puts time and effort into crafting a vision statement and defining its mission. We work hard to state our values, and we build nifty offices, decked out with all the cool things that we hope will create an engaging culture.

Then we meet, and things gets real. All those beautiful values—is that really how you treat each other when you talk about your work? The ambitious mission and inspiring vision: are they what you're focused on in your meetings?

Meetings embody our true culture and clarify our real priorities.

Regardless of what we've pasted into our organization's brochure, what we actually talk about, and the length of time we spend talking about it, tells everyone what really matters. Who talks and who doesn't, and how they treat each other's contributions, shows us whether that group lives its stated values, or whether the group's members are really more concerned with personal power and safety.

Meetings provide the first, the most frequently repeated, and the most pervasive opportunity we have to walk our talk. If we don't talk together first and foremost about the work laid out in our mission and vision, those things don't happen. If how we speak to our coworkers and our customers during meetings doesn't match up with the values poster up on the wall, everyone can see that our organization lacks integrity.

Meetings are where the action is.

When you get that new job, it's because you did well in an interview (a meeting) and the team decided to hire you (in a meeting). When that scrappy startup gets funded, it's because it presented itself well during the pitch (a meeting), people they know vouched for them (in meetings), and then the investment group decided to approve the funding (in a meeting). When our leaders decide to send troops to fight in foreign lands, or instead to send diplomats, they do so in a meeting. When peace talks happen, guess what? Those are meetings too.

It is in meetings that we agree on how we will make or break the future.

If your meetings are not working well, designing meetings with intention—to explicitly support your mission and codify your organization's cultural values in day-to-day practice—is the most powerful way you can effect change. It's also not that hard to do.

I know a lot more about meetings now than I did when I started my career. I'm a generalist, so that means that there's a lot more that I don't know. Let me share my journey so you will understand what I mean.

When my younger self first realized the important role meetings play, I was working in a software company. I believed most meetings were a waste of time run by skill-free people. Naturally, I believed that the way to improve meetings was to figure out the rules and then automate as much of that as possible, thereby bypassing all the incompetents on the road to efficiency. I'd seen several successful boards of directors using Robert's Rules. Rules provide structure, and structure is useful. Meeting running too long? We need an automated timer and an alert. Unclear what the result was? Obviously people need a better tracking mechanism. Is someone in the group confused by the process? We can use software to give them tips! I believed "the solution" to meeting problems was better mechanics.

The first books on business meetings that I found reinforced this belief. Several people recommended reading David Strauss and Michael Doyle's *How to Make Meetings Work*, a classic meeting manual first published in 1976. The authors talked about the importance of using an agenda, of encouraging open dialogue, and of keeping the whole affair zipping along on time. As I had suspected, they seemed to be saying that running good meetings was mostly about getting these mechanics right.

We launched the first version of the Lucid Meetings software platform in 2012. It didn't take long to discover that we were wrong. Better mechanics weren't enough on their own. It wasn't enough to simply "have an agenda"; it turns out there's an artistry to creating an agenda that increases your odds of meeting success, and lots of ways to put out a lousy agenda that won't achieve diddly.

Stinging from this disappointing realization, I looked next to the realm of professional facilitation. Here I found all kinds of clever techniques for running powerful meetings. I learned new skills that felt like superpowers to me! Did you know that how you phrase a question at the beginning of your discussion can radically change not only what people say in response, but also what they then *believe* and act on going forward? You can literally change the future with the question you ask. Knowing how to ask that question—that's a superpower!

The facilitation world is full of people who do work-for-hire. Most of them specialize. Some run really great strategic planning sessions, and others focus on conflict resolution. They're often brought in for one day, or maybe a week, and then they go on their way. So while they held the keys to an arsenal of meeting superpowers, they didn't have much to teach me about how a team could build on that one good day and then run useful meetings not just as special occasions, but as an everyday habit.

This question of how teams could meet happily day in and day out led me to the coaches. Leadership coaches, team coaches, personal coaches: "It's all about relationships," they explained. "If the people in the room can't trust one another—if they're anxious, worried, or angry, no amount of fancy facilitation will work. Building relationships matters most." I found a lot of wisdom here that brought a more sustainable perspective to the facilitation techniques I'd learned.

And yet, I'm a small business owner. While I can understand the importance of relationships and I get how crucial they are to success, I just couldn't accept that this was all that really mattered. What about the business results?! Where is the accountability? Where are the useful decisions? What about all the legal requirements that impact our meetings?

I went in search of anything I could find from the business world and spent two years digging through acronyms, business model canvases, maturity models, and more proprietary business operating systems than you can shake a stick at. Agile, Scrum, Lean, PMI, EOS, KPIs, CMM, ISO-9000—an alphabet soup whirlwind of prescriptions for getting things done (GTD included). I found lots of certainty, lots of contradictory advice, and people using statistics to prove their point. When I dug into the numbers, I discovered that often people were just pulling these out of their... ears... which led me to the academic research community that's attempting to dig through all this too. More learning ensued.

From the business world, I learned how to run a Root-Cause Analysis Meeting, because you have to know root cause before you can really solve a problem! I also learned techniques for logically reviewing and weighing the options before making crucial business decisions, because the cost of a "wrong" decision can be fatal. Wow! How useful to have these tested ways that help a group make the right decision!

This was when I learned about complexity theory as it's applied to human systems.

We live in interesting times of change. An understatement, I know. "Root-cause analysis? Ha!" say the complexity folks. "Sometimes there *is no one root cause.* Sometimes there are many causes, and even if you could figure them out, you could never be sure they'd create the same problem in the future again. It's too complex!"

Okay—well, let's just move on to making the best possible decision, then. I know how to run that meeting....

"Hold your horses, there!" the complexity cohort cries. "How can you possibly predict which decision will work best when everything in the environment around you is in flux? There is no 'right' decision—your best bet is to run a bunch of small experiments instead, because there's no predicting what people might do in the future."

To which the social psychologists say, "Well, actually, you can influence people's behavior in meetings quite a bit if you—"

"Quite a bit?" interject the neurobiologists. "Heck, if you look down at the biochemical level, people are 100% predictable. We're discovering that free will is most likely a myth. It may all just be biology."

"Who cares about what *people* will do?" say the technologists. "All our banking decisions are being made by computers and algorithms these days. We're spending our meeting time trying to figure out how to navigate around the robots."

"People don't like meetings as much when they're cold," chime in the research grad students.

There's a lot to learn—more than any one of us can learn in a lifetime. This is because meetings are where the action is. Helen Schwartzman, a psychological anthropologist and among the first to take a serious scholarly look at meetings, said that meetings are sociology in action—in other words, meetings are those moments when all the things that make up our complex societies converge.

> It is argued that meetings exist within a sociocultural system, but they also play a major role in shaping this system, as they both create and then respond to the context that they have generated. Meetings provide individuals with a way to make sense of as well as to legitimate what otherwise might seem to be disparate talk and action, whereas they also enable individuals to negotiate and validate their relationships to each other. Finally, I suggest that meetings are a form that frequently stabilizes but can just as easily destabilize and transform a cultural system in ways that are often unrecognized and even unintended by actors in the system.
> —Schwartzman, *The Meeting*, 1989

To sum up my journey, I originally thought the "meeting problem" was that people lacked information, and if I could just educate them, they'd see what they'd been doing wrong and get their meetings on track. Simple, elegant, and unfortunately: baloney.

I know better now. The simple "teach them meeting skills" approach doesn't work. It's not because people already know meeting skills but refuse to use them. Although that's true for some, we see that even when people know the basic skills, they often forget to use them or they use them in a way that's kind of weird.

The simple fix doesn't work because meetings aren't simple. Success in meetings requires getting the mechanics right, *and* building the relationships, *and* producing useful business results. Success means balancing the needs of the individuals involved and the organizations they represent in a way that's appropriate for the environmental context in which they operate. Success means anticipating and navigating from start to finish through all the wondrous variety each of these realms brings to the party.

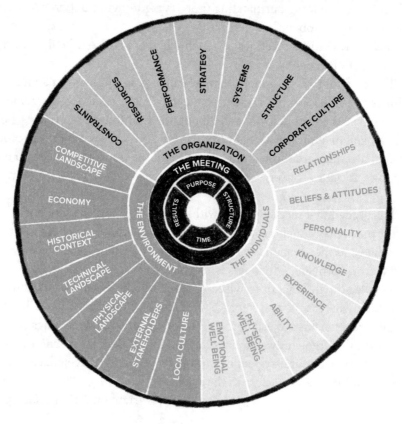

This is important, complex stuff.

We hold meetings to decide whom to hire, what to fund, what to do next, and why we're here. When we meet, we explore our work and our relationships with other people. Meetings are complex because the work changes and because relationships are complex. If I claimed there was a single skill you needed to learn to master every job, you'd think I was cracked. The same goes doubly when it comes to relationships. I know that if I told you there were "five quick tips" you could use to make all your relationships succeed—one approach that would work equally well with every one of your friends and relatives and coworkers—you'd know that I was a fool.

Since meetings involve work *and* relationships between multiple people, I was a fool for believing in a simple fix in the first place.

But here's what I know now.

There is no one, generic meeting problem and no one, simple fix.

For example, a problem with accountability in team meetings is not the same as trouble closing deals in sales meetings. These problems require different solutions. This doesn't mean you should start from scratch, however. There are many good examples and best practices to draw on that are specific to the different meeting scenarios.

The basics are just that: basic.

Using an agenda and sharing notes after a meeting are the equivalent of table manners. They provide just enough meeting etiquette to avoid embarrassment but not enough to bring mastery. You need to learn this stuff, just like you need to learn how to say "please" and "thank you." But just because you know which fork to use for the salad, it doesn't mean you'll be successful at a fancy dinner. Fork selection, like agenda creation, is just one of many skills on the path to mastery.

Most "meeting problems" aren't actually about meetings.

Bad meetings are almost always a symptom of deeper issues. Fortunately, getting specific about how to run better meetings is a startlingly effective way to identify those underlying problems. Trying to "fix your culture" is insanely difficult and rarely works; fixing your weekly leadership team meeting, on the other hand, is readily achievable, and has a big ripple effect on that culture challenge.

When designed and implemented with mastery, meetings are a keystone habit in world-class organizational cultures.
When an organization develops *The Way* it works, it always includes a series of meetings that embody that *Way*. These get so specific that they may no longer be referred to as meetings. Instead, they have the Daily Scrum, the Kaizen Event, the Town Hall, the Crush... that organization's way of uniquely describing what they do consistently and well.

These conclusions sound obvious to me now, but it took me 10 years as an "expert" to come to this understanding. Ten years filled with research, training, and painful conversations with people who ultimately set me straight and set me on the path to writing this book.

My goal with this book is to change what you think and how you feel about meetings, so you can master the ones that drive your world. I'm going to share a new perspective on meetings and teach you how to approach them in a more nuanced and successful way. As one of our consulting clients told me: "You put our meetings on *science!*" The research that backs this perspective comes from various disciplines, including business, social science, history, neuroscience, behavioral biology, economics, and more.

To illustrate the concepts here, I'll share the story of Pacific Bold, a fictional marketing company struggling to improve its meeting culture. While Pacific Bold and the people we'll encounter are 100% made-up, their story is informed by the many stories I've heard over the years. If you read about them and think it hits uncomfortably close to home—that perhaps Pacific Bold is just a thinly veiled reference to your organization— please know that I've learned about the challenges described in their story from companies big and small, public sector and private, young and old, and from all over the world.

Everyone meets, and at some level, everyone struggles to do it well.

The book is organized into four sections:

Part 1: Breaking the Doom Loop
In this introduction, you learned how I formed my beliefs about meetings. In Part 1, you'll take a look at your own beliefs, question why people meet in the first place, and explore why people react to meetings in all the contradictory ways that they do.

Part 2: Mastering the Work in Meetings
These chapters cover the kind of work that happens in meetings and the factors that contribute to a meeting's effectiveness. You'll learn the basics, and also some of the psychology behind why these basics have become standards. Consider this a condensed guide to running a better meeting.

Part 3: Mastering the Meetings at Work
Next, we'll look at how meetings function as part of an organization's larger operating system, and the levels of performance that can be achieved when an organization improves the maturity and skill with which it manages meetings. You'll learn how to assess your organization's performance level and where to start when you want to improve.

Part 4: The 16 Types of Meetings That Work
There's one message that you'll see fanatically repeated throughout the book: *You must get specific if you want successful meetings.* The final section describes the 16 major types of specific meetings from the Taxonomy of Business Meetings. This section will teach you how to tell one kind of meeting from another and recognize when the meeting you're in isn't the one you need to be having.

There's plenty of theory here, but also a number of practical checklists and a handful of special techniques that deliver big value. You'll get both the why and how.

Along the way, we'll witness Pacific Bold's journey as they break their own doom loops to save their company.

Part 1

Breaking the Doom Loop

Hello !

CHAPTER 1

The Bad Meetings Doom Loop

This is the Belief Cycle.

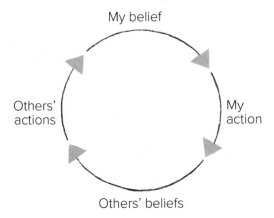

I originally learned about the Belief Cycle in Dave Gray's book *Liminal Thinking*. He learned it from someone else before that. Then I learned it again from Ari Weinzweig, co-founder of Zingerman's. He also learned it from someone else. It's one of those concepts that pops up over and over again because once you learn it, you know how to start tackling intractable problems.

Here's how the Belief Cycle works. Based on some past experience, you form a belief. This experience could be something that happened to you in the past, something you read somewhere, or maybe something you saw in a movie one day. Whatever it was, it stuck, and now you believe this idea to be true.

Let's say, for example, that you believe meetings are a waste of time.

This belief then informs your actions. If you are like most people, you don't put extra effort into things you believe to be a waste of time. That would be silly, just throwing good money after bad, as they say. So, if you believe that meetings are a waste of time, you're unlikely to waste even more time preparing for them in advance. You'll put as little effort as possible into planning and preparing for meetings.

Bloggers love to quote statistics claiming that leadership teams feel 50% to 80% of the time they spend in meetings is a big, fat waste of time. The leaders of our organizations publicly declare that they believe meetings are a waste of time. Hmm. Can you spot the problem there?

A leader with anti-meeting beliefs works to minimize the time they put into meetings. They do not do extra work to make meetings successful. Then, when everyone else shows up to this leader's meeting, they find themselves in a meeting that hasn't been well-planned. The leader demonstrates through their actions that advance preparation isn't required or expected, so no one else believes they should prepare either. Without a plan for running the meeting or much preparation on anyone's part, the conversation is listless, goes around in circles, and fails to reach any meaningful outcome.

The meeting ends up being a total waste of time, reinforcing the leader's original belief.

This is known as a **Doom Loop**. Here's how it looks.

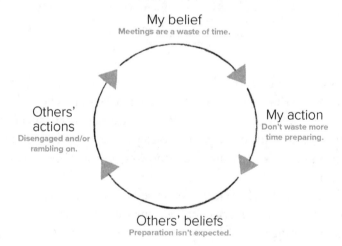

Meetings are a waste of time. It's a popular belief. Check out these quotes.

If you had to identify, in one word, the reason why the human race has not achieved, and never will achieve, its full potential, that word would be 'meetings.'

—Dave Barry, Pulitzer Prize-winning humorist

People who enjoy meetings should not be in charge of anything.

—Thomas Sowell, economist, social commentator, and author

A meeting is an event where minutes are taken and hours wasted.

—Bizarrely and falsely attributed to James T. Kirk, captain of the fictitious *USS Enterprise*

A party without jerky is just a meeting.

—The back of a bag of *Jack Link's Meat Snacks Beef Jerky, Original, 8-Ounce*

This meeting is bullshit.

—Statement printed on my socks

I got these socks for Christmas. They're orange if you want to look them up online. You know a belief must be pervasive if you can find it attributed to a sci-fi television hero, dried meat products, and socks.

So how do you break a doom loop? Start with a different belief. Dave Gray suggests considering the opposite of what you believe is true, then acting *as if it were*. It's an experiment: Act as if a different belief were true, and see "What then?"

Simple: *Act as if.* What then?

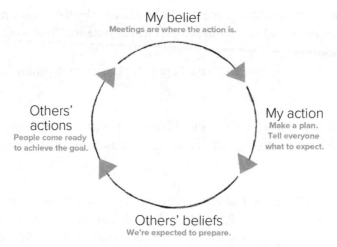

My belief
Meetings are where the action is.

My action
Make a plan.
Tell everyone
what to expect.

Others' beliefs
We're expected to prepare.

Others'
actions
People come ready
to achieve the goal.

Meetings are where the action is—it isn't a far-fetched belief. Just take a look at the news headlines. Here in early 2018, the news is full of reports about which world leader met with which other world leader, who might meet with whom, what they may or may not have said to each other in meetings, and on and on. Never mind that the polar ice caps are melting—there's an important meeting we need to know about!

The next time you watch a movie, keep a notebook and a pen handy. Count the number of meetings you see. Any narrative more sophisticated than G-rated kids' fare tells parts of the story through meetings, and I'm not just talking about the political dramas. The *Star Wars* movies are full of meetings. And apparently, Captain Picard never heard that James T. Kirk quote, because *Star Trek: The Next Generation* features at least one meeting—*in a conference room on a spaceship*—per episode.

Before moving on, I invite you to consider your own beliefs. What do you believe about your meetings? Pause a moment and write these down. Then look at each belief you've written. What kind of loop starts from that belief? And for every negative belief, what might happen if you acted as if the opposite were true?

What then?

CHAPTER 2

The Truth About Why We Meet

"Here's your challenge," the consultant says. "Make sure there are no meetings on your calendar for the next two weeks."

A pause.

"But we told you," the client replied. "We already tried canceling all our meetings. It didn't work. You think we should try it again?"

"Sorry, no. I don't want you to cancel anything, necessarily. This challenge is different. I'm asking you to get specific in how you use language. You should have no 'meetings' on your schedule, but you might have a 'One-on-One,' or a 'Working Session,' or a 'Project Kickoff.' I'm literally talking about *removing the word 'meeting' from how you invest your team's time.* Saying you'll have a 'meeting' is not clear enough. And if you can't figure out a more specific name for that event, then, yes, you should cancel it."

Say Hello to the Team at Pacific Bold

Pacific Bold is a marketing agency serving the food industry. They specialize in brand-building and advertising for small farms and organic producers, an industry that's grown to nearly $50 billion in U.S. revenue in the past five years alone. They're known for creating brands described as "clean," "crisp," "honest," and "vital"—all traits they prize in the products they help promote and in their company culture.

Hello!

Pacific Bold isn't a new company, but with all the growth and change in the last half-decade, it feels like one. When they were founded 20 years ago, back before *organic* went mainstream, the founding partners, Charla and Craig, were the only employees, and most business was won on a handshake. Since then, Pacific Bold's reputation in the industry and stellar service has attracted clients from all over the world. They now provide branding for farms on four continents and in 15 languages. Today, Charla and Craig oversee a leadership team that manages 144 employees working from four separate offices. Sixty-eight of those employees joined Pacific Bold within the past four years.

Charla and Craig care deeply about making sure Pacific Bold is a great place to work. They pay their employees well and provide great benefits, but more importantly, they work to create a sense of shared ownership and purpose in the work. They believe transparency is important to ensuring trust between teammates, and they encourage everyone to speak up any time they see an opportunity to make a change for the better. Many employees came to work for this niche firm because they believed they'd get a real opportunity to make meaningful contributions and that their opinions would be heard and valued.

But there's a problem. As the company has grown, Charla and Craig have found it harder to manage the business. They had hoped the competent experts they'd hired to lead each functional group would help smooth things out, but while each has certainly brought some rigor and polish to their department, projects are taking longer and longer to complete. This is frustrating for everyone.

Recently they turned to the team at Lucid Meetings, where we started by challenging them to eliminate the word *meeting* from their work. Talking with Lucid was certainly not the first thing they tried, nor the second, nor the fifth.

It all started with a simple question nearly 18 months ago.

It's 97 minutes into the Pacific Bold leadership team's "one-hour" weekly review meeting when Charla snaps.

"I don't understand what the problem is here," Charla says. "We keep hiring more designers to handle the client work, and more project managers to keep these projects on track, and yet these projects are taking forever. Don't tell me we need more resources! What are all these people doing with their time?"

Angie, the head of the project management group, responds. "I know they're working. My team starts by 9 AM and they stay until at least 5 PM—often longer. You all know we have people working evenings and weekends trying to catch up. We're not slacking off!" Angie is clearly frustrated, and now she's feeling attacked.

Craig jumps in. "Hold on—no one said anything about slacking. You're right. We do know people are putting in the hours. But Charla's got a point. Why is this happening? Five years ago we had less than half the people, and we were doing the same kind of work. There were times we stayed late and busted butts to hit a deadline, but not every week. So now that we've got more clients, but also more people here to do the work, why are so many people staying late and still missing deadlines? What else are they doing with their time now that we weren't doing five years ago? Is it Facebook?"

(Craig doesn't trust Facebook. He suspects Facebook is implicated in many of the confusing and frustrating changes in his world these days.)

Charla and Angie reply automatically and in unison, "It's not Facebook."

"Well, it's something," Bert, the finance director, says. "Utilization is sitting at 38% and dropping. If something doesn't change, we're going to have to dramatically raise prices, which I'm not sure is an option, or start laying people off."

Nelson, the leader of Pacific Bold's creative team, begins to panic: "Wait, what does that mean? Why are we laying people off? No one told me about this!" Nelson is a brilliant designer, a gifted motivator, and his team loves him. He's also pretty vague when it comes to the business mechanics.

"It means," Bert explains for what feels like the hundredth time, "that for every 40 hours we pay someone to work here, they're billing out just over 15 hours of client work. The other 25 is all overhead. Ideally, we need to see people billing closer to 28 hours to turn a comfortable profit."

Angie is distraught. "40 hours?! As if anyone here only works 40 hours anymore! My team is pulling 60-hour weeks easily!"

Charla steps in. "Okay, stop. We're not getting anywhere with this. We've obviously got a big problem, and we're not going solve it in this room by shouting and speculating. We need information. I need each of you to work with your teams and find out where the time is going. Let's not guess. Let's get some data."

"It's probably Facebook," Craig mutters.

It wasn't Facebook (or, not mostly). When Pacific Bold's management team dug into what was happening and pulled all the numbers together, the answer was clear.

It was meetings.

They found that nearly every Pacific Bold employee spent 12 hours or more per week in meetings. Meetings with clients, meetings about projects, meetings about sales, department meetings and team meetings and All-Hands meetings and Workshops and design reviews. The management group spent even more time in meetings: over 25 hours each week. Very few of these hours were accounted for when it came time to send client invoices. Too many meetings were sucking profitability out of the work and putting the company in jeopardy.

— PB —

Why are there so many meetings? Research shows that in 2014 there were somewhere between 55 and 65 million meetings every day in the U.S. alone, and this number is on the rise. The hours any individual will spend meeting varies. Estimates show that all workers spend at least two hours a week in meetings, often more, and managers meet an average of 23+ hours a week. Given the dramatic rise of technology-aided communication like email, chat, workstream applications, text messaging, and all the other ways we can collaborate, you might have thought that the number of meetings would be going down. It's not. Why is that?

The simplest answer is because people like to meet. Given the alternatives, meetings work pretty well. You may have heard that meetings waste time, meetings are drudgery, or that meetings are where good ideas and work goes to die. You may even have said something like this yourself. I know I certainly have. This belief—that meetings are a pox on productivity and an evil which we must combat—may even have inspired you to pick up this book.

It's because meetings suck, right? Sure they do. And yet...

> "The opposite of a correct statement is a false statement. But the opposite of a profound truth may well be another profound truth."
>
> —Niels Bohr, Physicist

Okay, I grant that "meetings suck" may not qualify as a profound truth, but I think you can see where I'm going. Before we look at the research, consider each of these questions:

1. How much time do you waste in meetings?
2. Do you like meetings?
3. What happens if you tell your spouse/parent/partner that you can't talk now because you have a meeting?
4. What do you hope will happen when you apply for your dream job?
5. What do you do when there's an emergency you need to solve quickly with your team?

If you respond to these questions like most people, your answers probably look something like these:

1. Too much! I can never get anything done because I'm always in a stupid meeting.
2. Are you kidding? I hate them. You want to hear a story about a terrible meeting? Why, just last week....
3. Oh, my family understands and knows not to disturb me in a meeting.
4. I want to be the first person they call for an interview. I'm ready, and I know I can rock it if they give me the chance.
5. If there's a problem, we get everyone in a room and crash on it. There's no time to waste sending email back and forth, and I can't risk misunderstandings here. We'll get together and figure it out.

Meetings suck! It's a popular sentiment, and even the title of a recent book by the international business consultant Cameron Herald. Research, however, shows the opposite.

"Overall, how effective or ineffective do you think each of these types of communication is at your company?" **When asked how well they think different approaches to team communication work, 84% of people rate meetings as effective and only 16% mark them ineffective.**

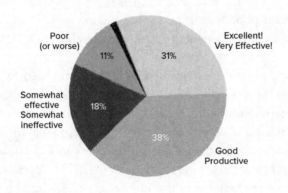

Most People Think Meetings Work
with ample room for improvement

Poor
(or worse)
11%

Excellent!
Very Effective!
31%

Somewhat
effective
Somewhat
ineffective
18%

38%

Good
Productive

A Researcher's Perspective

Steven Rogelberg is one of a growing set of academic researchers turning their attention on meetings. This excerpt from one of his team's recent papers perfectly explains what we see in the survey results.

What Do Employees Think About the Meetings They Attend?

The minute we tell an employee or leader we are studying meetings, many launch into what we refer to as the "meeting hell" lament: "If you want to know about bad meetings, you should shadow me for a day!" was a common response. Some of the data we collected was consistent with this anecdotal experience: More than half of the employees we surveyed said they publicly complain about their meetings. But there was an intriguing paradox within this self-characterization. The majority of the individuals in the "complainer group" actually admitted that they did not feel as negatively as they indicated publicly.

Indeed, in private surveys employees offered accounts of effectiveness in meetings that were quite favorable. When asked about meetings in general from a productivity perspective, a significant majority responded positively: in round numbers, 17% called them very good to excellent; 42% rated them good; 25% rated them neither good nor bad; and just 15% rated them poor or worse. When asked to rate the productivity of their most recent meeting, the responses were even more positive: 36% rated them as very good to excellent; 33% rated them as good; 16% rated them as neither good nor bad; and 16% rated them as poor or worse.

—Dr. Steven G. Rogelberg, meeting researcher from UNC Charlotte

Pacific Bold's problem starts here. When people need to share information, given the available alternatives, most of them will choose to meet. Meetings let you communicate with multiple people at once, deal with questions quickly and openly, and be reasonably sure that the other people in the room actually got the message. The same cannot be said for email.

So the first answer to the question "Why meet?" is, "Because people feel that meetings work better than the alternatives." Let's build on that. Work better for doing what, exactly? What are meetings good for?

This depends on the meeting. Most of the advice you'll find is true for certain kinds of meetings and not for others. With that said, there are underlying concepts and general rules that apply most of the time. These are the fundamental principles and basic manners you should know if you want to meet well.

Let's start with the idea that meetings are a tool—a means to an end. But to what end? When we work in collaboration with other people, we have two things we have to take care of to be successful: the work and the people.

In theory, the work should be something we can plan and manage logically. After each piece of work begins, there are a series of tasks to complete and problems to solve that continue until the work is done.

Also in theory, the people doing the work should be able to coordinate their efforts through a simple exchange of factual information. When Fred completes task A, he marks it done, and Betty starts task B. When Alan runs into a problem with the work, he could write down the facts of the situation and send them to others for help—help they could then offer in any number of ways that do not involve a team meeting.

Clean, efficient, and logical. When the work is well understood and routine, this approach makes sense. The people doing the work click along like a "well-oiled machine." In these situations, there is very little reason to meet.

Of course, the "well-oiled machine" theory of work only applies to jobs that could literally be replaced by one or more well-oiled machines. The order of tasks, environment in which the tasks are performed, and definition of success are all known in advance. The context and the players rarely change, everyone knows what they're supposed to do, and they just get on with it.

If the current technology trends continue, this well-oiled machine version of the workplace will soon have very few people in it. At the fall 2017 Gartner Symposium, analysts predicted that artificial intelligence will displace millions of jobs in the next five years. "Start thinking about how to divide tasks between your digital labor and your analogs," the analysts told the crowd at the opening keynote.

Yes, when those analysts said "analogs," they meant *people*. That's us, folks. Chew on that for a second.

The Gartner analyst also predicted that a whole new industry would arise, creating millions of jobs for data scientists and analysts and researchers. Human ones! All of these new analog jobs would involve making sense of complex data and complex problems.

The well-oiled machine theory doesn't apply to the work that can't literally be relegated to the machines, just as it has never applied to businesses that need to respond, adapt, evolve, and grow.

The well-oiled machine theory does not apply to collaborative work.

Pacific Bold engages in collaborative work. They help clients understand their market, craft their brand, and reach their customers. Their world is the world of color and feeling and nuance and the complex shifting of trends and the evolution of media. Pacific Bold relies heavily on its analogs—okay, that's enough of that—on its *people* to make sense of a situation and then make magic.

So, because they're human, when Fred completes task A, he may indeed mark it done. But let's say Betty's cousin is in town and she's taking a few days off, so she doesn't start task B right away. Then, when she gets back, she finds 239 new alerts in her inbox and never even sees the note from Fred. The "machine" breaks down. Later, when Alan runs into that tricky problem with the work, instead of writing it up so the team can help, he spends the first day thinking that he must have missed something and searches the web for answers. When that fails, he picks up a few side tasks to keep himself busy, hoping a solution will "come to him" while he's getting other stuff done. It doesn't, and now it's been days and other things are starting to stack up behind Alan's unfinished assignments. The machine is now truly broken. This team needs to meet.

We Meet to Find the Elephant in the Dark

Meetings have one core function. Specifically: **We meet to quickly create shared perspective in a group.**

It can be hard to care about "shared perspective" as an abstract concept. Each person might think they know everything needed to get on with the job, and that this time spent with the group is a waste.

The reality is that we are all working with blindfolds on. There is too much information flowing through the modern workplace for any one of us to fully grasp the "truth" of the matter.

This ancient parable illustrates our challenge.

Six people who have never seen nor heard of an elephant enter a dark room. They each touch the elephant hidden inside the dark room to learn about it. Each person feels only one part of the elephant; just the tail, or just the trunk, for example.

Each one forms a true, accurate, *and very limited* idea of what an elephant is. The person who felt the trunk believes an elephant is like a hose. The person who felt the side thinks it is like a wall.

When they compare their ideas, they find they don't agree at all. The disagreements get heated, and the whole thing devolves into a brawl.

By contrast, a properly structured meeting helps people share, compare, and merge what they each know independently into a more complete picture.

Together, we can all better appreciate the whole elephant.

At the most basic level, teams meet to **quickly create shared perspective** in a group.

Let's pull that statement apart, starting with the concept of a "shared perspective."

Before the meeting, we call the shared perspective we want to create the "**desired outcome.**" Desired outcomes take many forms: The outcome of a meeting can be a decision, a plan, a commitment, a new understanding, an intention, an apology, a resolution, and so on.

When they meet, Fred and Betty will figure out that it's time for her task to begin. If they meet soon enough, Alan will have to share the problem he ran into, giving the rest of the team a chance to either help him or adjust their plans around him before the whole project gets totally out of whack.

The shared perspective created in a meeting doesn't just include what the group agrees to on the surface. It also includes what they learn and believe that they didn't before, and how they *feel* about the whole thing.

When Fred, Betty, and Alan meet, they get a shared perspective on the *work*—what's done, what's not—*and the people.* Fred will learn that Betty isn't ignoring him, and they can both stop assuming that Alan's a slacker.

Meetings put focus on both the work and the people. The coaches at Leadership Strategies describe meeting outcomes in terms of the "Hand, Head, and Heart." They teach us to think through what each person should leave the meeting with "in their hand"—the tangible or documented result—"in their head"—new knowledge and understanding—and "in their heart"—meaning how we hope people will feel at the meeting's end.

There are other ways to create shared perspective. Email, reports, books, chat, and video can all work—and we certainly can't just meet with all the people all the time when we want to communicate our thoughts and feelings. **Again, given all the alternatives, why meet at all?**

The key is the word "quickly." Meetings quickly create shared perspective. When well executed, the other adjective I'd add is "reliably," as no other communication tool gives you the same level of clarity and control that a meeting can.

Let me illustrate that point. Like, literally, with pictures. Behold!

Direction, Momentum, and Force: A Visual Model for Understanding Meeting Function

I find it's easiest to understand what meetings do for teams with some simple visuals.

Before the very first meeting, people are all out there just doing their own thing.

During, they come together to explore the work at hand.

After the meeting, they leave with a shared perspective on the work and begin to move in a coordinated way toward a common goal.

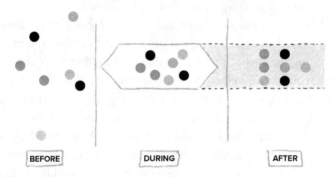

Individual perspectives get aligned in meetings so the team can move forward together.

Most effective meetings last less than one hour. On the overall work timeline, an hour is a blink. This is where the "quickly" part of our meeting function shines. Meetings *quickly* create shared perspective in a group.

By contrast, when we look at how long it takes for a team to get coordinated by email, our only guarantee that the total elapsed time required is less than an hour is if we have everyone constantly checking email. That doesn't bode well for their chances of getting much else done, does it? Most tasks require periods of uninterrupted focus—something group chat and email aren't designed to respect.

The Function of a Meeting

Because all the people start in different places, **effective meetings begin by focusing the group** and bringing them into the conversation. Once the group is focused, they can move into the main part of the discussion.

The path the conversation takes during the meeting depends on the desired outcome; it can get pretty messy while all those individual perspectives navigate their way to a mutually understood and agreed end point.

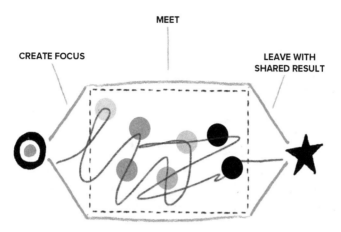

How meetings function: focus the group, find a shared perspective, and focus the outcome.

Once this desired outcome is achieved, **an effective meeting ends with a clear and focused review of the result.** You can visualize the meeting as a force that *pulls* people together, aligns them, and then *pushes* them toward a shared goal.

Everyone sets forth together, their goal clearly before them.

Why Teams Have Lots of Meetings

In a perfectly harmonious and stable world, our team could meet just once to get that shared perspective, then happily flow down that straight path to being done. This would happen naturally if people were indeed well-oiled machines.

That is not the world we live in. So naturally that never happens, and we need more meetings. If we visualize the schedule for a typical project timeline, it might look something like this.

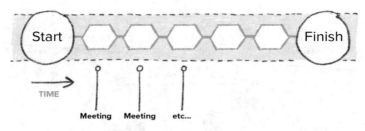

Meetings in a typical project timeline

(Note: I'm using the term "project" here to represent any goal-oriented work a group might undertake. The same concept applies whether your team builds products, drives corporate strategy, or hosts an annual bake sale.)

With our pull-push visual in mind, we can zoom-in on this timeline to look at what's happening with the team at the beginning of the project.

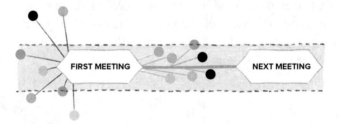

Zooming in on the first team meeting

Like we saw before, that first meeting pulls the group together and sends them out on the path. But this time, we can see that while all the people are headed in basically the same direction, they're not all moving at the same speed or along quite the same trajectory.

In other words, they are true analogs! People with all their individual skills and quirks and realities. So, before too long, the team has another meeting to pull that group back into alignment.

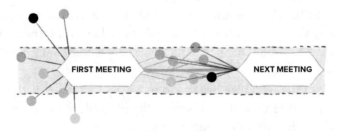

The second meeting pulls people back into alignment.

And this pattern repeats until the work reaches a conclusion.

For teams working toward a common goal, meetings are a forcing function for creating alignment around a shared perspective. Unlike email or chat or project records, meetings are hard to ignore. Obligatory, even. When team members are headed in wildly different directions, or someone is off in la-la-land, a meeting can bring them all together much more quickly and effectively than any other method.

Assuming it's a well-run meeting, of course. But we'll get to that later.

Meeting Strategy: Knowing When to Meet

In a later chapter we'll talk about when not to meet—about when to cancel a meeting rather than waste everyone's time. Now let's look at when you *should* meet, based on this understanding of what meetings do for our teams and our work.

When to Meet Rule 1: Meet to create momentum.

In between meetings, a team's sense of shared perspective gets fuzzier as each person learns new things, then encounters distractions, obstacles, and competing priorities. When meetings are fairly close together, there isn't much time for people to get too far off the path. Recreating that shared perspective is pretty easy. It's just a little pull back into alignment.

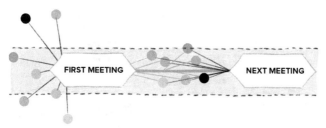

Meetings quickly re-establish shared perspective.

But the longer you wait between meetings, the more frayed that shared perspective gets. Those who move quickly have a chance to get way out ahead of the group. Those with slower motors get farther behind. Some get lost, and there's always a risk that someone has been completely knocked out by some outside factor. All of these risks may go unnoticed by the rest of the group in that big gap between meetings. The people on this team are no longer looking at the work from the same perspective.

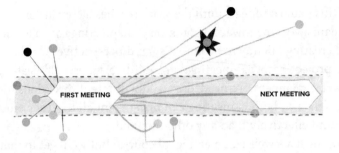

The group loses cohesion when too much time goes by between meetings.

In some ways, this group is farther apart than they were before the project started. The second meeting now needs to be just as long and involved as the first one in order to recreate shared perspective. **So mind the gap! Schedule meetings frequently enough to maintain momentum.**

When to Meet Rule 2: Meet to change course.

So far we've been focusing mostly on how meetings help us create a shared perspective between people. Sometimes, however, it's not the people who get out of alignment, but the work itself that goes all wonky. We live in a dynamic universe, and sometimes elements out of our control come in and blow our best-laid plans to smithereens.

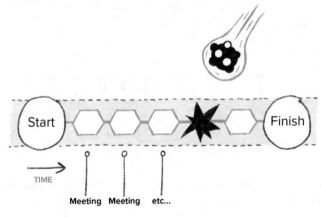

Time for a new plan.

When facing an unexpected dead-end, teams meet to reorient themselves and chart a new path. What just happened? What do we do now? How do we get back on track? These are important questions around which the team needs to form a new shared perspective—a shared answer—before they can move forward.

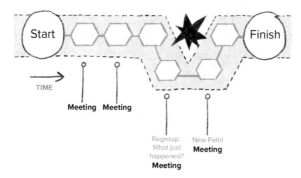

Meet to find a new path to success when circumstances change.

Catastrophes aren't the only changes that warrant a meeting. More often than not, the path that seemed so clear at the outset gets complicated along the way. The team may find itself at a crossroads, unsure which path will lead to the goal most directly. Other times, the team may glimpse an alternate route leading to an entirely new destination—one that they couldn't see before they started along this path.

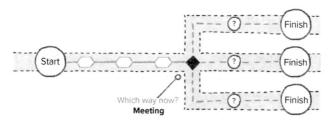

Meet to decide when the best path forward isn't clear.

Whenever you're facing a decision about a major change in how to proceed, meet. What constitutes a "major" change? Obviously that depends, but it's helpful to remember Rule 1: Meet to Create Momentum. Any change of course where a lack of shared perspective would be a momentum killer warrants a meeting.

To sum up:

- Meetings are used as a collaboration tool to quickly create shared perspective.
- Meetings function by pulling a group of people together, creating

alignment around their work, and pushing them out along a coordinated path toward a goal.
- Meetings must be held frequently enough to maintain this shared perspective and create momentum along the path.
- Meetings should be held any time the path becomes unclear and the whole team needs to shift to a new perspective on the work.

Metcalfe's Law and the Unchecked Organic Growth of Meetings

Now that I've talked about why people meet—the function and fun that is meeting—and we've seen some of the research that confirms that people do indeed prefer to meet when given a choice, we can start to see how Pacific Bold has grown into its "meetings problem."

When a company is small, it's pretty easy to maintain a shared perspective, and it's okay to simply schedule a meeting whenever you feel you need one. You're busy, you know everyone else is busy, and you have a good idea of what everyone else is doing each day, so you really only need to meet when you get stuck.

The problems arise as the company grows. I've worked with several companies that started out with five people, then became 20, and the next thing they knew, there were 200 people on the org chart. And all of the sudden they *had* an org chart!

Once you get beyond that first five people, you no longer have an intuitive sense of what everyone is doing, so you start meeting more to find out. It's often unconscious. Teams simply continue to operate like they always have; only now there are more people involved.

Pretty soon, they start feeling the implications of Metcalfe's Law. **Metcalfe's Law states that the value of a network is proportional to the number of connected nodes in the system.** Metcalfe was looking at computers in a network, but this has since been extended to illustrate what happens with large groups of people. The simple equation for expressing the possible One-on-One meeting combinations within a group looks like this: $(n * n\text{-}1)/2$. Personally I find that math to be far too abstract—an example works better.

When you have two people in your group, the possible combinations of people you might have in a meeting is exactly one.

When there are five people, you have 10 possible connections.

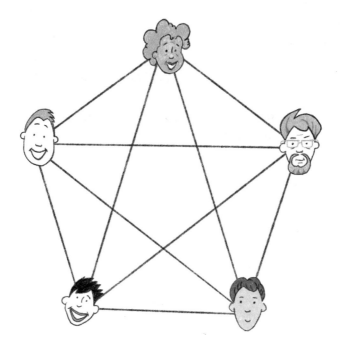

When there are 12 people, you now have *66* possible One-on-One meeting scenarios. When that same 12 people run meetings with more than one person, the number of possible combinations jumps dramatically.

As the number of nodes (people—*analogs*, even) in a network increases and the number of possible combinations increases with them, so too does the potential value of the network. The social media giants helped revise Metcalfe's thinking to express this growing value better for situations involving lots of people rather than those just involving multiple computers, but while this tweaks the math, the concept holds. More people involved should result in higher value—*assuming you can connect these people in a sensible way.* The challenge is that connection alone is not valuable; only connections that work to combine and build on each person's unique value serve your organization. The rest are noise.

A 12-person team is very unlikely to hold 66 One-on-Ones each week, but each of those people is likely to be interested in what's happening with the other 11. If the group doesn't find a way to share that information efficiently, then they risk spending way more time in unplanned conversation than they should, or conversely, isolating some of the people in the group. These two phenomena are so common they have names. If people don't know how to make progress and call a meeting any time they have a question or idea, you say the group has *meetingitis*. When someone in the group minimizes their participation in meetings and stays focused on producing work, they are said to have gone *lone wolf*. Both situations reduce the value of the network.

Pacific Bold passed the 12-person mark a long time ago. With 144 people, their network looks more like this.

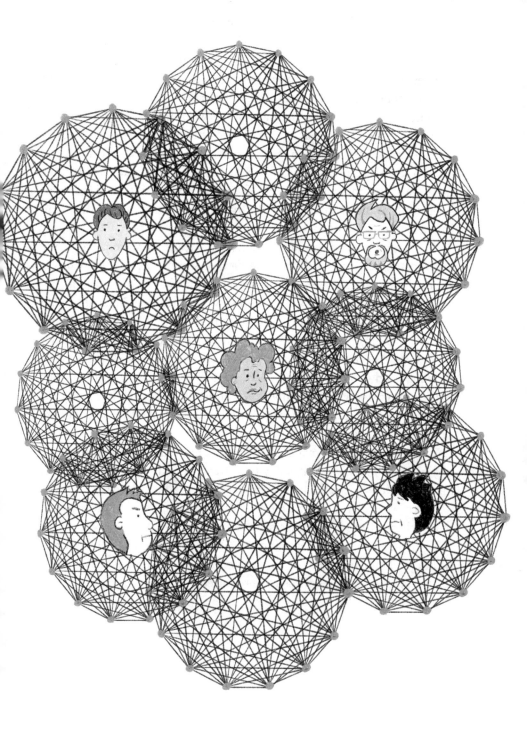

Think of organizations as a kind of collaborative organism.

For the collaborative organism—whether that's a company or a neighborhood or a movement—there are a set of required resources the organism needs to survive, just as there are for any other kind of organism. First, there must be people. No people, no group, no possibility for organization. Second, there must be communication between the people. No communication, the organism ceases to exist. We often use the word *organization* as if we're discussing a static thing, like a chair or a hockey puck. In reality, though, these are groups of people continuously *organizing*. Without this organizing interaction, you're left with a number of isolated individual people. Third, there should be collective action. No action and the organism fails to have an impact.

Of these, think of communication as a means of sustenance. To an organization, communication is the diet. It is entirely possible to sustain yourself on a terrible diet, and this is certainly what happens when organizations communicate in an unplanned way. When they start out, collaborative organisms don't really need much in the way of process or communication strategy. They can stay in contact all day and still be productive, very much like how my small children can happily snack on a pound of Halloween candy and then head out to play. As we mature, though, the "eat anything you want any time you want" approach has nasty side effects. This holds equally true for the all-you-can-eat buffet style of organizational communication.

With too much information flowing around in unstructured ways, the organization bloats and bogs down. Systems get out of whack and meetings proliferate unchecked, growing to fill the available space.

When we see an organization in a situation like Pacific Bold's, we say that their meetings have metastasized.

Pacific Bold needs a new plan, and they know it. Even though they hadn't yet benefited from my clever communication-as-diet analogy, they realized that drastic measures were required.

Craig thinks he has the solution, "That's it. Just cancel all the meetings!" he says.

Angie, Charla, and Nelson all grumble variations of, "Wait, what?"

Craig, fired up, continues, "Listen, this data is clear. Our meetings are clearly out of control. We've got a bad habit that's killing the company, and if we don't step in right now, we won't survive. We need to take bold action. Go cold turkey. Come on! Is our name Pacific Bold, or Pacific Maybe We Should Talk It Over in Another Meeting? Just do it!

"We spent all that money on a project management system, we've got chat, we've got email—we have all kinds of ways to communicate when we need to. We clearly can't afford to keep getting 10 people into a room for an hour every time we need to make a decision! At our rates, every one of those meetings is $1,000 we aren't invoicing and 10 hours farther behind hitting our deadlines. I want everyone's calendars cleared by this time tomorrow! In fact, this meeting is taking too long. We're done here."

If he had a mic to drop, Craig's mic would have dropped right into the stunned well of silence he leaves behind as he storms out of the conference room.

PB

CHAPTER 3

The Perverse Psychology of Meetings

Craig's suggestion is extreme, but it's hardly unprecedented. Basecamp, a software company based in Chicago, championed the "no meetings" movement back in 2010. In 2015, a VP at the technology firm Slack advised new startups to regularly cancel all their internal meetings, then see which ones turn out to be necessary by watching what hurts. Abstaining from meetings—going on a "meeting fast"—is a surprisingly popular approach to the too-many-meetings problem.

It's not an approach I recommend. Like dietary fasts, meeting fasts rarely last very long, and they don't help you learn healthy, sustainable habits. If meeting binges are at one end of the pendulum swing, fasts are at the other. Only, meeting fasts are harder than dietary fasts, because for it to work, you have to get all the other people to go on the fast with you. I think we'll see that Craig swung his pendulum a little too hard.

The binge/fast pendulum swing is just one of the extremes we see with meetings. Our relationship to meetings as a society is complex, and we lack a good way to talk about this complexity. This spills out into bizarre behavior, like the people who complain that they hate meetings then secretly confide to researchers that, actually, they kind of enjoy them. (Shh! Don't tell!) Like the companies that proudly declare themselves a "no meetings" zone. (This really has happened.) Like the people who complain that nothing gets done and they're wasting their time, then bristle when you try to take notes or follow an agenda.

People get all weird about meetings. I think I now understand some of why that happens.

One night when I was in the middle of writing this book, I went to dinner with a friend. She said, "It must be hard to sell people on better meetings when everyone hates them so much. Why do you think everyone hates meetings?"

"I don't think they do, actually," I replied. "The research backs this up. In fact—"

"Really?" she interrupted. "But then, why do you think people *say* they hate meetings if they actually like them? Is it because they've just never seen a good meeting, or what?"

I'm so glad she asked! (*It's possible that she wasn't.*)

As we know, the truth is that most people *don't* hate meetings. I believe people *say* they hate meetings because it's useful to do so.

A Great Excuse

Meetings provide us with a **usefully imposed obligation**. What does that mean? Any time we have a meeting on our calendar, that's an automatic excuse to say no to anything else that may come up. And because everyone knows how much we hate meetings, we don't even have to feel guilty about it. Heck, meetings are so broadly understood to be painful, it's likely that the person we just rejected feels sorry for us!

The obligating force of a meeting is so strong that we use it in nonsensical ways. Have you ever been in a meeting where someone stood up and apologized that they had to go because they were expected in a different meeting? It doesn't even matter what the current meeting is about or who's in the next one—the fact that there *is* another meeting starting trumps whatever you might be doing already.

This excuse is so powerful, so unquestioned, that using it when you don't have a meeting is cliché.

"Charlene, if my wife calls, tell her I'm in a meeting." What movie is that quote from? Frankly, does it matter? It's from pretty much every movie featuring a goofy boss, and you know it.

I believe any time we talk about meetings *in the abstract*, the powerful myth that meetings just waste time will persist. There is a strong and useful social shorthand we all understand when we complain about being "stuck in meetings" or "running from meeting to meeting" or "missing my family because I had to take a late-night meeting" that we're not going to give up without a fight.

Meetings' bad reputation gets people off the hook. This common perception that meetings are a waste of time is also a fabulous excuse for staying ignorant about how to make meetings work well. Effective meetings happen between people with skills that go beyond "talking at each other." There are levels of mastery to attain, and that's a fair chunk of work. Effort is required.

When untrained and inexperienced people tell me that all meetings are a waste of time, I put about as much stock in that as I do all the advice my retired nurse mother gives me about building software. It's not that she has no exposure to software—everyone does! It's everywhere!—but rather that she has no relevant skills, education, or interest in figuring out what it takes to do better.

This is one reason I advise people to never schedule anything called a "meeting." This generic term comes loaded with negative baggage, setting you on a path to mediocrity before you even begin.

PACIFIC BOLD

This abstraction is also what makes it possible for Craig to pull his "cancel all the meetings" stunt. *Meetings*, as a general concept, are universally loathed wastes of time, and by declaring all these awful obligations canceled, Craig finds that he feels like a bit of a hero as he strides from the room.

Buzzed on adrenaline, Craig looks out across the office at all the designers and project managers and developers he's brought into his company, and he beams. "Imagine how grateful they'll be when they realize I've freed them up to focus," he thinks. "They'll get uninterrupted time to do their work, and they'll be able to go home to see their kids or even meet their friends for a beer while there's still daylight! I bet they'll start to create even more brilliant campaigns than they did before, now that they can really concentrate without all those distractions. You know, we might need to start turning clients away! Oh, and the awards! I should start looking into how we can get a trophy case installed in the lobby...."

Craig's euphoria lasts exactly as long as it takes him to reach his office and check his phone, where he sees two alerts about the upcoming meeting with Pacific Bold's largest client.

Oh.

═══════════════════ PB ═══════════════════

People Who Don't Like People

Another, more serious, reason that I believe people may hate meetings is this: Some people don't like collaborating with other people.

A well-run meeting engages *everyone* in the discussion, not just the boss or the most charismatic individual. Powerful individual contributors do not always enjoy waiting to hear what others have to say. They believe they know everything they need to know, and that meetings are where they tell everyone else what to do. Consider a popular strain of business advice that tells leaders to keep most meetings to five minutes or less. Yes, the advisors admit, you do have to cut people off. Yes, the employees say, they were shocked and appalled at first, but they learned to adapt. Yes, another advocate says, it's good to "allow" your team to get together for a bit longer every once in awhile to "maintain spirits."

Just so we're clear between us here, **there is no such thing as a five-minute meeting.** You can have a five-minute conversation, sure. You can endure a verbal assault in well under three minutes. But *meetings* do more and require more.

While a well-run meeting engages everyone, **a well-structured meeting constrains dominant individuals.** A clear structure defines what will be discussed and how the discussion will progress. This leaves a lot less room for people to turn the conversation to their pet project. A well-structured *sequence* of meetings sets clear expectations about how to prepare and how to follow through, forcing mutual accountability toward shared goals between team members. Strong individual contributors can perform at exceedingly high levels, but they prefer to do so on their own terms, according to their priorities, and in their own time; they are not interested in following up on action items.

When we help a client start using agendas, inevitably they run into someone on their team who complains that they don't need "all this formality and structure!" Occasionally, this means that the agenda isn't right for the team and needs to be adjusted. More often, however, we find that the person complaining does not value collaboration, sees no reason they should be held accountable to the rest of the group, and has no interest whatsoever in working together toward a shared result. The structure and formality complaint is a feint, because the reality is every meeting has a structure. The real question is: who owns that structure? Habit? Mood? The alpha person in the room? Or does the team own it collectively? If the alpha gets to choose, let's hope they're a team-oriented alpha.

Dominant individual contributors are often unabashed self-promoters. They're totally ready to tell everyone else how they should think and act, including pearls of wisdom such as "cancel all your meetings," "complete every team interaction in under five minutes," and "go big or go home!" Their voices are loud, and we've all heard these messages, which feeds power to the myth that meetings suck.

A Lesson from History and Politics

In 1933, a fire ravaged the German Reichstag—the building where the German parliament met. Newly elected Chancellor Adolf Hitler convinced the government that the Reichstag fire was a secret plot by Communists who sought to overthrow the budding Nazi party. Within days, German President Paul von Hindenburg issued what has become known as the Reichstag Decree. Ostensibly necessary to "restore order," the decree immediately revoked many of the civil liberties that had previously been guaranteed by the German constitution, including the right of public assembly. This decree became the foundation of Nazi law, allowing Hitler to declare martial law both at home in Germany and in the lands his Nazi-controlled military later invaded.

Revoking the right of public assembly is clearly not the worst thing the Nazis did, nor is it particularly remarkable in the grand scheme of despots. All dictators who invade and impose martial law revoke the right of assembly. This is not a benevolent act. Dictators do not revoke this right because they believe the people they're dominating will be happier and more productive without all those waste-of-time meetings. Rather, they know that when people can't meet freely, they remain isolated, fearful, and easier to control.

Today, the rights of freedom of association and freedom of assembly are part of every major democratic constitution and the Universal Declaration of Human Rights adopted by the United Nations in 1943. In my home country, the U.S., the right of freedom of assembly is included in the First Amendment to our Constitution, alongside the right to free speech.

We all understand that the right to drone on during the weekly staff call doesn't warrant the same kind of protections that governments provide for protesters and political activists. Still, when I hear of a company that's banned all meetings or requires people to keep every conversation under five minutes, I shudder. These are tactics borrowed (unwittingly, I hope) from oppressors, dictators, and mass murderers everywhere. They have no place in a modern organization.

Happily, this is not the situation with Craig at Pacific Bold. Craig isn't trying to shut down collaboration or oppress anyone; he's trying to save the people who work for him from layoffs. No, an individualist disdain for collaboration isn't Craig's problem, but now that Pacific Bold employs 144 unique individuals, it's a sure bet that this is an attitude the leadership team will need to deal with at some point in its journey.

Meetings vs. Job Performance

The final reason I believe people say they hate meetings has to do with how we recognize performance in our organizations. Paul Graham famously spelled this out in his blog post *Maker's Schedule, Manager's Schedule*. In it, Graham explains that Makers get paid to make stuff, requiring big blocks of uninterrupted focus time. These are the software engineers and the nurses and folks in the factory. When these people are in meetings, he argues, it inhibits their ability to make stuff. At review time, if they have a number that's used to review their performance, it's going to be a number related to how much good stuff they made, and meetings are an interruption that keeps them from making good stuff.

Graham then posits that Managers, on the other hand, get paid to meet. They need to know what's going on in the business, and to do their job, they call everyone into meetings all the time without realizing how much these interruptions hurt their Maker friends.

As someone who has worked in the software industry since 1999, I know that this message resonated with my Maker friends in a big way. Some of them stopped showing up at meetings that they felt weren't deserving of their time. (Which would have been a way cooler move if it meant they used that time to actually write more high-quality software. Beware pulling this one, as it risks exposing your prima donna underskirts.)

Then something surprising happened. Our software teams adopted Agile methodologies. Suddenly, my engineering peers who couldn't spare their precious focus time in company meetings started holding their own meetings seven times each week. Seven meetings a week for one team! How was this possibly okay with them?

The engineers using an Agile process happily met seven times every week because that was the way they got their work done. *Meeting performance was job performance.* What they did in their meetings directly led to the production of higher-quality software at a faster rate. They also happily sat in meetings because they didn't think of it that way. Every one of those meetings had a special name and a specific function. The Daily Scrum kept the group in sync with work in progress. During Sprint Planning, they set the work queue for the week ahead. The Sprint Retrospective provided an opportunity to share lessons learned and refine their practice. They didn't waste a minute in useless meetings—come on, we all know meetings are the worst! Instead, they practiced their Agile rituals (*known to the rest of us as "meetings"*) so they could achieve more together.

I believe that Paul Graham was correct to point out that a meeting which keeps people from doing the work they're paid to do is a problem. The success of Agile shows, though, that it is not meetings *per se*, but rather it's *irrelevant* meetings that are the problem. If a meeting is not relevant to how a person's work performance gets evaluated, then they shouldn't be there.

Having said that, I think Graham made a mistake when it comes to the work of Managers too. It's a mistake I've heard repeated by many Managers, so I don't fault Graham for falling into this trap, but my rebuttal is: Meetings are *not* a Manager's work. Setting direction, clearing obstacles, developing skills, making decisions—these are a Manager's work.

Running an organization is the Manager's work. Meetings are a tool Managers use to do this work, but never the point. Managers who understand that their responsibility is a well-run business will learn how to use these tools well. They'll learn the difference between each type of meeting, and the situations that call for one type over another. The set of meetings a Manager needs to understand is larger than the set my Agile friends use but no less tailored.

Too often, Managers are hired from within and never receive the training they need in the specialized work of managing. They saw their Manager go to meetings all the time, so they schedule and go to meetings all the time. And the organization muddles along. And all too often, a well-intended program designed to improve the organization backfires. For example, Managers may be expected to hold a One-on-One with each person on their team every week. The intent is to ensure each person gets the support they need and that personal issues don't have time to fester or derail the team. Great idea, right? When the group includes six people this policy might even be manageable, but as the group grows, this one initiative can quickly become a lot of how a Manager spends their week.

When meeting performance is tied directly to job performance, the way Managers meet changes too. Where Makers end up going to more meetings, Managers go to fewer, more specialized meetings. Managers of larger teams find other ways to support those team members and a cadence for individual check-ins that ensures the Manager has time to do the rest of their job as well. Everyone becomes much clearer about how the meetings they attend help them achieve what they need to achieve, and you stop hearing people complain about all the time wasted in pointless meetings.

In Pacific Bold's case, this observation about tying meeting performance to job performance points to another possible approach to their problem. Currently their teams are spending a lot of time in meetings that they do not invoice to clients. They consider all meetings overhead. It is highly likely, however, that many of those meetings are held by teams collaborating on client projects. In other words, the meetings about client projects are work they are doing for clients, and potentially billable.

Checkpoint:
Why We Hold the Meetings We Love to Hate

Let's review the story so far.

First, we met the Pacific Bold team and learned that, while they are entirely awesome in many ways, they are facing a crisis that could lead to layoffs. After some initial investigation, fingers point to too many meetings as the main problem.

Then, we looked at why people meet. Namely, people meet because they think it works better than the alternatives. Meetings help teams quickly create shared perspective, and when run well, they establish a healthy work momentum.

Healthy matters. When meetings are scheduled at everyone's discretion, they tend to proliferate and consume an unhealthy amount of the organization's time. We say these meetings have metastasized.

Recognizing the need for drastic action, Pacific Bold's founder Craig declared that all meetings would be canceled immediately.

Organizations face a variety of challenges when they try to adopt healthy meeting habits:

- The abstract concept of a meeting comes with social baggage that makes it awkward to talk about publicly. We use meetings as an excuse, and the excuse doesn't work well when we respect our meetings. (Trust me on this one. I've had 10 years of awkward conversations!)
- Healthy meetings constrain dominant individual contributors, so these people often resist efforts to establish effective meeting practices.
- Meeting performance is often seen as separate from job performance, which disincentivizes people who want to improve meetings.

The challenges are real, but they must be overcome to unlock the greatest potential value in the organization. Individual people don't actually know very much on their own, which means we each need access to the knowledge and thinking power embedded in the people, tools, and resources around us.

To combat these challenges and establish effective meeting habits, organizations need to get specific and design the meetings that matter for their work. To do this, we first need to find a more specific way to talk about meetings.

CHAPTER 4

Introducing the 16 Types
of Business Meetings

PACIFIC BOLD

Okay, so when I said "Cancel all the meetings," what I really meant was....

Craig takes a few deep breaths, then turns around and heads back to the conference room. The rest of the leadership team is still there, engaged in an animated debate that goes silent the moment Craig opens the door.

"Okay," Craig says. "I apologize. I got carried away, and that was rude. I'm really sorry—we don't just shout orders here, and I'm the first one to call baloney on that kind of thing when someone tries to pull it on me. I guess... I mean, I realize we can't cancel every meeting, but I do think...."

Craig looks up and trails off when he sees the not-very-well-hidden grins on everyone's faces. Charla can't hold it any longer. Chuckling, she reaches out and gives Craig a hug. They've been partners for years, and Charla's a hugger.

"We know, Craig. It's okay," Charla says. "We were pretty sure you knew too, and that you'd be back. That was good, though! What flair! We're going to have to tell this story to the company when we roll out the changes."

"Oh, yeah!" Nelson agrees. "We can make a production of it! Maybe you rip a calendar in half after you say, 'Meetings? Cancel them all!' Do you think you could tear up a full-sized calendar, or should we get one of those day-by-day planner things and have you shred through that like some kind of crazed ferret with a roll of toilet paper?"

Angie isn't participating in the plans to dramatize Craig's earlier walk-out. Instead, she's making a list on the whiteboard. "Obviously we aren't going to cancel client meetings," Angie says. "The board meeting—that needs to stay too. What about us? Do we still need a leadership team meeting? Or can we get by with a check-in on video chat? I can cancel my weekly meeting with my team and all the One-on-Ones, and I'll have the project managers cancel all the internal meetings they're running. I'm not sure exactly what will happen, but I know a lot of people who will be very happy to see those status meetings go. What else? Is there anything else we absolutely have to keep?"

Within an hour, the Pacific Bold leadership transforms "cancel all the meetings" into "cancel most of the meetings and see what happens." At this point, they know there are too many meetings sucking up people's time, but they don't have a good way to see which ones work and which don't. This approach promises to shake up the system.

—— PB ——

What Makes One Kind of Meeting Different from Another?

When you want to run better meetings, two of the most useful questions you can ask are, "Do we need a meeting?" and, "Is this the right *kind* of meeting to achieve what we need?"

To answer these questions, it helps to understand what makes one kind of meeting different from another. At Lucid Meetings, we developed a taxonomy to help distinguish the different types of workplace meetings. Each type of meeting creates a different work result. Some meetings are clearly special. As Craig quickly realized, calling his client to cancel the upcoming account review or canceling the quarterly board meeting because "Meetings are a waste of time!" would be ludicrous. These meetings involve high-value stakeholders and can clearly make or break future business; this is obviously where the action is.

Other meetings aren't so clear. What should the Pacific Bold design team talk about in their weekly meetings? Should they discuss upcoming projects, or new hires? How about conferences they'll be attending? Is this the place to raise questions about getting new equipment? And when, exactly, is it okay for Nelson to tell yet another story about his dachshund, Floyd? The way the team had been meeting, any one of these topics might come up—or these topics plus three more—and the meeting would spill over into two more meetings. Other weeks, the only interesting discussion point really was Floyd the Wonder Weiner's latest adventure.

For most of the internal meetings at Pacific Bold, the reason each one mattered and what it was meant to accomplish wasn't clear. They had picked the hammer out of the toolbox and were just beating out all their ideas and problems the same way.

Learning how to distinguish between different types of meetings is akin to learning about the different tools in the toolbox. A performance evaluation is not the same kind of tool as a sales negotiation. These meetings have different business functions, just like a measuring tape has a different function than a hammer.

When we started Lucid Meetings, I believed that there was a general "meeting problem" that we could fix by helping people learn to use generic best practices. When we spoke with prospects about our platform, we said it could make "experts out of novices," helping people who didn't know an agenda from their elbow get proficient.

Now, instead of making experts out of novices, we focus on making novices out of generalists. That's because we found the generic "best practices" approach doesn't work. You cannot build a house when you only have a hammer, even if it's a really great hammer and you're really good with it, and we can't use blanket rules like "keep it short" to build an effective business communication system. Just like you can't succeed when someone tells you to build a better house. Better than what? For what? Where? We all have an idea of what a house might be, but the concept *house*, like the overloaded and much-loathed generic concept *meeting*, isn't very useful when it's time to draft up a plan.

The Meeting Taxonomy defines 16 types of business meetings. For each one, there are many levels of mastery to achieve. For example, the person leading a Training meeting may have been thrown into the room because they have some job experience and happen to be available, or you could find yourself in a Training led by someone with a doctoral degree in Instructional Design and 20 years' experience.

In this book, you'll learn that these meeting types exist, you'll learn what each one does, and you'll get just enough guidance that, should you find yourself suddenly in charge of one of those meetings, you'll know where to start. To extend the previous hammer/house-building metaphor—while you won't learn how to become a master carpenter, you will learn that carpentry and plumbing and architecture and structural engineering are all specialties that work together to make a cohesive whole. You'll learn enough to improve your practice in those areas where you have experience and how to start learning about those where you don't.

More importantly, you'll learn that those beliefs you wrote down about meetings earlier, back when we looked at the doom loop and the belief cycle, may only apply to a tiny sampling of the meetings in your life. I'll go into detail about each of the 16 types of meetings in Part 4. For now, let's look at the major factors that require us to approach each kind of meeting differently and get a quick overview of the taxonomy.

The Differentiators:
Intention, Format, and Participation Profile

Meeting Intention

The intention behind a meeting is most often expressed as the meeting's purpose and desired outcomes. In other words, why do people run this kind of meeting? What is it meant to create?

There are two major outcomes for any meeting: a human connection and a work product (more on this in the next chapter). When people first try to figure out all the kinds of meetings they run, they often look only at the work product. This sets up the conditions for bad advice.

For example, the intention of a Decision Making meeting is:

1. A decision (the work product) and
2. Commitment to that decision from the people in the room (a human connection outcome).

It is very easy to run a Decision Making meeting that achieves the first part (a decision) but fails to achieve the second (commitment), and therefore will fail to deliver the expected business result. If you have ever been in a meeting where you were discussing a decision you thought had already been made, you know this to be true.

We need to consider the meeting purpose and both kinds of outcomes when describing the meeting intention.

Defining your meeting's special purpose

Purpose: Why you're meeting.
State the meeting's purpose as a verb. It describes the main action. Examples:

- To decide on next steps for the big project.
- To learn more about each other and see if there are opportunities for working together.
- To share more about our services and answer questions.
- To brainstorm a list of possible locations for our next event.

Desired Outcomes: *What you will get* at the end of the meeting.
State the outcomes as nouns. Examples:

- Solutions for any project blocks and a list of next steps.
- A list of opportunities for collaboration.
- A date for our next meeting.
- Answers to your questions and documented next steps.
- A list of possible event locations to research further.

When you schedule a meeting, always include the purpose and desired outcomes in the invitation. If you can't figure these out, then your meeting probably won't line up with our taxonomy and probably will be a waste of time. Cancel it or work harder!

The Format

When I first started looking at meeting format, I used a standard breakdown of "formal" and "informal" to help distinguish between board meetings and team meetings, but I abandoned that pretty quickly because it doesn't hold up in practice.

In practice, I found that while boards have rules that they must follow by law, and they generally do, this didn't necessarily mean that the majority of the meeting followed any very strict structure. Many board meetings actually include lots of free-form conversation, which is then briefly formalized to address the legal requirements.

By contrast, I would have considered an Agile team's daily stand-up an informal meeting. Heck, I run those, and I don't always wear shoes to them. But despite this casual, social informality, the daily stand-up runs according to a very clear set of rules. Every update includes just three things, each person's update is no longer than two minutes, and we never *ever* problem-solve during the meeting.

It turns out that formal and informal told me more about a participant's *perception of social anxiety* than it did about the type or format of the meeting. I experience stand-ups and interviews as informal, largely because I'm in charge and am confident of my role there. I doubt everyone I interview considers it an informal chat, though, and I imagine our stand-up would feel pretty uptight to someone who wasn't used to it.

Instead of formal and informal, I found that **the strength of the governing rituals and rules** had a clearer impact on the meeting's success. By this measure, the daily stand-up is highly ritualistic, board meetings and brainstorming sessions abide by governing rules but not rigidly so, and initial sales calls and team meetings have very few prescribed boundaries.

This still didn't quite explain all the variation I saw in meeting format, however. When I looked at the project status meeting, I realized it shared some characteristics with the board meeting, but these project meetings aren't governed by rules and laws in the same way. And while the intention for project updates is always the same—to share information about project work status and manage emerging change—there's a ton of variation in how people run project status updates. Some teams are very formal and rigid, while others are nearly unstructured. This means our "governing rituals" criteria didn't work here.

The major characteristic all project status updates share, and that you'll also see with board meetings, is a dislike of surprises. No project manager wants to show up to the weekly update and get surprised by how far off track the team is, or how they've decided to take the project in some new direction. Board members hate this too. For these meetings, surprises are bad!

Surprises are bad for project updates, but other meetings are held expressly for the purpose of finding something new. The innovation meeting, the get-to-know you meeting, the Problem Solving meeting all hope for serendipity. Going into those meetings, people don't know what they'll get, but they work to maximize their chances of something super cool showing up by the time they're done.

So, when categorizing meetings based on format, I looked at both:

1. The strength of governing rules or rituals.
2. The role of serendipity and tolerance for surprise.

The Expected Participation Profile

Finally, I felt that *who* was expected to attend and *how* they were meant to interact had a major impact on what needed to happen for that meeting to succeed.

The question behind these criteria is: what kind of *reasonable assumptions* can we make about how well these people will work together to achieve the desired goal?

Remember: every meeting has both a human connection outcome and a work outcome.

This has many significant design impacts. For example, in meetings between people that know each other already, you can spend less time on building connection. We don't do introductions in the daily huddle; we assume the team handled that beforehand.

In meetings where the work product is arguably far more important than the human connection, it's not always necessary for people to like one another or even remember each others' names as long as the process used gets them to the goal in the end. A formal incident investigation does not need the person under investigation to know and like the people on the review board to achieve its goal.

By contrast, some meetings only go well after the team establishes mutual respect and healthy working relationships. The design of these meetings must nurture and enhance those relationships if they are to achieve the desired outcomes. Weekly team meetings often fail because people run them like project status updates instead of team meetings, focusing too heavily on content at the expense of connection, and their teams are weaker for it.

After much slotting and wrangling, I found there were three ways our assumptions about the people in the room influenced the meeting type.

1. **The expected audience.** Here the options were:

- A known set of people all familiar with one another. Team meetings fit here.
- A group of people brought together to fit a need. Kickoffs, ideation sessions, and Workshops all fit here.
- Two distinct groups, with a clear us/them or me/them dynamic, meeting in response to an event. Interviews fit here, as do Broadcast meetings and negotiations.

2. **The expected leadership and participation styles.** Every type of meeting has a "default" leader responsible for the design. This is usually the boss or manager, a facilitator, or the person who asked for the meeting. Most also have an expected interaction style for participants that, when encouraged, gets the best results. Some meetings are collaborative, some very conversational—like One-on-Ones—and some are very formal—almost hostile. Still others, like an All-Hands Broadcast, don't require any active participation at all.

3. **The centrality of relationships.** Finally, I looked at whether the meeting's success depended on the group working well together. Nearly every meeting that teams repeat as part of their day-to-day operations works best when team members get along, and becomes torturous when they don't. Outside of regular team meetings, there are also meetings designed explicitly to establish positive relationships, such as the first Introduction, interviews, and team chartering Workshops. In all these cases, a successful design must take relationships into account.

Now, given that extended lead-up, what types did I end up with?

The 16 Types of Meetings

I've broken the list into three main groups below. You'll find details for each type in Part 4.

Cadence Meetings

Organizations use Cadence meetings to **review performance, renew team connections, and refine their approach** based on what they've learned. All of these meetings involve an established group of people, with perhaps the occasional guest. Most happen at regular and predictable intervals, making up the strategic and operational cadence of the organization.

These meetings all follow a regularized pattern: Each meeting works basically like the last one, and teams know what to expect. Because the participants and the format are all known, these meetings often require less up-front planning and less specialized facilitation expertise to succeed.

Cadence Meetings include:

1. Team Cadence Meetings
2. Progress Checks
3. One-on-Ones
4. Action Review Meetings
5. Governance Cadence Meetings

Catalyst Meetings

New ideas, new plans, projects to start, problems to solve, and decisions to make—these meetings change an organization's work. Catalyst meetings are all scheduled as needed and include the people the organizers feel to be best suited for achieving the meeting goals. They succeed when following a thoughtful meeting design and regularly fail when people "wing it."

Because these meetings are scheduled as needed with whomever is needed, there is a lot more variation in format. This is the realm of participatory engagement, decision and sensemaking activities, and when the group gets larger, trained facilitation.

Catalyst Meetings include:

1. Idea Generation Meetings
2. Planning Meetings
3. Workshops
4. Problem Solving Meetings
5. Decision Making Meetings

Learn and Influence Meetings

These meetings are all designed to transfer information and intention from one person or group to another. They are scheduled by the person who wants something with the people they want to influence or get something from.

On the surface, that sounds Machiavellian, but the intention here is rarely nefarious. Instead, these meetings often indicate a genuine interest in learning, sharing, and finding ways to come together for mutual benefit.

Because each of these meetings involves some form of social evaluation, the format and rituals have more to do with etiquette than regulations or work product, although this is not always the case.

Learn and Influence Meetings include:

1. Sensemaking Meetings
2. Introductions
3. Issue Resolution Meetings
4. Community of Practice Meetings
5. Training Sessions
6. Broadcast Meetings

Meetings that Don't Fit into Any Category

This taxonomy has more types than your garden-variety meeting taxonomy, and yet, not all meetings fit nicely here. I hereby reserve the right to continue learning, and I acknowledge up front that it's very possible we'll need to update the taxonomy in the future.

People tell me a lot of stories about their work, and I'm finely attuned to noticing how many meetings appear in stories that aren't necessarily "about" meetings. While I freely admit that my taxonomy may prove incomplete, so far those meetings I hear about that don't fit this taxonomy have not inspired any changes to the 16 Meeting Types.

For example, at a recent gathering I asked friends for any fresh meeting stories and was awarded with this taxonomy-defying gem.

My friend—we'll call her Amanda, although that's not her real name—works at a nonprofit that employs five full-time staff. Recently, the board hired a charismatic new executive director to lead the organization.

"He's not the type who would ever use an agenda. Ever," Amanda says.

(Most of the stories people tell me about *Meetings Gone Bad!* start with this disapproving condemnation of those who venture forth agenda-less. They always sound quietly shocked, but I know they probably do it too. Everyone goes agenda-free when they think they can get away with it.)

Amanda continues, "And he shows up late *all the time*." Knowing nods ripple through the room. We all know his type. The looks on people's faces seem to suggest: "This leader can't be trusted. We don't want his type in charge of anything more complicated than a cactus. A small one!"

"So, in December, my new boss wrote the strategic plan, and got it approved by the board."

"Wait," I say. "He wrote the plan *by himself?*"

"Yep."

Gasps this time. That's taking it to a new low.

"In it," Amanda continues, "He decided that we were going to change the organization's name to make it more exciting to millennials. He'd asked the staff about this name change before and none of us thought it was a good idea, but he put it in there anyway. And the board approved it."

"Oh no."

"Oh yes," Amanda says. "So I heard about it, and I told him we needed to have a staff meeting. He said he wanted to tidy up the minutes from the board meeting first so the staff would understand it all better." Eyes roll. "And I'm like, 'Okay, so let me know you're ready, because we're running out of time.' We had two weeks left in the year, and our office closes the week of Christmas."

Amanda takes a deep breath, gathers herself, and goes on. "A few days later he still hadn't called the meeting, so I asked what was up. He said it was going to be too hard to get us all together—mind you there are only five of us, remember?—so instead of a meeting, he would just send out the new strategic plan by email on Friday. The Friday before we all leave for 10 days. And then, he didn't actually send it until *Saturday,* when everyone was officially gone."

This sinks in. "Wow," I replied. "So did you have the meeting when you got back after the holidays?"

"Yep," Amanda says. "He came to me a week after we got back and said he thought we'd better have a meeting. No joke. So we finally got everyone together—some of us in the office and two others on the phone—for this meeting. Of course, he didn't send an agenda for it, and clearly he had no idea what he was going to say. We all show up, and he says: 'Well, I assume you've all had a chance to see the new strategic plan, and I figured I'd get us together to see if there are any questions.'

"That was it! No explanation, no going over the plan—he didn't even mention the name change! So my coworker Sandy just ripped into him. She's been there 11 years, he's been there eight months, and he never consulted her even once. She started asking, 'Do you regret how you created this plan without discussing it with us? Do you realize how you've disrespected everyone in the office and undermined our ability to work for you? Do you regret the way you've communicated this so far?' and on and on. I'm sitting next to this guy, and he's just shrinking. It was really painful to watch—like, super painful—and I'm actually starting to feel a tiny bit bad for him."

Amanda pauses and looks me in the eye. "Sandy stopped, and it got quiet. Finally, this guy looked at me and said, 'Well, I don't know. Amanda, you were in some of those meetings. What do you think about it?'"

We gasped. In that moment, Amanda's sympathy for her new boss evaporated. She spent the next two weeks convincing her colleagues that, no, she wasn't behind the plan and, no, she hadn't betrayed them. That new boss, though—he could kiss any support he thought he was getting from Amanda goodbye.

That was offered to me as a particularly harrowing meeting story, and it is a truly awful example. I retell it here because it's also a good example for a few more reasons.

1. The problem in this story is not a meeting problem.

Well, at least not primarily. The real problem in this story is an incompetent leader. Clearly this fellow doesn't realize that leading an organization actually means leading the people who make the organization go. No people, no organization! The real problem here could be greatly improved by even a handful of quality meetings. Sadly, folks who are the root cause of most terrible meetings are also the least likely to recognize this.

2. It's not a unique story.

Crappy, but not rare. That's why everyone in my group of friends knew his type. We've all encountered those people whose unique snowflake brilliance cannot be confined to anything as "boring" as an agenda. They believe they have transcended agendas and plans. If only the rest of us could keep up!

3. This meeting doesn't fit in the taxonomy because it had no clear intention.

The boss in this story is meeting because he knows he needs to. Amanda told him they needed a meeting, the board probably suggested it, and in his gut somewhere, he knew he had to at least go through the motions. He obviously did not want to go to this meeting; it was a CYA meeting only. (CYA = Cover Your Ass, and is one of the more important business acronyms to know!)

If Amanda's boss had wanted to explain the plan to the staff, the reasoning behind it, and the next steps, that could have been a Broadcast meeting. There isn't much interaction or participation expected from staff in a Broadcast meeting, as these are typically used to share things that are a "done deal," but the presenter is expected to at least do some presenting.

If Amanda's boss had wanted input and to get the team started on implementation planning, they could have had a Planning meeting.

If he had acknowledged how upset everyone was and had the courage to take that on, he could have had an Issue Resolution meeting.

Instead, he led one of the many meetings run every day that fall into the soupy mess of meetings which defy categorization. They aren't held for a particularly clear reason, and they're often led by people who don't necessarily want to be there themselves. As one friend told me, "All my managers talk about how much they hate meetings. It's weird, because that seems to be mostly what they do!"

This is another reason why I recommend teams work to banish the word "meeting" from their calendars. It's a critical-thinking exercise. When you are forced to use a more specific name than "meeting," you automatically think through what else you might call this thing. Then, with the Taxonomy as a handy cheat sheet, you can get to the clarity required to make that time worthwhile.

Clarity about why you're gathering is the first and most important step toward running a better meeting. In the next chapter, we'll look at the other steps the experts from both research and practice agree matter most.

One Last Note

There is a second meeting in my friend's story: the board meeting in which the board approved the much-loathed strategic plan. For her organization, the board meeting is where the action is. That board meeting may have been well-run, it may have been enjoyable, and it definitely resulted in meeting notes. Unfortunately, the people most informed about the organization's operations and the people most impacted by the board's decisions, namely the organization's staff, were not invited and did not get a copy of those notes.

This lack of transparency is another major contributor to a poisonous meeting culture. Even in organizations where everyone claims to hate meetings, you will find people maneuvering to get access to a meeting they weren't invited to. You see people head to every meeting and never, ever turn down an invitation, for fear that they'll miss something important. We know that even when our meetings are lousy, they also make or break our future.

Part 2

Mastering the Work in Meetings

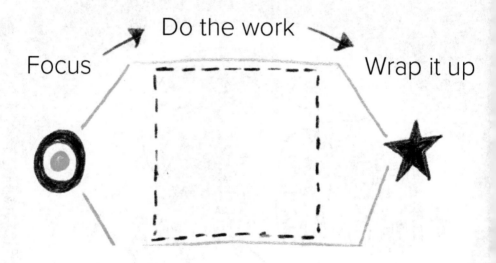

Focus

Do the work

Wrap it up

PACIFIC BOLD

The team at Pacific Bold now has far fewer meetings on the calendar. The weekly team meetings are gone, as are the internal project checks. There are no more One-on-Ones or Design Reviews, and the All-Hands scheduled for the last week of the month was canceled too. Everyone has a lot more undivided time on their calendar, which in theory they could use to focus on creative work. Everyone also has a lot more email in their inbox, and *a lot* more instant messaging to keep up with. A few of the more sensitive types are developing a nervous twitch whenever they hear a notification ding.

Reviews are mixed. There is a balance to be found here that they haven't hit yet, and it's pretty clear that text chatting all day long is not the solution they need.

They aren't eager to reschedule the canceled meetings, though, because the ones they kept on the calendar aren't working well. They're still meeting with customers and vendors, of course, and there was no legal way to cancel the board meeting. Now that the customer meetings are some of the only ones they have, it's more obvious than ever that these are not good meetings.

So they have a lot fewer meetings now, but they still aren't great. More importantly, only a handful of people are billing significantly more hours. The rest seem to have traded non-billable meeting time for non-billable time spent typing at each other.

Angie suggests that they establish a rule forbidding all non-work-related communication. "Stop wasting time on animated cat GIFs!" Angie grumbles. Charla suspects this would just push the problem somewhere else.

"No. That's a sucker's game of whack-a-mole," Charla says. "We need to rethink *how we work*."

PB

CHAPTER 5

The Core Competencies

I used to believe that following best practices—agendas, time keeping, minutes, etc.—was *the key* to running a quality meeting. Like many dearly held beliefs, when examined under the researchers' spotlight of critical inquiry, the flaws in this thinking became clear.

This is good news! While the research on what makes for a good meeting is young, it exists, it's accessible, and it's growing. This was not the case when I started my journey. Personally, I'm delighted I don't have to guess so much anymore.

You can divide the research findings into two major categories. We'll anoint these with the TLAs (Three-Letter Acronyms) you see below.

PMQ: Perceived Meeting Quality

PMQ looks at what makes people *feel* like the meeting they just attended was worthwhile. This research focuses on the practices and behaviors within individual meetings as isolated events. In other words, PMQ is concerned with what it takes to make the work done in meetings *feel* successful. This one is all about perception. Chapter 7 focuses on PMQ.

NPI: Net Positive Impact

NPI examines how what we do in meetings impacts what happens outside of meetings. In other words, NPI looks at how we can successfully use meetings in our overall work. NPI is all about the ripple effects of meetings on your organization. We'll pay special attention to NPI in chapter 9, but really, it's a central theme for the whole book.

In the coming pages, I'll highlight some studies that show the specific things you can do to increase PMQ and NPI. For those of you who prefer to cut to the chase, I've summarized the key guidelines that fall out of these studies in this list of core competencies.

The
Core Competencies
of High-Performing
Meetings

Train everyone who meets in your organization in these effective habits.

1. Know the meeting's purpose and desired outcome.

2. Structure meetings to achieve the desired outcome.

3. Respect the time invested.

4. Structure meetings for engagement.

5. Take visible notes.

6. Publish meeting records where everyone can find them.

At first blush, this list doesn't look all that different from any other list you may have seen on how to run better meetings. That's because it's not. The generic best practices are useful at a basic level, and they're important to put in place as a foundation. This foundation has a few unique features, though, that make it subtly more sound than similar lists.

Let's briefly explore each of the Core Competencies in turn.

1. Know the meeting's purpose and desired outcome.

To run an effective meeting, you must be specific. Clarify the purpose and desired outcomes. Why are you meeting, and what is the meeting meant to accomplish? This first competency makes success possible. Without this step, everything else is form without function. Your meeting may look pretty, but it doesn't do anything useful.

The next three competencies improve the efficiency and collaborative nature of the work done in the meeting, increasing Perceived Meeting Quality, or the way that people feel about the meeting.

2. Structure meetings to achieve the desired outcome.

Here's a subtle difference from your run-of-the-mill best practices list. Notice that I'm not saying you need to provide an agenda. For many meetings, that's a good idea, but it isn't always necessary. Every meeting, however, should use a process that helps the team achieve the goal, at the right time, in the right space, and with the appropriate people. All of these factors make up the structure of the meeting. Chapter 6 goes into more detail about meeting structure.

3. Respect the time invested.

Engage in temporal courtesy: show respect for the time invested. Starting and ending on time matters, as does sharing the time within the meeting fairly. Perhaps more importantly, considerate leaders work to schedule meetings that minimize disruption to other work, avoid inconveniencing unnecessary attendees, and rarely make people attempt to look professional at awkward times. Time is a major human currency we must spend wisely. We'll visit this theme in Chapters 7, 8 and 9.

4. Structure meetings for engagement.

Use teamwork to make meetings work: structure every meeting for engagement. Know how everyone present will contribute to the outcome.

This increases both the PMQ and the NPI. People enjoy meetings they actively participate in more, and when everyone actively participates, the meeting often creates a higher positive impact on the organizations. Chapter 8 focuses on what meeting engagement looks like and how to get everyone engaged.

5. Take visible notes.

This may be the first competency that you haven't seen before. It's also one of those master tips that trained facilitators know to be a prerequisite for success. Posting a visible agenda and taking notes that everyone can see makes progress visible; everyone in the meeting can see where you are in the process and what you've accomplished. Visual agendas and note taking improve engagement, clarify outcomes, and increase the meeting's potential positive impact.

6. Publish meeting records where everyone can find them.

When you centralize meeting records, the organization owns the results. Centralized notes mean that people no longer feel obligated to go to every meeting for fear they'll miss out. It also means that the group no longer needs to rely on fallible memories and each person's interpretation to know what was decided. This final competency is all about Net Positive Impact. Central records make it possible to build on results, reuse successful meeting designs, and keep meetings small. Perhaps equally important, transparency about what happens in meetings helps everyone recognize that this isn't a time for personal politics, but rather the work of the organization done on behalf of and belonging collectively to the group. It's not my meeting—it's our meeting.

CHAPTER 6

Functional Meeting Structure

Previously, I asserted that meetings should "quickly create shared perspective." We meet to make sense of that elephant in the dark. Let's unpack that one further: *What do you get* from teams that have a shared perspective?

Shared perspective produces:

1. Clarity regarding the work.

- What's done.
- What remains.
- Who's doing what next.
- Which option the team is going with.
- What problems need to be solved.
- Which questions still need answers.

2. The seeds of trust.

- When you hear other people's ideas.
- When other people listen to your ideas.
- When you learn about the context of other people's work.
- When you learn about other people's lives beyond work.
- When other people make commitments.
- When other people report back on completed commitments.
- When the agreements you make and commitments you keep are appreciated by others.

To achieve this shared perspective, you need two things: Clarity about why you're meeting and what you need to accomplish (the purpose and desired outcomes), and a structured plan for achieving that goal as a group. When a meeting fails to create this shared perspective, it's usually because the meeting wasn't structured to do so—which is sad, really, because once you understand the basic framework needed for any productive meeting, there's just no reason to ever spend time in an unproductive meeting again.

The Essentials of Meeting Structure

Meeting structure is a fancy way of saying the plan for running the meeting. Structure covers all the *how*:

- How you'll invite people.
- How you'll arrange the meeting room.
- How people will introduce themselves.
- How you'll organize the topics.
- How you'll guide the discussion.
- How you'll review presentations.
- How the group will make decisions.
- How you'll capture results.

...and so on.

Using the appropriate meeting structure for the type of meeting you're running prevents dysfunction and ensures results. For example, how you run a One-on-One with your mentor will look quite different than the board meeting or a crisis resolution with a major client. That said, **every functional business meeting shares a common, underlying structure.** You can think of this underlying structure as a basic outline for a functional meeting.

When you understand this core structure, two things become possible.

1. You will plan better meetings.
2. You will make unplanned meetings better.

Meetings 101: Creating a Mental Model

If there were ever to be college major in leading effective meetings, coursework should start here.

Why start with structure? Because research has debunked the idea that "natural talent" is all you need to excel. Instead, expertise and mastery come from deliberate practice and having a mental model readily available for tackling the work in front of you. This chapter will help you build a basic mental model you can use to structure any meeting.

To understand this basic structure, let's start way up at the stupid obvious level. From here, we see that for each meeting there is a before, a during, and an after.

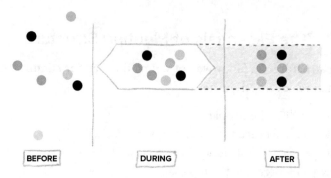

Before: everyone doing their own thing. After: aligned and moving forward together.

Zooming in, we can see the structure of the meeting itself. Every meeting has a beginning, middle, and an end.

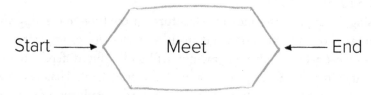

Meetings start, then later they end. Still pretty obvious.

What distinguishes a functional meeting from a waste of time?

In a meeting that works, the team focuses 20%-30% of the meeting time on the beginning and end phases. Rather than just blips in time, the start and end of a meeting are dedicated phases in the process. A meeting that is all middle doesn't work as well.

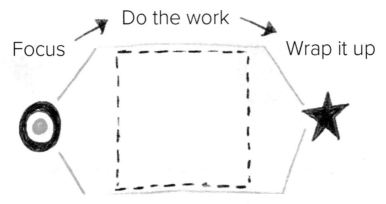

Focus · Do the work · Wrap it up

20%–30% of the total meeting time spent opening and wrapping up

The 3 Non-Negotiable Phases
of a Meeting That Works

At the most basic, rock-bottom level, a meeting needs these three distinct phases.

1. **Focus and Become Present.**
2. **Do the Work.**
3. **Wrap It Up.**

At this *minimal functional level,* we're talking about a meeting that isn't a total waste of time. Teams that go through these three stages *will* achieve a shared result. They may not have any fun doing it, but at least they'll get something out of the time spent. Here's what that looks like.

Phase 1: Focus and become present.

The meeting begins by getting everyone into the conversation at the same time, transitioning them successfully from wherever they were before onto the task at hand.

It starts with focus. A functional meeting must secure the attention of the team before the work can begin. This is why many meetings begin with some form of welcome, roll call, or other activity designed for everyone in the meeting to literally declare themselves "here." A focused opening ushers the group into the rest of the meeting, assembling the team together and guiding them into the main show.

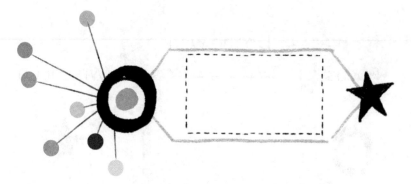

A focused opening pulls the team's attention into the meeting.

People who are multitasking, preoccupied, or otherwise "not really there" cannot participate effectively in creating or understanding the work of the group. Unfortunately as a meeting leader, you can't guarantee that the people in your meeting will really "be present" for the discussion. If you fail to clearly open the meeting, however, *or to even ask for this presence up front*, you greatly increase the likelihood that the meeting will fail. We live in an incredibly busy and distracted society. If you don't do the work to transition people into the meeting and engage them in the topic, don't assume they'll do it on their own. They won't.

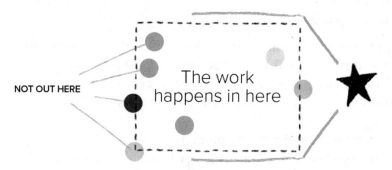

Without a clear opening, some people never bring their attention into the meeting.

Connect with Why You Need to Connect

It used to be hard for me to understand why I needed to care so much about how I start meetings. I find small talk incredibly frustrating if it lasts more than a few minutes, and I loathe getting-to-know-you games like "two truths and a lie." Why start off a meeting by lying to each other about non-work-related trivia? I find time spent this way both unprofessional and counterproductive. My favorite way to begin used to be, "Everyone here? Great. First topic…" and then I'd drive to get everyone done and out of the room as quickly as possible. The best meeting is a short one, right?

My original approach to running better meetings was about eliminating errors and waste. Reduce wasted time, reduce unnecessary presentations, reduce poor decision making, reduce repetitive discussions, and most importantly, reduce the number of meetings altogether. Can you tell I spent some time in project management?

I've since learned that my favorite "all-business, no chit-chat approach" was also shockingly counterproductive. Now I always begin meetings spending some time creating interpersonal connections, and I've learned a host of techniques so I can tailor these openings to the type of meeting and the group. Why the change?

Partially, this change of heart is informed by research findings from cognitive science. We now know that task switching—the mental work involved in turning your focused attention from one thing to another—is mentally taxing and takes time. We also know that people experiencing stress have limited access to the higher-reasoning functions of the brain, and running to make a meeting on time or sitting with a group of people you may not know well are both stressful experiences. Need to report a missed crucial deadline to your team? That's a situation perfectly designed to trigger the fight-flight-or-freeze emotions that make clear thinking inaccessible.

Knowing this, leaders can begin a meeting by *clearing*. Clearing is the practice of intentionally letting go of whatever other work or concerns you bring with you into the meeting and that interfere with your ability to fully engage in the discussion. Some teams clear by chatting, some do it by explicitly asking if anyone has something they need to clear, and others begin important meetings with a short meditation. Before you scoff, the meditation example comes from a team of investment bankers. This is not just hippy-dippy stuff—each of these approaches has been demonstrated by research to help set up favorable conditions necessary for critical thinking in the brain.

Like many of the deeper truths concerning how people work and what it takes to successfully connect, our ancestors knew the importance of this dedicated time at the beginning of a meeting even without the scientific benefit of the hormone readings from saliva swabs used by modern researchers.

One indigenous community in South America starts every meeting breathing deeply and "taking a moment for the soul to arrive." Quaker meetings begin similarly. Everyone enters in silence and sits in silence, listening quietly for the presence of the divine. Meetings in feudal Europe often began with those assembled marking out a clear meeting space— ringed with swords and lances placed in the ground—within which every- one spent a long moment in silence before joining in the communal pledge to maintain peace within the circle. Like the giving of thanks before a meal, these moments of clearing and connection at the beginning of a meeting bring an important focus and clarity into the room.

The cognitive psychologist Gary Klein stated elegantly and simply that increasing performance is not just a matter of reducing errors. Instead, he wrote:

> Increased performance = reducing errors + increasing insights

In other words, while you can make something better by making fewer errors, you can also make it better—and more joyful—by adding more that's insightful, engaging, and positive by nature. To do that, you have to start by connecting.

Phase 2: Do the work.
Once everyone becomes present, they can work together to get aligned. When we draw this part of the meeting, it can look a little messy.

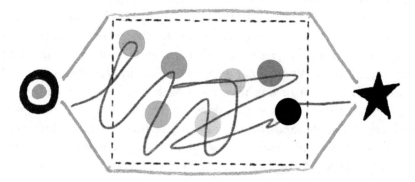

Lots of back and forth during a meeting.

Functional meetings result in some tidy outcomes: a decision, a plan, a set of action items, a date for the next meeting, and a feeling of time well spent. The creation of that outcome requires everyone in the group to move from whatever they understood the situation to be beforehand to this new shared understanding. They need to assemble the elephant. There are questions to answer, conflicts to unravel, egos to navigate, and a smattering of "aha!" moments to enjoy.

People arrive at conclusions at different rates, and as new ideas emerge, the group can get pulled back into the soup. While you can work to tidy up this part of the process, the creation of alignment will always be a bit messy.

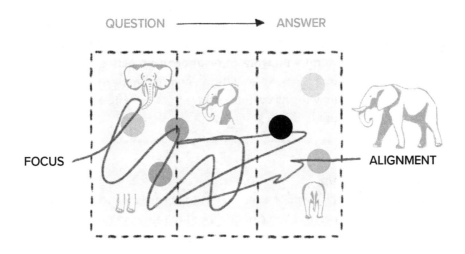

People start to see the full picture at different rates.

Every meeting I've ever seen has a "do the work" phase. Groups always manage to *talk* about something in a meeting, but they don't necessarily hear what's said (because they weren't really present) or walk away with any noticeable result. Meetings fail when they *only* focus on doing the work. That's why functional meetings always end with a clear review of what the group just created.

"TIME OUT!" I HEAR YOU CRY.

"Work doesn't happen in meetings! Meetings are where we go to avoid work. Meetings are what keeps us from getting our real work done. I do all my work outside of meetings!"

Oh, you Maker, you. For you, I have two replies:

1. Rethink what you consider "work."

Of course tangible production matters—but only if you're producing something useful, valuable, and/or desired. You need to know what to produce, how to do it, by when, with whom, and for whom, and these things often get decided in meetings. If no one does the *deciding and coordinating work,* your "real" work goes nowhere.

2. If there is literally no work to be done in a meeting, cancel it. This is not a book on how to over-think complicated ways to waste time. It's about how to structure meetings to make sure they do the work they're meant to do.

Phase 3: Wrap it up.

Remember, the *whole point* of a meeting is to ensure the group walks out with a shared perspective. You can only be sure this worked if you ask.

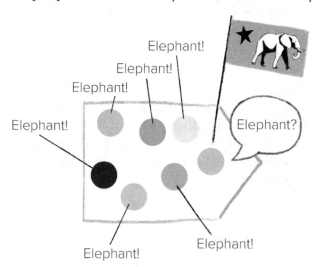

Elephant!

Elephant!

Elephant!

Elephant!

Elephant?

Elephant!

Elephant!

Don't assume you have an agreement. Ask and be sure.

Before the group leaves, decisions need to be restated, each person must confirm that they understand what just happened, and more importantly, that they know *what will happen next* as a result.

It's an elephant! Let's take him back to the savanna.

Many groups who *think* they achieved their meeting goal skip this step, especially when they're rushed for time. Groups that skip this step assume the decision they think they heard was clear to everyone else. Close perhaps, but unlikely.

Hmm. It looks like they don't have the same idea about that elephant after all.

And when a group fails to check commitments at the end of a meeting, each person leaves with whatever they felt was most important and heads off in the direction that seems best to them. Individuals take responsibility for whatever actions they think they own and remember only the details that directly and immediately impact them. Even if they share the same picture, they may not share the same beliefs about what they're supposed to do about it.

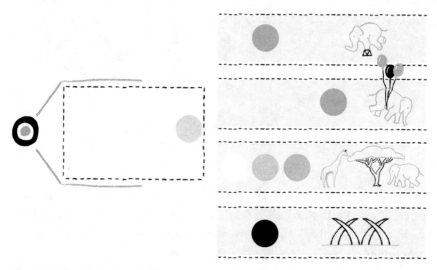

Because they didn't explicitly agree on next steps in the meeting, each person may have different ideas about what to do with an elephant.

People often assume that "someone else" will take on any tasks identified in the meeting, then quickly forget most of the discussion. This can leave your elephant just sitting there in the dark, mucking up the place and waiting to be set free. Not ideal.

From Functional to Successful

So *at a minimum*, every meeting must start by getting the group really "present" for the discussion before they can work together. Then, once the work is done, the meeting must end by wrapping up to make it clear exactly what's supposed to happen next.

That's really a minimum, though. More successful meetings approach these three phases with vigor! Successful meetings:

1. **Engage!** Go beyond "present" and get the group involved!
2. **Co-Create!** Don't just do the work and punch the clock—work together to co-create something new! Combine unique ideas and insights to create a shared perspective that's more complete, more ambitious, and more everything than what any one person could do on their own.
3. **Commit!** Don't just recite a list of outcomes! Commit to acting on the agreements made in the meeting. Every action has an owner, and every owner commits to seeing that action through. Meetings that end with a new shared perspective *and* strong commitments to act upon this outcome are not a waste of time.

Symptoms of a Mangled Meeting Structure

What does it look like when a meeting lacks this basic functional structure? Poor structure is behind many of the common problems you'll see.

Signs of Failure to Focus at the Beginning

Problems you'll see when there is no opening or "ask" for engagement at the beginning of the meeting:

- People using cell phones or checking email during the meeting.
- People who don't speak up or participate; who aren't really "there."
- Confusion and false starts, as people try to figure out why they're there.
- Sloppy and/or uncomfortable moments when it's not clear where the chit-chat ends and business begins.

Signs of Failure to Structure the Work

Problems you see when the process for doing the work isn't clear:

- Rambling discussion; people talk and talk.
- Inconclusive discussion.
- Running over time.
- New topics pop up.
- Teams revert to safe answers or give up.
- The creation of long lists without owners or priorities.

Signs of Failure to Wrap Up

Problems you see when the meeting isn't wrapped up at the end:

- No written communication afterwards.
- Only the people in the meeting know what happened.
- Nothing much happens afterwards or changes as a result.
- Agreements made in the meeting don't stick.
- You have the same conversation with the same group again later.

Does any of this look familiar?

Meetings at Pacific Bold suffered from all of these problems at one point or another. Most lacked any semblance of structure. No rituals, no agenda, no stated purpose, and no written results.

Not all the meetings were structure-free, though. Angie and her team of project managers ran infamous project status updates that always had an agenda, but those agendas didn't include room for "extra nonsense" like a friendly check-in. If the rest of the organization was going to be critical, they may have pointed out that these agendas didn't really have room for all the supposedly *very important* details they did include.

Every week, the project managers ran each team through a rigorous gauntlet of reporting: every deadline, risk, issue, open action item, and possible thing which could impact either the budget or the timeline was checked and updated in a spreadsheet.

Yes, these meetings had an agenda. They also always ran long and were universally loathed. You could see each project manager visibly steel themselves at the start. They believed they were a brave squad of warriors fighting the unpleasant but necessary battle to keep it all together for the team. Each one dreaded the meeting but took solace in the knowledge that if it wasn't for their valiant sacrifice, the whole organization would fall apart.

Angie was right. People were thrilled when these meetings were canceled.

PB

Personally, I've worked with a number of smart, dedicated project and program managers in my career who lead meetings like the ones led at Pacific Bold. These managers are like bulldogs with spreadsheets—tenacious, dedicated, and committed to getting the job done. This kind of meeting seems even to be the recommended best practice of several prominent project management methodologies.

Unfortunately, this command-and-report style is terribly dehumanizing. It's designed to serve the needs of the spreadsheet and the reporting structure, making sure all the rows are up to date and the higher-ups get their numbers. It doesn't serve the people doing the work particularly well.

Tool: A Single Topic Agenda

Here's a simple, useful example of the basic structure at work.

What It Is

The Single Topic Agenda provides a quick way to turn any unstructured short meeting into a decent use of time. If you watch carefully, you'll see experienced facilitators and leaders follow this basic structure in nearly every work conversation they have.

The Single Topic Agenda comes in especially handy when:

- You're in a working session with literally a single topic, e.g., confirming plans for a conference, or coordinating schedules.
- You know the meeting's purpose but don't have time to pull together a full plan.
- You find yourself invited to a mystery meeting, where the purpose isn't clear and it's not your meeting to cancel.

How It Works

The Single Topic Agenda follows the basic structure underlying all well-run meetings. A quick refresher:

1. Focus and Become Present
2. Do the Work
3. Wrap It Up

When you share this in an agenda, it looks like this:

1. Welcome (or Introductions)
2. Discussion
3. Review and Next Steps

Whether you're the meeting leader or an invited participant, all it takes to follow these steps is asking a few questions and capturing a few notes.

Step-by-Step Instructions

Step 1: Welcome.
When the meeting starts, ask: How much time do we all have?
It's easy for an agenda-free meeting to get sloppy and run over time. Without any structure to the conversation, people can get into all kinds of interesting tangents, only to discover they have something really cool to work on just as time runs out.

You can help prevent this up front by asking: Is the scheduled time fixed, or is it okay if the meeting runs long? Or, if you must end on time yourself, saying so up front helps everyone focus on achieving something before time runs out.

Then ask: What would you consider a good result from this conversation?
Put them together, and it sounds something like this.

"We have 30 minutes scheduled today. I want to be mindful of time; do you need to end right on time today?" or

"We have 30 minutes scheduled today, and I need to end on time to fulfill other commitments."

Then:

"In the time we have together, what would you most like to see happen? What would a really useful result from this meeting be for you?" or

"I'm hoping we can achieve X in the time we have. Is that also what you'd like see, or are you hoping for something else?"

The Critical Step for Success: Write down what people say!
You do not need permission to take notes in a meeting, and you should not expect anyone else to do it for you if they haven't volunteered already. When you write down what everyone wants to achieve—Bam!—you've just clarified the purpose and desired outcome for your meeting.

Step 2: Discuss.

Once you have a better idea of what everyone wants to accomplish, you can dive into the discussion. Watch the time to make sure you can wrap up in time for step three.

Step 3: Next steps.

In the last five to 10 minutes, ask: Did we get the result we wanted?

Because you asked about this result earlier and wrote it down, you can now reference your notes and check this one with the group.

Then confirm: What happens next?

This is the moment to confirm any new decisions and action items. These two questions together might sound like this.

"Okay, you said you wanted to achieve [whatever it was]. Do you feel we did that?"

Then:

"Can we take a minute to make sure we're clear on what happens next? I want to make sure I've captured my tasks before anything gets lost."

Small Changes, Big Ripples

The Single Topic Agenda tool shows how asking a few quick questions at the beginning and then the close of a meeting can create focus and clarify results. Without these questions or something like them, it's easy to leave with no clear sense of what was accomplished. Asking a few well-timed questions is a small change that can have a big impact.

In their book *The Surprising Power of Liberating Structures*, Henri Lipmanowicz and Keith McCandless define organizational macrostructures as the big things like the buildings and the strategic plan and the org chart, and the microstructures as the small ways in which the people within the organization interact.

Often when an organization wants to make big culture changes, they start with the macrostructures: a new values statement, a new performance program, perhaps a series of interventions with consultants. Sometimes this works wonders. More often, these initiatives benefit from an initial burst of energy but then fizzle as old habits reassert themselves.

By contrast, changing microstructures is relatively easy. Meetings are full of microstructures.

For example, to encourage more open dialogue, the boss can choose to sit along one side of the table rather than at the head of the table. Or better yet, the boss may hold the meeting somewhere that the group can sit in a circle. Instead of passively listening to a series of presentations, the group can read the material in advance then spend meeting time exploring what they've learned. Working to change microstructures—those ever-present small ways in which we interact—is work that directly shifts the entrenched habits of behavior that can otherwise undermine our loftier goals.

As Lipmanowicz and McCandless detail in their book and on their website, changes in microstructures can have outsized impacts. By focusing on how the group treats each other in meetings, how they encourage participation, and how they talk about both success and failure, leaders can encourage culture change in a powerful, effective, and, perhaps most importantly, *easily implemented* way.

Read the case studies in *The Surprising Power of Liberating Structures* or on their website for some fascinating examples: www.liberatingstructures.com/field-stories/

The Meeting Canoe™

The basic structure of Focus, Discuss, Wrap Up underlies all successful meetings, but it is decidedly basic. When I work to design a new meeting—whether that's a sales demo or half-day Workshop—I prefer to start with an outline that has a bit more going on.

There are several useful models out there, all of which provide a richer scaffolding to build on. The one I find myself using most often is The Meeting Canoe™ from Dick and Emily Axelrod, organizational designers and authors of *Let's Stop Meeting Like This*.

First, let's get this out of the way: "Canoe" is not an acronym. It's a reference to a canoe, a type of long boat.

The name describes the shape of a successful meeting, and how designing meetings that follow this shape will propel a team forward toward a common goal, as if they were all rowing the same canoe. You can read The Meeting Canoe as moving left to right in time.

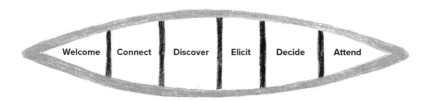

The Meeting Canoe: Welcome, Connect, Discover, Elicit, Decide, Attend.

The Meeting Canoe has its own description of the phases in a meeting. The Axelrods understand the importance of getting people engaged with each other before diving into the work. The Meeting Canoe model dedicates two full seats—"**Welcome**" and "**Connect**"—to becoming present.

The next three seats break the work into explicit "Discover, Elicit, and Decide" steps. Separating the work into these segments tidies up what can otherwise be a messy process.

Discover the way things are. In other words, make sure the group understands the situation under discussion so you're all working with the same information.

Elicit people's dreams and ideas. Spend time exploring the range of possibilities to get the best possible chance of finding a good one.

Decide on next steps.

The last seat on the Meeting Canoe is reserved for the wrap-up. **Attend** to the end, where you confirm the decisions you've made, ensure any new tasks are clearly understood, and express appreciation for each other's time.

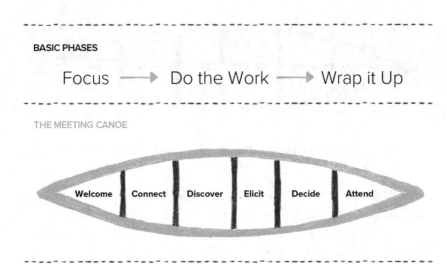

Focus ⟶ Do the Work ⟶ Wrap it Up

THE MEETING CANOE

Welcome | Connect | Discover | Elicit | Decide | Attend

Here's how the six parts of The Meeting Canoe™ line up with the three basic meeting phases.

Think Structure, Not Agenda

All this talk about structure: isn't that just a pretentious way of saying that people need to use an agenda? And what is an agenda anyway?

If you'd asked me this 5 years ago, I would have thought it a silly question. An agenda is simply a list of topics to be discussed in the meeting, right? Since then, I've seen a lot of things called agendas, and they're all over the map. Content might include:

- Subjects to discuss, e.g.. 1. Marketing, 2. Finance, 3. Sales, etc.
- Process steps for discussing a single topic, e.g., 1. Introductions, 2. Brainstorm, 3. Sort ideas, 4. Vote
- A mix of the two, e.g., 1. Announcements, 2. Review Finances, 3. Review Issues, 4. Real-Time Agenda (what?), 5. Next Steps
- Detailed documents with attached reports, speaker bios, timing requirements, and more.

Agendas come in all kinds of formats, from bulleted lists to multi-column tables to full-on booklets. Then there are unconferences and meetings like them where attendees propose the topics for discussion when they walk in the door. The leaders tell everyone that there's no set agenda; they'll create the agenda together at the meeting.

Yet even in these no-agenda meetings, the organizer absolutely sends pre-work for participants and follows a specific process. Agenda-free in this case does not mean unstructured, unprepared, or winging it.

The truth is there are a lot of good ways to structure a meeting and put together a meeting agenda. So what should an agenda contain? Roger Schwarz, author of *The Skilled Facilitator*, says it well:

> An effective agenda sets clear expectations for what needs to occur before and during a meeting.
>
> —Roger Schwarz

In other words, a good agenda contains information that helps people prepare for the meeting and understand where they are in the process during the meeting. Here's the definition I use when writing meetings guides: **The agenda is the version of the meeting plan you share with attendees.**

It may include specific topics for discussion, it should include any required pre-reading, and it may explain the process you'll use at a very high level. The agenda is not, however, the place to go into all the details about how someone should lead the conversation. If you've never seen or used a detailed facilitator's guide, this may be a surprise. Your past experience led you to believe that putting together a bulleted list was really all there was to planning a meeting.

The big news here: many meetings run according to a more thoughtful and detailed plan than we see on the agenda. The agenda is just the tip of the iceberg, my friends.

Given that, it's a little misleading to call the tool on the previous pages The Single Topic Agenda because, really, this structure gets used most often for those meetings that don't have an official agenda sent out in advance. It works pretty well, too.

You may have been told that every meeting needs an agenda. Angie at Pacific Bold believes this. The people who tell me their sad meeting stories believe this. All the acquaintances who helpfully offer "Well, Elise, you know the problem with meetings is that people never bring an agenda!" clearly believe this.

Too bad it's not true. That would make this a heck of an easy book to read, though, eh?

It is not absolutely necessary to share a document called an agenda in order to have a high-quality meeting. It is important, however, to:

1. Have clarity of purpose (in other words, know why you're meeting) and
2. Use an appropriate meeting structure designed to get that result.

For example, daily standup and shift-change meetings do not rely on an agenda. Instead, they follow the same structure every day. Everyone knows what to expect and what to discuss during the meeting without the need for an agenda.

Consider also the last Workshop you attended. It's possible you saw an agenda before the Workshop, but it's more likely that you were simply given a Workshop description. You didn't need to see a detailed plan of exactly how the Workshop would go before you registered; you just needed enough detail so you could come prepared and could reasonably assume that you'd learn what they promised to teach you.

A multi-day Workshop and a 15-minute daily standup meeting sit at opposite extremes of the meeting landscape, but neither one requires leaders to distribute an agenda in advance to succeed. While these are radically different types of meetings, they both follow a very clear *structure*.

Every meeting has a structure. The Single Topic Agenda provides a way to put a solid functional structure in place for a meeting that doesn't otherwise need an agenda. In my practice, I follow this Single Topic agenda structure all the time without ever mentioning the word "agenda" once.

I also encourage you to root yourself and your team in this idea of structure because at Lucid Meetings, I've seen firsthand how the belief that you "must have an agenda" has been misunderstood and misused, leading to even worse meetings than the bad meetings the agenda is meant to fix.

People mistakenly believe that an agenda is just a list of topics to be discussed at the meeting. It is not. To repeat: **The agenda is the version of the meeting plan (or structure) you share with attendees.**

People asked to create an agenda who do not understand meeting structure think to themselves: "Well, okay. The topics we'll discuss at the meeting. Let's see. There's the budget, and risk, and timeline, and work status, and updates from the board, and..." and they create what's known as a "laundry list"—a long list of possible discussion topics, possibly in a logical order, that may or may not lead the group to any meaningful result.

At Lucid, we get support requests from people asking if we can make the text smaller on our online agendas, because they have to scroll too much when they try to read their 72-item weekly team meeting agenda.

Multi-line eye-doctor charts are not what the experts meant when they taught everyone to always have an agenda! Data from our users show that teams with laundry-list agendas do not actually look at most of these agenda items during their meetings. Our observations are consistent with research showing that this perversion of the agenda is widespread. In a 1999 study examining how people used tools for planning and managing meetings, Volkema and Niederman found that only 50% of the meetings that had agendas completed the items on that agenda during the meeting.

So I must ask: *Why?* Why go to the work of creating an agenda you won't use?

Please don't misunderstand. I am not against agendas. I love agendas! I believe an agenda can be a very useful artifact for communicating the plan for running the meeting, just like an invitation is a useful artifact for communicating the time of the meeting, and directions make it easy to find the meeting location. But just as the map is not the territory, and the directions are not the location, a meeting agenda should not be mistaken for an adequately planned meeting structure.

Structure comes first. The agenda is then a simplified document used to talk about this structure.

Checkpoint:
Structuring Meetings for Success

Let's review what we've covered so far.

Our heroes at Pacific Bold quickly realized that they couldn't cancel all of their meetings, because some are just too important for making the business function. They used their intuitive sense of relative meeting importance to decide which meetings needed to stay, and canceled all the rest.

When you determine that one meeting is more important than another, the next question is *why?* What is the intention of that meeting?

Getting the answer to this question—*Why do we need this meeting?*—is the first step to success. A complete answer to this question has two parts: the purpose (a verb) and the desired outcomes (nouns). In other words, why you're meeting and what you expect to get out of the meeting at the end.

Once the meeting intention is clear, meeting leaders can use a basic meeting structure to connect everyone to each other and this intention at the beginning of a meeting. Then following the discussion, leaders must ensure they leave time to wrap it up by reviewing and confirming what the group achieved together.

The basic meeting structure I've discussed in this section prevents outright meeting failure. With clarity of intention and the basic structure in your pocket, you can run the Single Topic Agenda process any time to get a reasonable result.

Moving beyond the basics, more interesting structures help meetings become engaging tools for changing organizational habits and culture. Rather than starting from scratch, you can start by referencing the 16 types of business meetings in the Meeting Taxonomy. The taxonomy provides clues that help leaders refine their meeting intention, and once you know which category your meeting falls within, you can find many example structures specifically designed to achieve those goals.

And that's when it gets fun! When you're working with a team to achieve a clear goal, you know when to break out the high-fives! You know what you need to do, and you can experiment with the most engaging, playful, and effective ways to do it!

Speaking of engaging, playful, and effective, let's talk about what it can look like when you get meetings right.

CHAPTER 7

Pumping Up Perceived Meeting Quality

PACIFIC BOLD

"We need to start having the project status meetings again," Angie says.

Angie, Charla, and Nelson are enjoying lunch at their favorite ramen spot just around the corner from the Pacific Bold office. Charla considers ordering just a cup of miso soup and a side salad. Now that they aren't *officially* meeting anymore, it seems she finds herself out to lunch with some part of the leadership team every day, and it's starting to impact her waistline. One look at the glum expressions on her colleagues faces, and she opts instead for noodly comfort food.

Nelson groans. "I thought we'd agreed that was the one meeting everyone was happy to see go! Heck—happy isn't strong enough. Thrilled! Titillated! Jubilant! Personally, I'm delighted to have those hours back. Project status meetings are the worst!"

Angie glowers and prepares to retaliate, but stops when she notices Charla's raised eyebrows. Instead, she takes a deep breath, pokes at a few floating noodles, then quietly lays her chopsticks across the bowl. "Okay, then. What do you suggest we do? I need help."

This was a tough admission for Angie. She's the one who always helps everyone else. In her view of the story, she's always the rescuer; asking for help is uncomfortable.

"What exactly is the problem?" Charla asks. "Why do you need the project status meetings back?"

Angie sighs. "I know that the project status meetings aren't anyone's favorite, and that they're not fun, but it's the only way we've found to make sure all the project plans are up to date. When we get everyone together in one place at one time, we can pin down the people who never update their tasks in the project system and find out what's going on. We can also make sure everyone knows about any schedule or requirements changes when we read through the updates. That's the *one* time we look at the whole task list and make sure it's accurate. Without the project status meetings, my project managers are running around to every different person on their team trying to figure out what's going on with their projects. I know a lot of people already thought of us as nags, and now it's a hundred times worse because we're doing a lot more nagging."

Charla nods and says, "But isn't that what the project management system is for? When I want to see what's going on with the projects, I log in and take a look at the dashboard. Everyone tracks their progress there—that's why we bought the thing. Can't your project managers do the same?"

Angie is truly surprised. "You think everyone adds their project updates to the system themselves? Really? Boy, wouldn't that be nice. Nelson, tell me, have you ever updated your own tasks? When was the last time you logged in and reviewed the Gantt chart? Never mind—don't answer that."

Angie continues, "Maybe some people do keep their status up to date, but, no—for the most part, that's what the project managers do. We talk to all the people on the team and update the central records so that when you log in, Charla, your executive dashboard has all the current information. And before, a status meeting was the one time we could catch anything we missed. Now, the more we email and text people for updates, the more they ignore us. We're falling farther behind. Yesterday, I nearly lost Belinda. She said she was in a client update meeting when she found out the team was going to miss a deadline by a full week—in a meeting in front of a client! The client was upset that they didn't get more notice, and Belinda was mortified. It's her job to make sure that kind of thing doesn't happen, and despite all the email and requests to the team to let her know what was going on, she missed it."

Angie concludes, "We've made it too hard for the project managers to do their jobs without those meetings, and if we don't make a change soon, I think some of them are going to quit."

"I hear you," Nelson says, "but your project managers spent so much time in those status meetings reading the silly task list at us that we never had time to actually do anything about it! Every time I want to stop and solve a problem, I get shut down because there are always 20 more things we have to watch you all type into your spreadsheet. Half the time when I try to make it more interesting, I'm treated like a naughty child. It's patronizing! To have me just sit there until I need to make my report is not only boring, it's a waste of my time!"

"Well," Angie replies, "if people would pay attention instead of checking their email in the meeting, it would go faster! And what if people would just fill out their sheets in advance like Charla thinks they do? That would make that meeting go way faster—but good luck with that! Don't you think we tried to do it all by email so we could make the meeting shorter? Half the time, I know no one even reads my reports—much less acts on them— so this is the only way I can be sure they know about a deadline change!"

Angie is right. One estimate shows that only 70% of internal email messages are even opened. And even when people do open the message, only 40% do more than briefly skim the contents. Email can work, but it can also be a black hole.

Charla breaks the tension by taking a long, loud slurp of soup. Then she sets her bowl down and declares, "Well, this won't do. Angie, those meetings were awful and Nelson's right. There has to be a better way. Nelson, you know and I know that we can't be missing client deadlines without warning if we want to keep our clients. We rely on repeat business and referrals, and we aren't going to get those if the clients feel they can't trust us to deliver."

Charla continues, "Angie, if you've tried to manage the projects without the meeting, and you say you need that meeting back, I believe you. You can reschedule the status meeting on one condition: You have to figure out a way to make it so Nelson, his team, and all the engineers don't hate it. You're going to have to find a way to make that meeting work for everyone."

Then, softening a bit, Charla adds, "Don't worry—we'll help! We're creative people, after all! How hard can it be?"

— PB —

Research on Perceived Meeting Quality

Have you ever been told that:

- Good meetings are short.
- Good meetings have an agenda.
- The only reason to meet is to make a decision.

Guess what? As you might suspect by now, those are myths! A good meeting may be short, it may have an agenda, and it may be about making a decision, but none of these is required.

A 2011 study by Cohen, et al. titled *Meeting Design Characteristics and Attendee Perceptions of Staff/Team Meeting Quality* examined how variations in meeting practices made people feel about their meetings. In the study, participants were asked to rate various aspects of meetings, ultimately coining a quantifiable measure they called Perceived Meeting Quality—that's where I got the term.

Here's the short version of their conclusion: **When someone feels that** *they participated* **in a** *high-quality meeting,* **they feel that the meeting time was well spent.**

Let's get into the specifics.

What makes for a "high-quality" meeting?

The Cohen study looked at a bunch of criteria, ranging from how the meeting was structured, how people prepared, the temperature in the room, whether anyone took notes, and so on. Cohen and his colleagues found a handful of things mattered most.

A high-quality meeting is one where the leader sets and meets expectations. How, exactly? For one thing, **a high-quality meeting starts and ends on time.**

Much to everyone's surprise, the Cohen study showed *no relationship between meeting length and perceived meeting quality.* Whether short or long, either could be equally great meetings. What they did find, however, was that it was crucial for the meeting to start and end on time. Now, that doesn't mean that if you finish a meeting five minutes early, you need to sit around and wait for the clock before you can end it. But if you're routinely ending much earlier than expected, you need to schedule shorter meetings. It also means that you shouldn't wait around for people who arrive late. Don't punish the punctual!

Beware the Cultural Relativism of Time

It's worth noting that most of the research we have on meeting quality was conducted in Western organizations. The researchers behind the Cohen study were all based in the U.S., where our relationship to time is hurried and precise—a Western attitude toward punctuality might be stated as, "Early is on time, on time is late, and late is inexcusable." Growing up, I heard this quoted frequently as an inviolable truth and moral imperative. This is not the attitude in lots of other cultures, however. As one member of a First Nations board explained to me, "Here, we use island time."

I believe that rather than a hard rule about starting exactly at the scheduled time, the real key is to treat everyone's time with respect. Realize that every meeting is an interruption for someone there and that the people in the room deserve to have the time they invest together used respectfully.

Another study referred to this respect for each other's time as "Temporal Courtesy," and after I finished cleaning up the coffee I blew out of my nose laughing at how weird that sounds, I decided I love it. I believe Temporal Courtesy is just weird enough to be memorable—to make you stop to think about it—which is exactly the point. When it comes to the time you spend in meetings, stop and think about it, and for goodness' sake, be polite.

People also need to understand why the meeting is being held. At minimum, this means sharing the meeting purpose and desired outcomes in advance. Specifically, why are you meeting, and what will the team get out of the meeting at the end? Is it a plan, a decision, an update? Be clear up front.

For shorter meetings, that's enough. For any meeting that your team runs often, that's enough. There's really no reason to send an agenda for a 15-minute call, or a 30-minute discussion on a single topic. That's why "you must have an agenda" is on my list of myths.

But for any meeting longer than 30 minutes, you're generally better off having an agenda, and if you do, you need to send the agenda in advance. Sending the agenda before the meeting is vital—it's part of "setting and meeting expectations." You can't just show up to the meeting with an agenda and put it up on a slide.

To repeat: An agenda presented during the meeting doesn't cut it. In fact, Cohen, et al., found that in terms of people's feeling that the meeting was worth their time, *an agenda shared during the meeting was no better than having no agenda at all.* At that point, the agenda is just another slide; it's simply the opener to your one-person show.

After that, the only other thing they found to have a significant impact on meeting participants' perception of quality was how comfortable the room was or wasn't. In the case of a virtual meeting, this is where decent communication tools come in, and making sure people have adequate opportunity to practice so they can use whatever tool you choose.

To sum up, it's not how long a meeting is or what it's about that matters. It's about being clear up front about the plan for the meeting and then following through on that plan—setting and meeting expectations—if you want to help people feel a meeting is high quality.

Let's not forget the other big factor that led people to rate a meeting as a good use of time....

Participation Propels PMQ

This one is *huge*. We know that when people aren't actively participating, they tend to multitask. So while whoever is doing all the talking might think they're achieving something, if the rest of the meeting participants have their attention elsewhere, the group can't get to a shared result. You cannot have a meeting of the minds when most of the minds aren't actually in the meeting.

And before you jump to the wrong conclusion—while the survey I show below points out what people do when they're "tuned out" on a remote call, similar surveys about face-to-face meetings had answers like "daydreaming" and "pretend to take notes" for ways people escape when they're not engaged.

Otherwise? Multitasking

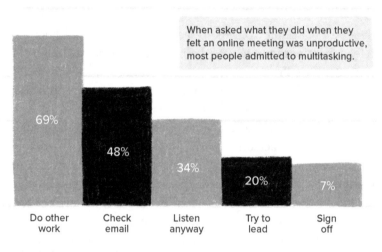

When asked what they did when they felt an online meeting was unproductive, most people admitted to multitasking.

69% — Do other work
48% — Check email
34% — Listen anyway
20% — Try to lead
7% — Sign off

2013 Leadership Strategies survey of 438 North American executives and managers
www.leadstrat.com/virtues-of-virtual-survey-results-2013

To compound the problem, once someone's focus is distracted, you lose them both for the time they spend focused elsewhere and for the time it takes them to return their attention to the group. Studies conducted on distracted driving—another event during which we are meant to be giving our full focus to the task at hand—found that people can take up to 27 seconds to regain full focus after interacting with the electronic systems in their car. If that doesn't sound like too long to you, try pausing here now for 27 seconds before you read on and imagine how that will feel to the rest of the group as they wait for a distracted person to try to answer a question when they weren't really listening.

Let's sum up what we've got so far. If you want to run good meetings, the research says that you need to:

1. Be clear about the meeting purpose and desired outcome up front. (That poor horse! I know we're beating this dead equine pretty thoroughly. Be forewarned: The beatings will continue until meetings improve!)
2. Only invite the people needed to achieve that purpose—those who will actively participate.
3. Send any material in advance to help everyone prepare.
4. Start and end on time.
5. Make sure everyone has an opportunity to participate.
6. Make sure everyone *can* participate: get the environment and the technology right.

Here's a final tidbit from the research that you should know: **People who lead meetings tend to rate their own meetings way better than the people attending them.**

Said another way: if that was your meeting, you probably thought it was pretty good. The people attending it often do not agree.

Given what we just learned about meeting quality, this should make sense. If you're the person who scheduled the meeting, there's a pretty good chance you know why, that the meeting is relevant to you, and that you're at least somewhat prepared. You know what to expect, and you will automatically work to meet your own expectations. Also, as the leader, you're guaranteed an opportunity to participate.

This leads to lots of bosses and managers who remain blissfully unaware of how painful their meetings are for everyone else in the room. So don't assume that you can ignore effective meeting habits because your meetings work fine and you've got other things to do. **You are not qualified to objectively judge your own meetings.** You have no idea. Knowing that is the first step toward fixing it.

"Okay," Nelson concedes, "I get that you need the project status meeting. I understand that we can't miss any big stuff, and if we're going to be realistic, I don't see how we can guarantee that everyone will just fill in their updates online. Besides, even if they did, they would have to read everyone else's update to really know there was a problem. I was in that meeting with Belinda when we found out we'd miss the review deadline, and it was a surprise to me too. I guess we just didn't realize how much those few days Ernest was out sick knocked us off track. I still don't want to sit through an hour of watching you guys update a spreadsheet, though. You know, what if we didn't go over *all* the tasks in each meeting and instead just covered the most important ones? Maybe whatever we can do in 20 minutes?"

"20 minutes?" Angie replies, "I don't know—that wouldn't get very far down the list. And I'm not sure it would have helped in this case, because the stuff Ernest was working on wasn't rated mission-critical on the sheet. It only became mission-critical when it didn't happen."

Charla intervenes, "Well, obviously that was the important task to talk about last week even if it wasn't marked important on your spreadsheet before. Do you think there's a way you could decide together what the most important issues are each week in the meeting? That way, you don't have to guess in advance, and everyone else will have a say in what you talk about in your time together. Maybe then they'd also be more willing to fill in the other details outside of the meeting if it meant the meetings became more interesting."

== PB ==

Tool: The Real-Time Agenda Technique

The Single Topic Agenda saves the day when you have a single topic to cover, but what do you do when there are a lot of things people want to talk about? Especially when you have limited time, like Angie's project teams do, and can't invest in a full-on Workshop?

What It Is
The Real-Time Agenda is the second tool you can use to turn an unstructured or disengaging meeting into a success on the fly. This tool gets everyone involved right from the start. Working together, groups prioritize and focus the discussion in real time, then walk away with documented results.

When to use a Real-Time Agenda:

- When the specific list of topics isn't clear in advance, and you know the group has more to talk about than they can cover in the time available.
- When the topics are clear, but again, there are too many to address and the priorities can't be determined in advance.
- As part of a larger meeting as a way to work through a list of issues or other sub-topics.

How It Works

Step 1. Welcome.
Greet everyone and, if this process is new, provide a quick overview of how the meeting will work.

Step 2. List all the possible topics.
When meeting in person, you can write these on a whiteboard or have people add their own topics using sticky notes. Groups meeting online can use meeting management software or a shared online document.

Step 3. Prioritize the topics.
Your group may come to a natural consensus here, but if the list is very long or the group very large, consider "dot voting." Each meeting participant gets a fixed number of votes (or dots) that they can cast however they want; they can place all their votes on the same item if they wish, or vote for several different items. When in doubt, give everyone three dots. This allows everyone to vote for multiple options and reveals relative priorities rather than declaring any single item a "winner." Everyone votes at once. Then, the leader counts the dots to identify the preferred options. The topics with the most dots rank highest.

Step 4. Discuss topics one at a time, and record the outcome.
Now that you have the priorities, you work through them one at a time, starting with the highest-priority topic. When a topic is complete, document any decisions or action items the group arrived at, then move to the next topic on the list.

Working this way, while you probably won't get through the whole list, you will get through some of it and have tangible results to show for your time.

Continue working through topics, stopping when 10 minutes remain in the meeting.

Step 5. Review and confirm next steps.
Stop the discussion with 10 minutes left in the meeting. This may mean that the group is just part-way through a topic. In that case, first decide how you want to handle that. For example, the group could agree to let the meeting run late, or they could assign the topic to a few individuals to finish up. Or, for teams who use a real-time agenda as part of their regular meeting cadence, they can agree to pick up that topic first thing at the next meeting.

Once you've decided how to handle any conversation mid-flight, review the list of documented decisions, action items, and notes, and confirm that these capture the agreements made in the room. Then you're done!

The Real-Time Agenda in the Wild
You may encounter several variations of the real-time agenda under different names, such as:

- *The Unconference*: for large events, conferences, and Community of Practice meetings.
- *Lean Coffee*: for Team Cadence and smaller Community of Practice meetings.

And then, literally, Patrick Lencioni (author of *Death by Meeting* and the *Five Dysfunctions of a Team*) calls one part of his recommended leadership team agenda the "real-time agenda." If you like the Real-Time Agenda Technique (I know I do), I recommend looking up these variations to learn more ways to use it well.

CHAPTER 8

The Spectrum of Meeting Engagement

Participation propels perceived meeting quality. We call it participation when we are attending a meeting—as in, "I had a chance to participate." Meeting leaders often use the term engagement to describe the same thing.

Engagement is about getting the individual into the meeting, about breaking through the noise and fog of whatever may be going on for each person so they can focus their will on the collective goals. Meeting engagement is observable behavior; you can see whether or not someone engages in a meeting. This engagement falls across a spectrum of behavior that looks something like this.

At the bottom end of the spectrum, you have the **Disruptive** behavior—things like:

- Arriving late or not at all, or leaving early
- Side conversations
- Interrupting
- Complaining
- Excessive negativity and personal attacks

Next, you have the inattentive people: these are the folks checking email or doing other work in the meeting, the multi-taskers, the people who are spacing out, and those who nod off.

Then, we start getting into the range of acceptable behavior with people who are paying attention—actively listening and perhaps taking personal notes.

The tricky thing is that it's very hard to tell the difference between someone who is actively listening and the person who's looking at you but thinking about something totally different. From the outside, there's no telling.

This is why we look for people who are actively participating in meetings. A person participating is answering questions when asked, talking with other participants, and following instructions. It's a reactive way to engage rather than proactive, but it's also obvious to see that this person is truly in the meeting.

Moving past participation, we come to those who are contributing by helping to shape the meeting outcome. People presenting reports, offering ideas, and raising questions are working to improve the meeting results.

Finally, at the highest level of engagement, you get the people taking ownership for the meeting result. This includes the meeting leader for sure and also anyone who's really driving a decision or setting the topic. Those folks are invested.

But meeting engagement can come in many forms. Someone who offers to take notes is engaged, but so is the person who loudly bullies everyone else into submission. One provides productive, generative energy to the group; the other destructive energy.

Generative energy drives forward momentum. Destructive energy kills it. In the middle, we get inertia, which we all know from our basic physics lessons devolves into entropy. A body at rest stays at rest.

The core competencies and the use of an effective meeting structure work to encourage meeting engagement and productive energy. Beyond these basics, there are five key steps meeting designers can follow to increase meeting engagement.

Five Steps to Improving Engagement in Meetings

1. Define what you want people to contribute.

2. Ask for engagement.

3. Make space for people to engage.

4. Acknowledge contributions.

5. Use what you receive.

1. Define What You Want People to Contribute

The first step is to clarify what kind of engagement you want to see. What do you want people to contribute and what will you do with those contributions?

I hear from many leaders who want to "get their teams more engaged" in meetings. When I ask for details, they talk about all the things that they *don't* want people to do.

- They don't want people to show up late.
- They don't want anyone checking their cell phone or email.
- They don't want a bunch of side conversations going on.
- They don't want folks to tune out.

This is a clear picture of disengagement, but the vision for engagement boils down to "paying attention."

I am always surprised by the number of meeting leaders who come to Lucid Meetings looking for ways to "get their team engaged," then describe meetings where they have everyone in a room, spend 20 minutes talking at them, and finally ask for input. There is nothing in that approach which tells people that they should expect to provide input before the meeting, and after 20 minutes, there is very little chance that anyone will still be paying attention. A go-around at this point often results in "Nothing to add" from most of the group.

If you define engagement in your meetings as having people simply pay attention, then you'd better plan to be entertaining. Unless your financial reports are chock-full of cinema-worthy drama, I recommend seeking a clearer path to engagement.

Also, do not anticipate that people will rate a meeting highly where they simply paid attention. "Paying attention" does not qualify as "participating" from an attendee's perspective.

To truly engage in a meeting—beyond just paying attention—people need an active part to play. They need a job to do. These jobs can be simple, like raising a hand to indicate agreement, or helping the group keep track of time. These jobs can also be complex, like they are when participating in a collaborative Workshop or building a complicated decision matrix together.

Too often we assume that people know we want their participation. To break out of these assumptions, ask yourself:

- What will it look like when someone engages in your meeting? What are they *doing*?
- Why would someone engage in your meeting? What's in it for them?
- How could you *know* that they were engaged?
- After they've engaged, then what? What happens with whatever they've contributed?

The answers will depend on the meeting. You may want people to share any concerns they have about a plan, or ideas for solving a problem. You may want to know what they like about how the group works, and where they're having a hard time. Perhaps the team needs information, or simply a chance to connect.

To increase participation, each person must have a *reason* to be there. When you schedule a meeting, only invite people you explicitly expect to actively participate. If you're inviting someone just because you're not sure who needs to be involved, or you're afraid to hurt someone's feelings, what you're actually doing is creating the conditions for a bad meeting because those people have no good reason to participate.

2. Ask for Engagement

Once you know how you'd like people to engage, it's time to ask for that engagement.

The simplest way to engage someone is by asking a question, then waiting for an answer. This works well in a one-on-one dialogue. The structure is:

Question → Answer

In this case, the job you've asked of the other person in the meeting is to answer the question. In a group, however, this *question → answer* structure often falls flat. Just like with any task you throw out to a group, you're likely to see several people keep quiet as they wait for someone else to answer.

A better structure for groups is:

Question → Go-around

Here, the meeting leader goes around the room and asks each person to answer the question one at a time to ensure all participants contribute.

Question → Answer or *Question → Go-around* are the most straightforward ways to ask for engagement, but not always the most useful or—frankly—the most engaging. After you figure out what kind of engagement you want, you can ask for that specifically. The *asking* can come at several times and in many forms. These meeting techniques all provide other ways to ask for engagement.

- **Meeting pre-work**: asking people to complete tasks assigned before the meeting so they can arrive informed and ready to engage. For example, you can ask people to read a report in advance and come prepared with the specific feedback you need.
- **Ground rules**: these are code-of-conduct rules that the group is asked to respect during the meeting. For example, "turn off cell phones" or "commit to stating objections in the room" are ground rules which ask people to stay in the conversation.
- **Activities**: participants are asked to complete these together during the meeting.
- **Meeting roles**: jobs individuals are asked to perform in the meeting.

Finding the right way to ask for engagement is an overwhelming task if you lack clarity about the purpose of the meeting. Once you know why you're meeting, however, and what you need to accomplish within it, it gets a lot easier to figure out what to ask.

Tool: Meeting Roles

What It Is
Meeting roles are predefined jobs that can be assigned to people in a meeting. People who take on a meeting role actively engage.

The most common roles you should know are:

Meeting Leader or Owner: responsible for the meeting content. This person is responsible for making sure the meeting purpose and desired outcomes are clear and that the right people are involved.

Facilitator: responsible for the meeting process and participation. This person officially starts the meeting, guides the group through the discussion, ensures everyone has an opportunity to participate, and helps keep the discussion productive.

Note Taker: responsible for recording the key decisions, insights, action items, and other results from the meeting.

Time Keeper: responsible for ensuring all time limits are respected, including time for discussing specific topics, for individual speakers, and for ending the meeting on schedule.

Contributor: responsible for contributing to the desired meeting outcomes. These are all the remaining people who should rightfully expect to participate in some meaningful way.

How These Roles Work Together

In theory, teams will assign different people to each of the meeting roles. This divides the work, gets more people involved in making the meeting a success, and helps each person do a better job since they're not trying to juggle all the things at once. In practice, the person who scheduled the meeting often takes on all of these roles at once.

This is not heroism. One person can't do a good job driving for a useful outcome (a leader's role) and making sure everyone gets to participate equally (a facilitator's job) while capturing key notes (the note taker) and watching the clock (the time keeper) all at the same time.

When one person takes all the roles, this is a sign of poor planning and inadequate training. The leader didn't get their job done in time for anyone else to pitch in. Each role is dependent on the others. Consider:

Before the meeting

1. The leader determines the business value the meeting needs to create: purpose, outcomes, timing.
2. Then the facilitator can design a structure that will achieve that goal. The facilitator can't determine how to get the job done if the leader hasn't clarified what that job is. The facilitator then shares this structure with everyone else.
3. Finally, once the purpose and process are clear, the contributors can prepare.

During the meeting

1. The facilitator runs the process and gets everyone involved.
2. The time keeper watches the clock so the facilitator can focus on the discussion. The time keeper can't keep time if the facilitator doesn't tell the time keeper how long each part of the process should take.
3. The note taker writes down key decisions and action items. The note taker can't know which things are important enough to write down if they don't understand what the meeting needs to achieve.

If there is no clarity about the desired outcome or the process in use, contributors can't contribute effectively. They will add whatever each of them individually feels like adding at the moment, perhaps an irrelevant monologue, or more commonly, nothing at all.

For any regularly occurring meeting, the business function should be known in advance. In Lucid's regular team meetings, we use pre-defined meeting structures, which makes it easy for us to take turns acting as the facilitator or time keeper. This gives everyone a chance to sharpen their skills. Because we use collaborative meeting software, while we assign a designated note taker, we can also all pitch in to help take notes when we're contributing. We consistently have different people in each of the core meeting roles because our meetings are intentionally structured for this by design.

3. Make Space for People to Engage

This step is simple, often neglected, and powerful.

If you ask for engagement, you must make sure there is time for people to give it to you.

The Five Hippopotamus Rule is a simple technique that illustrates this point. After you ask a question, remain silent for at least five seconds (the time it takes to count in your head, "one-hippopotamus, two-hippopotamus," all the way to five) before speaking again. This gives everyone time to consider your question. The silence also shows them that you really do expect to hear someone else provide an answer.

Too often, leaders will tell a group that they want to hear everyone's feedback on a new proposal, then spend 90% of the meeting presenting the proposal and leaving only minutes for the Q&A. To the people invited, this feels like a sham. Clearly, these leaders didn't actually want input, because if they did, they would have made space for it. Many well-intentioned presenters have insulted and alienated meeting participants by not allowing adequate time for the engagement they asked for.

As you consider the kind of engagement you want (the ask) and work to plan your meeting accordingly, you will find that making time for engagement is a forcing function, often requiring teams to plan meetings involving fewer people or addressing fewer topics. For example, if you ask for feedback on a presentation and give each person only two minutes to talk (which isn't very long), a group of 10 people will require 20 minutes just to go around the room. Then, you had better anticipate that some of this feedback will lead to further discussion, since differing opinions will warrant clarification, debate, and building upon. Twenty minutes is not a problem if the whole meeting is dedicated to feedback, but it's a huge time commitment if it comes after a 40-minute presentation.

Making space for engagement in a meeting means that:

A. Each person must have the opportunity to contribute.

One reason you need to be selective with your invitations: research shows that the more people present in a meeting, the less each person partic-ipates—or at least, the less most people *feel* they participate—and the harder it is to keep everyone coordinated. It's easy for someone to feel that they are not needed (or, worse, like they're wasting time) whenever the group gets larger than 5 people.

B. Each person can come prepared to contribute.

We all know not everyone feels the need to be prepared—or even informed—before they'll happily offer up their opinion. But then you've got a meeting dominated by people who like to talk, which doesn't make anyone look good.

So as a meeting leader, you want to make sure participants have any pre-reading or information they need to get prepared beforehand. This means not only do you have to make space during the meeting for engage-ment but also on the calendar preceding the meeting. Happily, when peo-ple come informed and ready, you'll also get a better result in the end. (Here's where that agenda comes in handy!)

Engaging meetings will need to include fewer people and/or cover fewer topics, or get blown up into full-on facilitated Workshops. In other words, structuring meetings for engagement will force you to run a tighter ship.

4. Acknowledge Contributions

"Thank you." At the very least, people who make a contribution to the meeting deserve thanks.

For many individuals, speaking up in a group means taking a personal risk. Some people are shy, and some environments are hostile. Whether the risk arises from internal or external factors, it still takes courage and effort to overcome. When this contribution is then glossed over, when it's dismissed, or when you haven't made time for it, people learn that the risk was not worth the effort. It is not safe to risk making a contribution in a group that does not appreciate that effort.

To encourage more engagement in a group that is still getting used to it, make a point of acknowledging and expressing appreciation for the effort. This makes everyone feel valued, reinforces the behavior change you want to encourage, and increases the likelihood that the team will contribute more going forward.

Visible note taking, the fourth core competency listed in Chapter 5, provides a simple and useful way to acknowledge contributions. When a person adds to the conversation, the note taker records what that person said where everyone can see it. You've probably seen facilitators do this in a Workshop when they write down replies on a flipchart. In everyday business meetings, it's often more useful to write down replies in a shared electronic document that everyone can access.

Visible note taking acknowledges people's engagement by literally writing it down. It also makes it radically easier to get to step five....

5. Use What You Receive

Finally, to get more engagement in meetings, make sure that the engagement matters to what happens outside the meeting. Engagement for engagement's sake is a mistake.

A meeting is never the point—it is always a means to an end.

Strategic Planning Workshops are notorious for creating a significant outcome that never gets used, and not because they fail to engage participants. It is possible to run a fabulously engaging Workshop to build out your company's strategic plan, only to then have that plan sit on the shelf for a year.

If all the exciting thinking you did in the meeting doesn't actually change what you do when you leave that meeting, it is wasted effort, and everyone involved will know it. Later around the water cooler, your meeting will be derided as a boondoggle.

When it comes to engagement, the rule is use it or lose it. No one appreciates making a good-faith effort to help a group, just to have this input ignored. It's disrespectful, patronizing, and a waste of their time.

On the bright side, if you know how you will use the group's contributions after the meeting (which you do, because defining this contribution is step one), this makes it much easier to figure out what kind of contributions you need. And if you take visible notes during the meeting, everyone can confirm that what you've written is what they intended, reducing the chance that you'll hit resistance later.

Getting clear about why you're meeting and what you will get at the end—the purpose and desired outcomes—is the most important step in creating a great meeting that not only engages your team but also serves your business.

CHAPTER 9

Designing for Net Positive Impact

PMQ looks at the quality of an individual meeting. Learning to run a meeting well is a worthy accomplishment! Leading one good meeting matters, but as we all know, most meetings are not solitary beasts. Only bad meetings stand alone; failed sales calls and botched negotiations are not joined by a second meeting.

The rest of our meetings travel in packs, each connected to and reliant on the success of the meetings that surround them. One good meeting is a start, but any success created there can quickly be lost in a crowd of otherwise unproductive meetings.

Some organizations understand this. They know that the way meetings work has an outsized impact on how the organization works. Some organizations put this understanding to work and actively shape the meetings that shape their culture. They know that how they meet largely defines who they are.

These organizations approach meetings as part of the larger operating system for the business, designing each one to serve a specific function in their work process. Meetings are a core part of the communication system in an organization. Taking a systems approach to meeting planning is not the same thing as simply setting up a series of recurring meetings on your team's calendar. That's a land-grab attempt to reserve time, rather than a thoughtfully considered attempt to maximize the investment of that time.

Instead, a systems approach looks at how meetings function within the larger context of the organization and works to ensure each meeting leads to an improvement in that environment. This brings us to our second quality acronym: NPI.

Design Meetings for Net Positive Impact

The concept of Net Positive Impact comes from the global environmental sustainability movement. The *Guardian* summarized it like this:

> "The aim of the net-positive movement is to encourage businesses to leave the world a better place than they find it."
> —Oliver Bach for the *Guardian*

This should also be the aim of every meeting: to leave the group in a better place than they find it. Corporate sustainability is all about responsible use of resources, where NPI can measure water usage, electrical production, carbon output, and the use of other natural resources. In the case of meetings, the "natural resources" they deplete can include time, energy, intellectual stimulation, emotional satisfaction, money, and forward momentum (to name a few!). Effective meetings create more of these resources than they use up.

At Lucid Meetings, we use the benchmarks on a Meeting Performance Maturity Scale to understand how well an organization minds its meeting NPI.

Organizations with low meeting performance maturity do not run consistently effective meetings. For these organizations, truly effective meetings are like rainbows; you see them every once in awhile, and when you do, it's always surprisingly delightful. For the most part, however, meetings in organizations with low performance maturity interrupt productive work and deliver unequal benefits to the people attending them.

Organizations with high meeting performance maturity run consistently effective meetings that establish a continuity of purpose and identity while also helping the organization adapt to changing circumstances. In these organizations, meetings are a fully integrated and necessary part of the way work gets done. Each meeting is designed to deliver a specific value with recognized benefits for those participating and for the larger system in which they operate.

What Is an "Effective" Meeting?

There is an online forum for meeting enthusiasts at Kunsido.net full of academics, facilitators, and other practitioners, where all kinds of questions and observations about meetings come up. One researcher asked the group: "What do you mean when you talk about an *effective* meeting?"

It turns out that the answer is not so obvious, and we don't all agree. So to avoid any confusion, here's what I mean when I talk about effective meetings in this book.

- Meetings are a tool. Their function is to connect people and move work forward. So, like a spatula or a vacuum cleaner, you can evaluate a meeting's effectiveness based on how well the tool did the job.
- For any specific meeting, the job to be done may be expressed as a set of explicit desired outcomes.
- An *effective* meeting achieves meaningful outcomes. These may or may not always exactly match the desired outcomes, but they will be related and they will have moved the group forward.

An effective meeting may be an *efficient* meeting, but that just means it didn't take up too much time. Efficiency is a lousy measure of quality when used in isolation.

An effective meeting is also different than a "good" meeting, because people will call any meeting that they enjoy a good meeting, regardless of whether there are any meaningful outcomes.

To be effective, a meeting has to be both "good"(enjoyable) and sufficiently productive to warrant the energy spent on it. In other words:

Effective = PMQ + NPI.

Here are a few examples from the research that HR and management folks will find interesting:

1. The quality of the meetings an employee has with their manager can have a dramatic impact on employee engagement and retention.

> Specifically, as managers make their workgroup meetings relevant, allow for employee voice in their meetings where possible, and manage the meeting from a time perspective, employees appear poised to fully engage themselves in their work in general. Thus, workgroup meetings are sites where engagement can be fostered or, if not conducted properly, sites where engagement can be derailed.
> ...When Perceived Organizational Support or Leader-Member Exchanges in meetings was high, high-Negative Affectivity (NA) employees were no more likely to quit than low-NA employees.
> —Allen, Rogelberg, 2013

In other words, when people saw that the organization cared about them because of how they were engaged and treated by leaders in meetings, they were more likely to stick around, even if they otherwise expressed negative opinions about the job.

2. Meeting satisfaction has a direct and meaningful impact on overall job satisfaction.

> On average, it appears as if meeting satisfaction is both a statistically and practically meaningful predictor of over-all job satisfaction. Importantly, we found that meeting satisfaction is not simply a proxy variable for the conceptually related constructs (taken independently or concurrently) of satisfaction with work, pay, supervision, advancement, coworkers, team members, horizontal communication, organizational integration communication, role ambiguity, overall communication, positive attitudes about the organization in general, and negative affect.
> —Rogelberg, Allen, Shanock , Scott and Shuffler, 2010

In other words, the way that people feel about meetings shapes and reflects how they feel about their organizations. Positive meeting experiences have a positive ripple; negative meeting experiences generate unwelcome waves.

Tool: Team Ground Rules

Ground rules act as the code of conduct for a meeting, explaining the behavior that's expected of all participants.

What It Is

Team ground rules extend traditional ground rules. It's very common for Workshop facilitators to establish ground rules at the beginning of a Workshop. What's less common—but which has a higher NPI over time—is the establishment of ground rules at the team, department, or organization level that apply across all meetings. Team ground rules give you a way to set some basic shared expectations around meetings at a higher level. They become boundaries about how to treat each other and how to run the process in a way that works for your organization.

While the ground rules you use should be developed collaboratively with your team, it's always helpful to start with some examples. The sample ground rules below reinforce those things that contribute most directly to perceived meeting quality.

Sample Ground Rules

Respect our commitment to making meetings enjoyable and productive.

- We adopt these ground rules as our shared commitment to doing great work in meetings. These are *our* rules; we can and will change the rules together if we feel there is a better way.
- Everyone is responsible for enforcing the ground rules. Notice when we have strayed, and speak up.
- Respect everyone's time.
- Start on time; end on time.
- Communicate well in advance about any meeting times that need to change.
- Share the time; do not monopolize the discussion or rob others of the time they need to share their perspective.

Respect the work of the meeting.

- Know the meeting purpose and desired outcomes. If these are unclear, ask.
- Come prepared and ready to engage.

- Information is the raw material of results. Be ready to contribute any information you have that will improve the results in this meeting.
- Document clear commitments, then follow through: walk your talk.

Respect each other as humans.

- Assume best intentions, but do not assume anything else. Ask questions to better understand anything that is unclear or troubling.
- Listen when others speak. Remember that no one has all the information, and don't interrupt.
- Share your views and concerns in the room. Show each other courage and respect by having tough conversations directly.
- Treat each other with kindness and tolerance first. We all have tricky days when we aren't at our best. You will appreciate this tolerance when that tricky day is yours.
- Take care of yourself. If you need to step out or take a break, do it. The group values your participation, so do what you need to do so you can devote your full attention.
- It's okay to have fun! We give ourselves permission to refrain from taking everything too seriously.

How and When to Establish Team Ground Rules

Teams typically develop ground rules during team formation or as part of a meeting improvement initiative. Teams that are just forming can set their ground rules as one part of their larger working team agreement by asking "What agreements or ground rules do we want to set for our meetings?" as one item on the agenda. Existing teams that want to improve their meetings can create ground rules together in a short, focused meeting.

How to Use Ground Rules

> The problem with ground rules is that they are often set but rarely used. ... But how do you actually use your ground rules to manage group interaction? By invoking them. Don't let the rules sit idly in front of the team.
>
> —Adams Spann, Means, and Spivey,
> *The Project Meeting Facilitator*

Ground rules are used to train and adjust meeting behavior. The most impactful and dramatic use of a ground rule is during a meeting when someone says:

"Sorry, but we agreed to [some specific item] in our ground rules, so I think we need to..."

For example:

"Sorry, but we agreed to have one conversation at a time. I think Ted wasn't quite finished with his point."

Or:

"We agreed to come prepared to meetings, but it looks like we aren't ready to have this discussion. What should we do? Would you like to reschedule, or should we add 10 minutes to the meeting now so everyone can read the pre-work?"

Ground rules can also be:

1. **Shared with new team members and employees as part of the onboarding process.** This helps new people know what to expect. Ideally, the new person will learn the ground rules from another team member rather than the boss, as this doubly reinforces that these are everyone's rules to enforce.

2. **Posted in meeting rooms as a reminder** (and as a way to demonstrate your organization's values to visitors). Several startups and technology companies have prominent Meeting Rules posters in their conference rooms to both remind their employees and impress outsiders with their professionalism. You'll find a picture of the startup Urban Airship's original ground rules on the Lucid Meetings blog.

3. **Written to include special language and rituals that express your team's character and unique culture.** For example, some teams use the "Vegas Rule"—as in "what happens in Vegas stays in Vegas" to establish that meeting discussions are to be considered confidential.

4. **Shared in your organizational marketing and recruitment as an example of your team's dedication to quality results.** Yes, companies actually do this.

Ground rules are useful, but they won't matter if the organization doesn't have any specific meetings to use them in. Right now, the team at Pacific Bold is still struggling to figure out which meetings, if any, they need to bring back. Craig feels personally responsible for how far they've gotten off track, and he's particularly obsessed with this problem.

At the deli the next day, Craig asks Charla, "When you think of all the meetings we used to have, which ones did you believe actually worked well?"

"Oh, I don't know," Charla says. "I didn't really mind our meetings the way they were. You know I like talking with everyone—that's what makes our work friendly. And I really don't feel like I have a handle on what's going on when I can't look people in the eye.

"But if I had to say which ones worked—what were the meetings where it seemed we were really getting things done—I'd have to say it was the prototyping Workshops. Those are fun! I love seeing all the ideas the designers come up with, and when we can get the client in there too, we always find some little gem that helps us get at their vision so much faster than we do when we just work from paper requirements. Do you remember that Workshop we did with the cucumber farmers who wanted us to create ads with a dancing cucumber for them, but all the designs kept coming out looking vaguely phallic? If we hadn't had them in the room, I don't know how long it would have taken to convince them otherwise—but that sure changed quick when you did that little dance in the beanie cap!"

Craig blushes. Yes, his improvised cucumber jig was remarkably persuasive, but it isn't his proudest memory. Besides, that isn't the point. "Yeah, okay," Craig says. "The Workshops are fun, but those take five hours to run. And sometimes—let's be honest—most of what happens there ends up getting thrown away. We can't exactly turn all our meetings into creative Workshops anyway—that would sink productivity for sure!"

Charla just smiles. She knows Craig has more to share. Craig has always cared about getting it right in all things and has always worked hard to stay current so he can advise clients on all the latest marketing techniques. He cares about getting the Pacific Bold corporate culture right too. He's the driving force behind the company's value statements and the selection of new locations. The current situation at Pacific Bold has him frustrated because clearly they aren't getting it right. It feels to him a lot like the Facebook conundrum the company faces: Craig believes that social media like Facebook is doing irreparable damage to society—especially to young people like his two teenage sons. He also knows as a marketing professional that there's a lot of money to be made by advertising through the social media platforms, and this has put him in a place of crisis. Is Facebook evil, or is it simply a tool? And what about business meetings? Are they an important business tool or a subversive force that drains company profits?

When Craig finds himself in a situation that's outside his core competence—but that he also thinks is his responsibility—his backup behaviors come out. His normal professional and pleasant conversational style turns snappish. He starts scouring the internet and the Amazon bestseller list for advice, usually finding lots of overwhelming and contradictory guidance that leaves him even more aggravated. Today, he's clearly aggravated.

Craig continues. "I've been doing some reading on meetings, and I'm trying to figure out how to make sense of it all. I read *Death by Meeting* by Patrick Lencioni—everyone says that's the best one. He seems to agree with you that meetings should be more fun—or at least more dramatic—but that book really just deals with the meetings held by the leadership team. It's a good one, and I can see some ways that we could make our leadership meetings better now, so that's something. It isn't dealing with our big problem, though. We canceled all the meetings to give everyone else more time to do billable work. It's everyone else's meetings we need to fix. Yes, we know how to run successful Workshops—after we spend at least a week preparing for them in advance. That's not going to work for the other meetings."

Craig takes a bite of his sandwich and continues, "So then I picked up a few more general books on running better meetings. You'd be amazed how many there are! They're all saying we need to create an agenda for every meeting, and then like a hundred other things. As if every meeting we have is a board meeting or something. I can see how we'd have better meetings if we followed all that advice, but I can't see how we'd get anything else done! We don't have time to turn everyone into professional facilitators, and that's not why people hire us anyway. They hire us to make sure they get an awesome brand out there! They hire us to prevent dancing cucumbers! How are we supposed to do all this work to fix our meetings and still do our jobs?!"

— **PB** —

The Impact of Meetings on Productivity

There are many people who feel that meetings and productivity are natural enemies—that every meeting is simply a stinky, hungry lion that devours the graceful gazelle of awesomeness they would otherwise be creating.

Argh! Your meeting ate my hopes and dreams!

Certainly this was the conclusion that our friends at Pacific Bold came to before they decided to cancel most of their meetings. They were spending a lot of time in meetings, and they weren't getting as much work done,;therefore the hungry meetings must be eating the work. Craig's research on what it would take to make their meetings more effective isn't doing anything to shift this perspective either, since now he's worried that they'd just be trading time wasted in ineffective meetings for too much time prepping for effective meetings.

Regardless of whether you believe meetings eat work or, rather as I do, that meetings *are* work, it's useful to see what we can learn from research on productivity and the implications this has for getting to meetings with a Net Positive Impact.

Let's start by clarifying the kind of productivity we're discussing.

Some jobs consist of the repetitive execution of known tasks. My eldest son got his first job as a grocery clerk, where he worked a shift fetching the shopping carts from the parking lot and taking out the trash. When he was called into a meeting (which never happened), it was clearly affecting his trash-emptying productivity.

Information is the raw ingredient for a meeting, and new agreements are the product. After completing his initial training, my son did not require any new information. He had agreed to empty the trash, his employer didn't need him to understand or agree to anything more, and his meeting days were done.

The productivity of repetitive jobs and service work is not the kind of productivity we're concerned with here.

Most jobs, unlike my son's, require regularly updated agreements to stay relevant and productive. For example, Pacific Bold's graphic designers cannot make a career by agreeing to design a single logo for a single client. Properly designed meetings are an excellent way for them to get new agreements.

The *productivity* that meetings may jeopardize is focus time spent by individuals in creating something new. Maker time. Here's what the research can tell us about that precious focus time.

It takes up to 25 minutes to get focused after an interruption.

Meetings are always interruptions, but they are hardly alone. Instant messaging (chat), email, phone calls, and simply sitting in a noisy open office can also interrupt someone's focus. In fact, while "too many meetings" always rates high on the list of interruptions people feel keep them from work, studies find that the rise in always-on communication technology is worse.

One study carried out at the Institute of Psychiatry found excessive use of technology reduced workers' intelligence. Those distracted by incoming email and phone calls saw a 10-point decline in their IQ—more than twice that found in studies of the impact of smoking marijuana, said researchers. "'Infomania' worse than marijuana," the press declared.

Even more alarming, that study was from 2005 and predates the introduction of Twitter (2006), the Facebook News Feed (2006), the iPhone (2007), and the latest always-on darling at the time of this writing, Slack (2013). How many IQ points do you think Pacific Bold collectively lost when they went all-in on email and chat?

Here's a personal example to show how this adds up. I spent two days locked in a hotel room to work on the first draft of this book. In that two days, I wrote for eight hours each day and completed nearly 20,000 words of my draft. I write pretty quickly and had the outline for the full book complete, so when I get uninterrupted time like that, I write like the wind.

By contrast, I've been working on this section from my home office, fitting it between meetings and frequent visits from my five-year-old who insists we all go by our magic names and join her on a quest. Today, I've ostensibly spent six hours writing, and I have just over 1,000 words to show for it.

In my case, the interruption penalty means it takes nearly 8 times longer to complete this task. Yikes!

There is an unmistakable hit to productivity when people are interrupted, and if you look at the pure math of it, the situation looks dire. And yet, we're all clearly more distracted than ever before, and still the world turns. Work gets done. It took forever, but I finished this book—and who really cares that it took six months longer than I had hoped?

So how can this be? Distraction and interruptions are at an all-time high, and work still gets done. Does that imply that we don't need to worry about these interruptions after all?

It turns out that humans are adaptable creatures. In studies looking at the impact of task-switching on productivity (what happens when you're interrupted, or when you try to multi-task), researchers found that people are pretty good at compensating for interruptions. Writing email, reading reports, cooking—those of us who are interrupted frequently during these tasks compensate by typing, reading, and chopping faster than ever!

At the organizational level, your employees' ability to compensate for interruptions may be mitigating some of the big productivity hits, but that doesn't mean there's no impact.

> Surprisingly our results show that interrupted work is performed faster. We offer an interpretation. When people are constantly interrupted, they develop a mode of working faster (and writing less) to compensate for the time they know they will lose by being interrupted. Yet working faster with interruptions has its cost: people in the interrupted conditions experienced a higher workload, more stress, higher frustration, more time pressure, and effort. So interrupted work may be done faster, but at a price.
>
> — Mark, Gudith, and Klocke
> *The Cost of Interrupted Work: More Speed and Stress*, 2008

Even though work still gets done, it's stressing us out! I can tell you for certain that while charming, my constant visits from Sparkle Hearts Zephyr (my daughter) in her quest to free the fairies from the trash monster are driving me freaking bananas.

The most obvious relationship between meetings and productivity is this: **Meetings can negatively impact productivity by interrupting other tasks.**

But...

Meetings drive work completion.

An old adage says that a meeting will expand to fill the time you give it. In the software world, when someone asks how long it will take to complete a project in the very early stages, they'll hear, "How long is a piece of string?" It's an unanswerable question.

Creative work can always be refined. Knowledge work can always achieve a deeper level of truth. Athletes can set new records. That report can always include a shinier chart. We are never really done, so sometimes we need an external constraint to get us there.

Research into creativity and productivity found that, contrary to expectations, teams with severely restricted resources actually produced more creative work than the teams who had more time, money, and access to resources.

Constraints, it turns out, force us to figure out how to get things done.

Meetings can act as a necessary constraint. Meetings set a deadline on the calendar when people are expected to report on progress. Just like a homework due date in school, the meeting date forces people to stop procrastinating and get stuff done.

Project managers know this pattern well, and it's one reason the project status update is a workplace mainstay even though it is also one of the most universally loathed meetings. Many project teams see a dramatic increase of productive output the day (and night) before an important milestone.

In fact, in our Meeting Taxonomy chart, there is whole row of meeting types dedicated to Cadence meetings, all of which are in part designed to impose a useful constraint on how long a team can spend before they need to report some progress.

Meetings as deadlines work extremely well, which is one reason you can see meetings metastasize across an organization. It's a tricky balance, but one that we need to try to get right because…

Too many meetings block the flow. So do too few.

I started this discussion of meetings and productivity by clarifying that we're not talking about the kind of productivity that my teenager needs to achieve in his grocery cart job. Instead, we're more concerned about the impact of meetings on the productivity of modern knowledge workers and skilled professionals.

Next, I shared research that showed how interruptions like meetings could make it take longer to complete tasks like writing an email, and the time penalties paid when we task-switch. But then on the other hand, there's nothing like a deadline to force a project into action. Anyone who's spent any time in the business world knows that many reports are completed exactly 10 minutes before the meeting starts. Deadlines force completion.

Composing email, finishing the report: often important work, but not exactly world-changing. For truly inspiring results, organizations need highly skilled people working in the flow.

"The Flow" is the name given to a skilled individual's peak productive state. Great work happens when people are in the flow, a state of deep concentration and productive output that, when achieved, temporarily suspends time. Research conducted by positive psychologist Mihaly Csíkszentmihályi and his international team found there are 10 components of the flow state.

1. Having a clear understanding of what you want to achieve.
2. Being able to concentrate for a sustained period of time.
3. Losing the feeling of consciousness of one's self.
4. Finding that time passes quickly.
5. Getting direct and immediate feedback.
6. Experiencing a balance between your ability levels and the challenge.
7. Having a sense of personal control over the situation.
8. Feeling that the activity is intrinsically rewarding.
9. Lacking awareness of bodily needs.
10. Being completely absorbed in the activity itself.

In the flow state model (shown below), you can see that Flow occurs when a highly skilled individual engages with a challenge that's just at the edge of too challenging. From the list above, you can see that getting into the flow requires a big chunk of dedicated time.

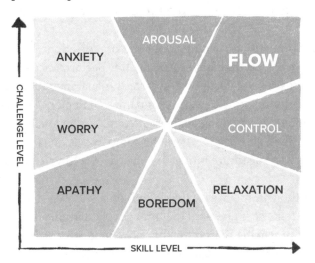

People describe the flow state as a feeling of euphoria or ecstasy. Researchers believe that's because when people are in the flow, they focus all the brain's available resources on a single activity and, in doing so, lose any sense of their mundane problems, the people around them, and even of their own bodies. It is a wonderful feeling arising from a fundamental cognitive limitation: our brains can only pay attention to so much at once!

Personally, I seek the flow state whenever I can. It's a deeply rewarding experience to engage successfully with a tough challenge. And productive! So many more pages written so much faster! That's bank money, friends.

As a business owner, I also want to create the conditions that give my employees access to the flow, because the results that come from people working in the flow can exceed any expectations. When people are deeply engaged and appropriately challenged by their work, they're happier, they spontaneously put in more effort, and they continuously improve.

Workplaces optimizing for flow must make sure high-skilled employees have adequate uninterrupted time to focus. Make sure to reserve several large meeting-free blocks on the calendar to maximize the opportunity for flow.

People require uninterrupted time to achieve flow, but that is not the first item on Csíkszentmihályi's list above. The first item is: *1. Having a clear understanding of what you want to achieve.*

This clear understanding will often emerge from a meeting. Again: We meet to quickly create shared perspective in a group. Shared perspective is the prerequisite to setting clear goals.

Use meetings to ensure people understand the organization's goals.

I've noticed something striking about the organizations Lucid Meetings sees that have achieved a high level of meeting performance maturity. Each one of them uses some form of pervasive transparency to encourage distributed decision making. Several companies champion open book management, giving every employee insight into the organization's detailed financials. "Vivid visioning," where the company vision is written as a full narrative view of the future rather than just a few pithy lines, is a common theme.

At first I thought this was a striking bit of nobility—I'd found the good guys! These folks care about all the little people! Digging deeper, I discovered a more pragmatic reason for this extreme openness: access to information dramatically increases employee performance. If people know the organization's current goals, understand the longer-term vision they're being asked to help build, and appreciate the current conditions affecting their work, *they have a clear understanding of what they need to achieve.* Flow becomes possible, and high-maturity meeting practices are a primary tool used to get there.

A final point about flow: uninterrupted time does not mean solitary time. Chess players achieve flow in a match with an opponent. Musicians and dancers achieve flow during group performances. Computer programmers achieve flow when working together on solving challenging software problems.

For some work tasks, it may be in a meeting where the group achieves flow. Highly skilled business leaders meeting to respond to a strategic threat will lose track of time and forget to eat while they're meeting "in the thick of it."

Sometimes supporting the flow means you meet more, not less.

Tool: Time Blocking

I believe you need to have regular meetings to maintain work momentum. But that doesn't mean these meetings need to be boring, and they definitely should not be allowed to pop randomly across your calendar like bad acne.

What It Is

Time blocking works exactly like it sounds: you schedule time on your calendar for focused work, thereby blocking out any other interruptions like email, meetings, coffee dates, etc. Consider using time blocking to keep meetings productive and minimize disruption to the rest of the work week.

I love time blocking as a personal productivity tool and have found applying it to our whole company incredibly beneficial.

Apparently I'm not alone. You can read more about this in Cal Newport's book *Deep Work*, in Kevin Kruse's research conducted on productivity experts detailed in *15 Secrets Successful People Know About Time Management*, and all over the web.

How It Works at Lucid Meetings

- All weekly meetings, for all departments and projects, happen on the same day. This means people attend several meetings that day, getting into "meeting mode." Tuesday is our Meeting Day.
- One day a week is designated as "No Internal Meetings" day. Everyone can plan to spend the full day focused on completing their part of the work. For those of us who meet with clients, that's part of our work, and now I have several days clear for those.

6:30a workout	6:30a workout	6:30a workout	6:30a workout	6:30a workout
8a–9a Email/Support	8a–9a Meeing Prep	8a–9a DC client meeting	8a–9a Email/support	8a–12p Writing
9a–12p Development	9a–10:30a Leadership Team Meeting	9a–10p Email/support	9a Marketing check in	
		10a–12p Template design	10a–12p Partner meeting	
	11a–12p Marketing Weekly			
12p–1p Lunch	12p–1p Lunch	12p–1p Lunch	12p–1p Lunch	12p–1p Lunch
	1p John one-on-one	1p–4:30p Development	1p–3p Email/support/ administration	1p Email/support
1:30p–2:30p Chicago client project update	1:30p Email/support			1:30p–5:30p Hike
	2p–3p Product review			
2:30p–5:30p Prototype dev	3p Amy one-on-one		3p–5:30p Writing	
	3:30p–4:30p Sales update			
		4:30p–5p Email/support		
	5:45p–7p Elise yoga			

Internal meetings are held on Tuesday. Other days have time blocked out for focus work and client meetings.

We know it takes an unfortunate amount of time to get back on task when we're interrupted, and meetings are always an interruption—unless that's the main focus for the day!

A designated meeting day makes it easier to embrace the work required to make those meetings productive. And planning to spend your day in meetings is a lot easier when you know you'll have a day without any meetings soon.

CHAPTER 10

The Game Changers

I introduced the Core Competencies in chapter 5. Those were the skills and habits that help organizations run quality meetings that people generally enjoy attending. The Game Changers build on the Core Competencies, so let's take another look at those here.

The Core Competencies of High Performing Meetings

1. Know the meeting's purpose and desired outcome.
2. Structure meetings to achieve the desired outcome.
3. Respect the time invested.
4. Structure meetings for engagement.
5. Take visible notes.
6. Publish meeting records where everyone can find them.

On to the Game Changers. These are the practices we've identified at Lucid Meetings that we feel can most quickly and dramatically shift an entire meeting culture, establishing meetings as a practice with a consistently high Net Positive Impact. The four practices work together to establish checks and balances on your meeting system and are most successful when implemented all at once.

The Game Changers

1. Banish abstraction: no "meetings."

2. Every meeting is optional.

3. Time blocking: ensure every employee has inviolable time for focused work.

4. Make meeting performance job performance.

Let's dig into these a bit deeper.

1. Banish abstraction: no "meetings."

Never schedule a "meeting." Instead, clarify your intention, and put that on the calendar. Use the Taxonomy of Business Meetings as a reference to get you started. Getting clear about your intention radically simplifies the work needed to figure out everything else you need to do to make that time successful.

2. Every meeting is optional.

Anyone can opt out of a meeting at any time. This one rule forces several behavior changes:

First, leaders will need to consider how to ensure their meetings are valuable and relevant to attendees. What's in it for them?

Second, meeting records become mandatory. When people do not have to sit physically in every meeting to know what happens, they can choose to stay in the flow rather than attend a meeting that only marginally relates to them.

3. Time blocking: ensure every employee has inviolable time for focused work.

It may not be realistic nor desirable to block out a meeting-free day for your whole company, but you can work with each person to ensure they have an appropriate time block for their position. For front-line employees, this may only be a few hours a week. For teams like mine where everyone has deep focus work to complete, we found it easiest to block out two full days. With these blocks in place, I can schedule any meetings we need on the non-blocked days without worrying that my team will suffer from the loss of focus time.

Also, with dedicated time to focus guaranteed, people are more interested in and willing to engage during meeting days. Time blocking means that most employees don't need to opt out of meetings to get work done; opting out is then reserved for extreme situations and inappropriate meetings.

4. Meeting performance is job performance.

Finally, tie meeting performance to job performance. Do people come prepared to meetings and contribute what they know, or not? Are meetings expected to produce a documented result that will get used to further the work of the organization? In short, are people making sure that what they do in meetings serves the business?

This is an expectation you can set, track, and manage. At Lucid, for example, we review goals and metrics in our weekly Cadence meetings. Should someone fail to report their numbers in advance, we'd be talking about that with them right away because it impedes our ability to manage the business. Should my salespeople regularly botch demos with new clients, we would swiftly intervene. Poor performance in these meetings is not acceptable for our business.

Part of Angie's frustration with the Pacific Bold teams arises because everyone outside the project management group treats the status meetings as something that interrupts their work, rather than as a part of how their work gets done. Should the designers and engineers get a personal visit from their bosses any time they failed to provide their update in advance, or any time they sat in a status meeting playing on their phone, that behavior would change. And, triple bonus, if they actually participated in the meeting, they might find that it became more interesting and useful to everyone.

Checkpoint:
Should you cancel your next meeting?

Before we go further, let's take a moment to review what we've learned so far and then apply that learning in an immediately practical way.

Our friends at Pacific Bold continue to struggle with their meeting problem. They've realized that they have meetings they enjoy but which aren't consistently productive—like the creative Workshops—and meetings they hate which seem necessary for running the business, like the weekly project status meeting.

The Workshops have all the ingredients required for a high Perceived

Meeting Quality. They start and end on time, cover the material everyone expects to cover, and most importantly, they get everyone participating together in the creation of a shared result. They're fun. But, because the Pacific Bold team doesn't always decide in advance what will happen with the work created in a Workshop, these Workshops can sometimes have a negative long-term impact on the business when a client or a new designer feels that the ideas they shared there weren't respected or used.

The project status meetings have clarity of purpose but lack many of the features needed for a high Perceived Meeting Quality. They do follow an agenda, so that's a plus, but it's not an agenda the project manager can ever keep on track. The meetings start late, go long—and should anyone decide to perk up—often veer into tangents. Because tangents are so deadly to the group's time, the project managers work hard to lock down all contributions to the bare minimum, effectively shutting down participation. These are unpleasant meetings, but when they don't happen, the project teams lose the thread of what's happening. Teams miss deadlines, they fail to communicate requirements changes, they're forced to re-do work, and both timeline and budget get blown out of the water. Overall, the Pacific Bold leadership is forced to recognize that these hated meetings have an overall Net Positive Impact on the business.

======================= **PB** =======================

What, then, is a leader to do? The answer: design a system for meetings in your organization that ensures they are both enjoyable and useful.

With that goal in mind, I shared relevant findings from research and some generally useful tools like the Single Topic Agenda and Team Ground Rules. We established the Core Competencies your team needs to learn so they can create quality meetings. And then I shared the Game Changers that your leadership and management groups can use to dramatically shift your meeting culture.

In the rest of the book, we'll dig deeper into how to evolve and scale meeting performance maturity and how to use the Taxonomy of Business Meetings, learning how each type of meeting works on its own and as part of an organization's overall meeting system.

Before we wade into the details, let's take a moment to put what we've learned so far to use. Please take a look at the meetings scheduled on your calendar for the next two weeks. **Ask yourself, given what you know now,**

do you believe those meetings will result in a high PMQ and NPI?

Maybe there are meetings that you're too busy to work on. Maybe your coworkers are too busy. Maybe there's one that's a big interruption that will keep you from more important work. Or maybe the meeting is really important, but you're simply not ready.

Whatever the reason, you now wonder, should you cancel your next meeting? And if so, how can you do that without looking flaky in front of the group?

Some meetings do more harm than good. If a meeting lacks a clear purpose, or the people you need aren't prepared, then the meeting just wastes time and can drain a team's energy. These vampire meetings prey on the productivity and goodwill of a group, leaving them de-energized and frustrated. Cancel those suckers!

A Thinking Person's Guide to Ensuring Meeting Quality Now

Not sure if your meeting is one of the living dead? Here's a handy process to help you and your coworkers spot vampire meetings and drive the cancellation stake through their lifeless hearts. Starting at the top, answer each question in turn.

If you are the meeting organizer: These questions assume you're the person in charge of the meeting, and therefore the one responsible for using the meeting time wisely. If you answer "No" to any of these, you should either cancel the meeting or do the work required so you can answer "Yes."

If you are a meeting participant: If you didn't call the meeting but suspect it's a waste of time, use these questions to request more information from the meeting leader. When that's not possible, refer back to the Single Topic Agenda and consider engaging in a bit of volunteer facilitation.

Question 1: Do you know the meeting's purpose?
Do you know why you need to meet, and why meeting would work better than chat or email in this situation?

Yes! Great! Next question.

No? Cancel it.

Making a decision, kicking off a project, figuring out how to handle an emergency—there are many good reasons to meet. "Just because" is not a valid reason to meet. Because you always meet on Tuesdays, because it's on the calendar, because you're not sure and afraid to ask, because you don't have anything better to do—if you don't know why the meeting matters and can't find out, cancel it.

What to Tell the Group
"Good news! It wasn't clear that this meeting would be a good use of time, so it's been canceled. If you feel the meeting was important, please contact me, and we can discuss a plan for rescheduling it. Otherwise, enjoy your meeting-free time!"

Question 2: Can you describe the desired meeting outcome?
Make sure you can fill in the blank.
Once we have _____, the meeting is over.
(*Examples: a decision, clear next steps, a list of issues to resolve, a plan.*)
Yes! Excellent—on to question 3.
No? Cancel it.
The meeting purpose explains *why* you need to meet. The intended result, or desired outcomes, covers the *what*.

What, specifically, will the team get out of attending this meeting? A new plan, a list of action items, a documented decision? You need to get this figured out. It doesn't have to be fancy or overwrought, but you need to know what you're asking the group to create before you take up their time.

What to Tell the Group
"Sorry, but I need more time to prepare for this meeting to make sure it's worthwhile. I'm canceling this meeting for now to make sure we don't waste anyone's time."

Question 3: Do you have a plan for getting that result?
The plan covers *how* the group will achieve the intended result. Your plan can be simply to ask a few questions, or it could be more detailed. For anything longer than 15 minutes, this usually means you'll have a version of that plan to share with the group in the form of an agenda.
Yes, of course. You're on a roll! See question 4.
No? Make a plan, or cancel the meeting.
Unless you're working in an improv troupe, your colleagues have better

ways to use their time than to get in a room and watch you wing it. And as someone with a Bachelor's degree in Theatre, I can tell you that good improv always begins with a goal, a basic plan, and an underlying code of conduct.

So I retract the theater exception. Pure "winging it" is just plain unprofessional. Bonus: when you work on the plan, you may find that *you can achieve the desired result without meeting at all!*

Question 4: Are the people and resources you need prepared?

If you have questions people need to consider in advance, they've been considered. If there are reports to read or presentations to create, that's done too.

Yes! Looking good... you might just have a worthwhile meeting in your future!

No? Cancel, then reschedule.

You can't have a successful lunch meeting without food. You can't impress a client if you're not ready to talk about the project. You can't make a good decision if people don't understand the options.

If your plan for achieving the meeting result is shot for now, work with the group to find a better time.

What to Tell the Group

"Sorry, but it looks like we're not ready to have this discussion. Let's reschedule for _____ to make sure everyone can come prepared."

Question 5: Did the people you need show up?

Yes. Awesome! Have a fabulous meeting!

No. Ouch!

Don't waste everyone else's time—cut the meeting short and reschedule. And that person owes everyone else a *huge* apology, ideally including chocolate.

What to Tell the Group

"So sorry, but we need _____ here to be effective. Let's not waste any more time today. I'll find out what happened with _____ and try to reschedule as soon as possible."

Only You Can Prevent Bad Meetings

If you are the meeting organizer or leader, cancel the meeting if:

- The purpose, expected outcome, and plan are not clear.
- The group is not prepared.
- Critical people can't or don't attend.

As a meeting participant, ask the leader to fill in any gaps above. If that's not possible, use what you know about the basic structure of an effective meeting to rescue a worthwhile result from an otherwise wasted time.

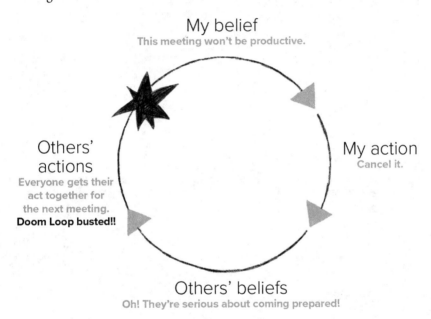

My belief
This meeting won't be productive.

My action
Cancel it.

Others' beliefs
Oh! They're serious about coming prepared!

Others' actions
Everyone gets their act together for the next meeting.
Doom Loop busted!!

Part 3

Mastering the Meetings at Work

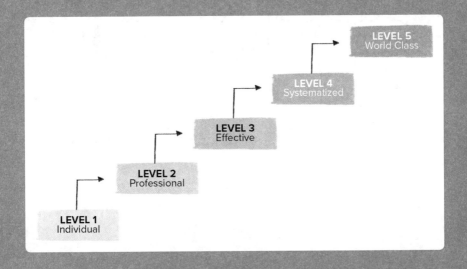

Everyone on the Pacific Bold leadership team shows up for breakfast at the bakery on Tuesday. Once everyone has their espresso and pastry, the conversation turns to work.

Charla clears her throat. "So! Angie, Nelson—how's your project status meeting working out? You've had a few weeks with this new approach. Is it better?"

"Yes," Nelson says.

"Well..." Angie says.

"*Mostly*," Nelson admits.

"Yeah, sort of. I guess," Angie agrees. "I'm still getting used to it. It just seems like we never get through everything we're supposed to get through. So far, we've only had time to talk about two or three issues each week, which leaves a lot more on the list that we never talk about. I always leave feeling like something's incomplete."

"I don't know about that," Nelson says. "I mean, sure, we don't get through that whole list, but do we really need to? I love that the meeting is shorter and, even better, that it's not boring! Last week when everyone really dug in and figured out how to rearrange the photography schedule to fit in both the eggplant people and the goat farm in the same day— that was genius! That's going to save us a week on the goat project and bring both of those campaigns in under budget. And who knows? Maybe there's another magical symmetry there. Do you know if goats eat eggplant? I had goats growing up and I know they'll eat clotheslines, but I've never seen a goat with an eggplant. That could be a cool photo! We don't get to use that deep purple in our work very often; that's a treat. Even if eggplant isn't."

Craig interrupts Nelson's veggie reverie. "That sounds like the kind of thing I've been reading about in these meeting books. Everyone says you have to keep meetings on time, and that you should encourage healthy debate—even conflict! It sounds like you guys are getting there!"

Angie still doesn't look happy. "Yes, we're sticking to 30 minutes as promised, but I worry that we're going to miss something by not looking at the whole list."

"Have you missed anything?" Charla asks. "I know you were caught off guard on Belinda's project when we canceled all the meetings, but since you've added these shorter meetings in, have there been any other big misses?"

"No, not that I know of," Angie says. "Not yet, at least. That's not my only challenge, though. After talking with you and Nelson the other day, I'm now worrying about how everyone else feels about these meetings. I hate the idea that people think we're intentionally trying to waste their time. It's not at all true, of course, but now I can't help noticing when some of the people who show up look like they'd rather be somewhere else. All the project managers are trying hard to make sure that these meetings are valuable to everybody, not just for us, and when we have people playing on their phone or ignoring us in the back of the room, it's super frustrating."

"I'll put a stop to that," Nelson growls, much to his colleagues' surprise. Growling—and frankly any sustained interest in discipline—is deeply uncharacteristic for the creative director.

"Whoa, tiger!" Craig smiles and puts a friendly hand briefly on Nelson's shoulder. Then he continues, "I have another thought. What if you made those meetings optional? Stick to the approach you're trying now, and if someone doesn't think they should attend, let them skip it. If they're not going to participate anyway, what's the harm? Making meetings optional is another tip I read recently, and I think it's worth a try."

"Wouldn't they miss out on the updates, then?" Charla asks. She's intrigued but not sure how this could work.

"Not if there were notes they can review afterwards," Craig says. "You do publish notes after every meeting, right?"

"Um, not really," Angie admits. "We update the project management system, but I already know that people don't check it regularly."

Nelson adds, "I don't think checking the system would do it anyway. The changes we made to fix the eggplant and goat photo shoot involved rearranging dates on five different projects. There's no way anyone would figure that out by just looking at each project's schedule. You kind of had to be there."

"Not if there are notes from the meeting, you wouldn't," Craig says. "You need to take notes and send them out after *every meeting*." Craig says this as if it's obvious. Craig hasn't sent notes out for any of his meetings in the past, but he's been studying up. "All the books say you have to document meeting results. I don't know that we're ready for formal agendas or minutes or anything, but we should at least send out some notes afterwards. That'll help for the people out on assignment too—not just the folks who decide to opt out. Frankly, that should be a new rule. All meetings get notes sent out afterwards."

"What a great idea, Craig!" Charla chimes in. "As you say, you've been reading all the books, and it seems like you've learned a lot of good ideas for what we should be doing in meetings. Why don't you write these up? Create the official Pacific Bold Meeting Rules!"

"Uh…" Craig hasn't considered this.

"Maybe 'rules' is too harsh," Charla continues. "How about 'guidelines'? A Meetings Manifesto? Or maybe something more organic—a Pacific Bold Certified Meeting Checklist? Okay, that doesn't work, but I'm sure you can find the right name. This will be so helpful!"

Craig tries to interject, but Charla is too excited to stop. "Once we get some of these things written down," she continues, "we can start scheduling meetings again just as long as they abide by The Code. Aha! That's good! I like the idea of having a Code! And I, for one, am quite ready to get a few more meetings on my calendar instead of all these lunches. Not that I dislike breaking bread with you all, but my wallet could use a break and I'm sure we're missed in the office."

Charla beamed. "Oh, this is just fabulous! When do you think you can have those ready, Craig?"

"Uh…" Craig sighs.

Craig spends the better part of a week creating the meeting guidelines. He scours the internet for examples and flips through a pile of books before settling on the ones that seem most likely to help the Pacific Bold team. On Friday, he runs the new guidelines by the leadership team, and then together they roll them out to the whole company the following Monday.

While researching his list, Craig is pleasantly surprised to discover that many large and successful companies like Intel and Boeing post their expectations on conference room walls. He works with Nelson over the weekend to make posters for all of Pacific Bold's meeting rooms.

They hang up the posters with pride. Then Nelson fetches Charla to admire their handiwork.

"Yep. This will do it," Craig declares with a grin. "No more lousy meetings at Pacific Bold. We're getting our act together!"

"Looks great, guys! Well done!" Charla says, then pulls them both into a congratulatory hug. "I'm so glad we've got this one handled."

═══════════ PB ═══════════

CHAPTER 11

The Meeting Performance Maturity Model

In Part 2, I talked a lot about how to run a meeting well. Now I'm going to zoom out and look not at individual meetings but rather at the collective set of meetings that organizations run as part of their everyday work.

At Lucid Meetings, we developed a standard performance maturity model to measure how well an organization manages its meetings.

The team at Pacific Bold was operating at what this model considers Level 1. Level 1 organizations don't put any organization-wide focus on how they run meetings, leaving individuals to do the best they can on their own. Level 1 is far and away the most common level of meeting maturity across organizations today. Pacific Bold gives us an example, and I'm sure you have many similar examples in your own experience.

The development of a set of meeting guidelines begins an organization's transition to Level 2. Pacific Bold is maturing—a change forced by a looming financial crisis.

Standard meeting rules (or guidelines) create a consistent foundation of essential skills and shared values that make it possible for organizations to then develop more nuanced approaches to their meetings. At the higher levels of performance maturity, this nuance can get pretty interesting.

Tolstoy's *Anna Karenina* begins with the famous line: "Happy families are all alike; every unhappy family is unhappy in its own way."

When it comes to how an organization meets, however, we find the opposite to be more true. Unhappy organizations are all alike; every happy organization meets in its own way.

The organizations that provide the case study examples for organizational excellence, cultural cohesion, and that achieve that enviable combination of economic performance and a healthy workplace have all created or discovered ways to meet that are uniquely tailored for them. I'll tell you about Zingerman's, one of these high-performance organizations, in the next chapter.

Those organizations that enjoy a high level of meeting performance maturity rarely set out with that as a goal. Just like our friends at Pacific Bold, they design more effective meetings in response to an unavoidable shift in the business. Meetings are never the point; they are simply one tool among many that we use to achieve our goals. Instead of a laser focus on meetings, these organizations have a clear vision and shared values which shape the way they meet. The meetings become the way that the organization practices these values, and the cultural container for the organization's shared identity.

Here's an example of an organization operating at the peak of meeting performance maturity.

Ray Dalio is the founder of the Bridgewater Associates investment management firm and the author of the bestselling business book *Principles*. In his TED Talk, Dalio shares his company's work to create an "idea meritocracy." Their goal is decision-making clarity, radical transparency, and aggressive effectiveness. It works. At the time of this writing, Bridgewater Associates has over $150 billion in assets under management. The culture they've created is extreme—he admits some employees find it doesn't work for them and leave—and their performance is phenomenal. When asked to describe how they practice this idea meritocracy, Dalio describes what happens in their meetings. Ray Dalio's TED Talk shows video from a meeting, there is a picture and description of a team meeting on Bridgewater's home page, he talks about meetings in interviews, and he's writing articles for *Forbes* about running better meetings. Meetings are a major mechanism of their success!

At both of the extreme ends of the meeting performance maturity scale, organizations run highly custom meetings. Low-maturity organizations run largely unstructured conversations—each meeting is a custom, mostly unplanned, and undocumented discussion that can run quite differently between teams and times of day.

High-maturity organizations run well-designed and structured meetings custom-tailored to fit each team, each work stream, and the unique situations they often encounter. In the middle, organizations pass from custom/chaotic into the realm of standardized best practices. (Those

Level 2 Rules that Pacific Bold just developed are the first step in that standardization.)

Organizations in the middle have enough maturity to use appropriate meeting structures but do not yet have enough mastery to transform these meetings into the specialized embodiment of their strategy and values that they could be.

Let's take a look at the Meeting Performance Maturity Model and explore what it means for an organization to operate at each level in more detail.

The Meeting Performance Maturity Model (MPMM) builds on the framing concepts found in the well-established People Capability Maturity Model® (P-CMM®) Version 2.0. The P-CMM has been used since 1995. The latest update came out in 2010, giving us 20+ years of lessons learned by the P-CMM's developers from which we can benefit. Like the larger P-CMM, the MPMM embraces the following ideas.

1. Capability must be developed in stages.

These stages can be described as significant levels that, once achieved, make it possible to progress to the next stage. For example, it isn't possible to consistently monitor and evaluate meeting outcomes (a Level 3 practice) until the organization consistently *documents* meeting outcomes (a Level 2 practice). Similarly, it isn't possible to harmonize meeting practices across business units until after the business units have meeting practices to harmonize.

2. Each maturity level can be the optimal maturity level for some organizations.

Level 1 maturity, where the organization relies on the individual skills and preferences of meeting leaders rather than a set of documented shared expectations, can work beautifully in small organizations with skilled workforces.

This is one reason Pacific Bold got caught off-guard by how much of a negative impact meetings had on their business. When it was just Charla, Craig, and Nelson, Level 1 ad-hoc conversations worked just fine. It doesn't scale very well, though.

Even when you take meetings very seriously, you still might not operate at the top levels of performance maturity. At Lucid Meetings, we operate at Level 3 because we're simply not big enough to warrant Level 4 practices.

Lower maturity levels do not necessarily lead to unsuccessful outcomes.

3. There are many right ways to do meetings.

The capabilities an organization needs in place to achieve each level may be implemented in many different ways. For example, to achieve Level 2 maturity, an organization needs to demonstrate that "Meeting records provide evidence that the expected meeting practices were followed." This might be in the form of formal meeting minutes, follow-up notes in an online system, or in updates to the sticky notes posted on the team's wall. The specific form and contents of the records are determined by the organization and its circumstances.

In addition to these framing concepts, our team also agrees with the performance benefits to be gained when embracing the principles espoused in the P-CMM, such as self-managed teams, decentralized decision-making, access to training across the organization, reduced status distinctions and barriers, and transparency through extensive sharing of performance information. You can find the evidence that an organization follows these principles when you observe their meetings. As I mentioned in the discussion about productivity, all the Level 5 organizations we've encountered espouse these values and benefit as a result.

Unlike the P-CMM, however, the MPMM doesn't seek to overhaul the entire organization. The MPMM focuses narrowly on meeting practices and performance, which, thankfully, makes it much shorter! The P-CMM is a 750-page book on its own—too long for a weekend read!

Here's a quick overview of the five levels.

The Five Levels of Meeting Performance Maturity

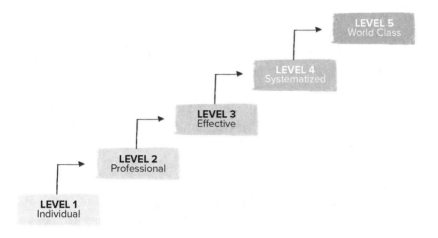

Level 1: Individual
Meeting competency is not an area of organizational focus. Success is dependent on the preferences and abilities of individual meeting leaders.

Level 2: Professional
The organization establishes professional standards for meetings. Leaders take responsibility for ensuring meetings adhere to these standards. At this level, meetings consistently have a clear purpose and documented results, although there may be no further standardization from meeting to meeting beyond these basics.

Level 3: Effective
Meeting processes are defined and implemented to achieve specific outcomes for each business unit.

Once they establish standard professional meeting practices, each team or business unit can focus on making sure the meetings they hold support the specific work they do. Level 3 organizations can successfully apply the Taxonomy of Business Meetings to differentiate between meeting functions and predetermine appropriate meeting structures. Teams and business units often adopt practices described as part of brand-name industry methodologies such as Scrum (for software development) or Six Sigma and Lean (for manufacturing teams).

Level 4: Systematized

Meeting processes are integrated and harmonized across the organization. Systems monitor and evaluate meeting performance data in support of continued process improvement.

The work of this level focuses on process improvement. With documented processes and outcomes in place, organizations can consider which meetings work well, how to handle areas of cross-functional overlap, and how to develop systems that support and automate repetitive tasks (such as agenda preparation and metrics collection) that have been standardized across the organization.

Level 5: World Class

Meeting practices embed the organization's values and strategic priorities. Meetings are continuously improved to optimize strategic outcomes.

Level 5 organizations have achieved mastery over their meetings. These meetings often work so well that other organizations seek to emulate them. These are the organizations from which Level 3 organizations learn best practices.

Meeting Performance Maturity in Practice

Moving beyond the basic definitions above, what does meeting performance maturity look and sound like in an organization?

First, meeting performance maturity is rarely equal across an entire organization. Larger corporations may have varying degrees of maturity by department or location. When Lucid's consulting team works to evaluate a group's performance maturity, we look at *how they operate most often*. Here, the exceptions quite regularly prove the rule.

Level 1 Organizations

New and small organizations may operate here, and that can be entirely appropriate. A Level 1 meeting is basically a pre-scheduled conversation: informal, adaptive, and free-flowing.

Level 1 meetings rarely have an agenda or a clearly stated set of desired outcomes. Groups come together at the appointed time to "talk about" one or more topics. Individuals may or may not take notes, and no one looks for a follow-up report.

Meetings usually involve five or fewer people, and expectations around timeliness are lax. People arrive late, meetings run long, and meetings get rescheduled or canceled often.

When a meeting involving customers, investors, or other high-stakes participants comes around, it's a big deal. These are special events that the team puts extra effort into planning, and this can cause significant anxiety. The agenda, presentations, and planning for these special meetings are treated as a one-off; they rarely result in models that the organization can use for future meetings.

When Level 1 Works
Level 1 meeting maturity can work if teams are small and either know each other well or all feel confident engaging in dialogue. Not coincidentally, these are also the conditions needed for an engaging conversation.

Most startups and new organizations begin at Level 1. These groups operate officially enough that they know they should schedule "a meeting"—but they aren't yet so structured that they're ready to do more than just get together and talk.

This free-wheeling approach puts faith in the concept of emergence, trusting that the key insights and right decisions will emerge when you get people sharing ideas together. That faith is rewarded for some groups.

When Level 1 Fails
Level 1 falls apart quickly and often. You may have noticed that the description of Level 1 meetings lacked many of the essential characteristics required for achieving a high PMQ (Perceived Meeting Quality). More than four people, more than a few hours spent that don't accomplish anything, and some team member will start looking for some structure.

Level 1 can also fail when it encounters the outside world.

Case in Point
For example, Lucid often works with outside contractors and independent vendors, and I cringe when I find myself working with a Level 1 group. These well-meaning folks will book a meeting with me. They don't say what the meeting will accomplish, who needs to be there, or even how long we can expect it to last.

At the appointed time, we'll get together and talk. This part is always pleasant enough. People talk until it feels like it's time to stop talking, and then they go their separate ways.

Then comes the most frustrating symptom of Level 1 "meeting" performance. Over the course of the next several days, I'll get a series of email and text messages all trying to establish what we decided in the meeting we just held and who's supposed to do what. It's like the meeting was simply a warm-up for the real work, all of which will manifest in disorganized fits and dribbles over the course of many extra hours.

I rarely recommend Level 1 vendors to others, which is too bad, because some of them are very skilled in their core offerings. For me, they're just too inefficient and aggravating to work with.

Level 2 Organizations

Many businesses operate at Level 2. At first glance, a Level 2 and a Level 3 organization may look very similar. In both cases, most meetings have an agenda, and that agenda may be roughly the same from week to week for recurring meetings.

After a meeting in a Level 2 organization, someone will usually send out notes by email. If they fail to do so, there's at least a chance someone else will call them on it.

The distinction between Level 2 and Level 3 is this: *The meeting structures you see in a Level 2 organization are entirely dependent on the person running the meeting.* This means that meetings in one group may work very differently than how they work in another group—it is left up to individual managers to decide how to run their updates. While all meetings adhere to a basic set of guidelines, there aren't established practices for running different *types* of meetings. If the person leading a team's meetings leaves or changes roles, the structure that person used rarely survives more than one or two sessions following their departure.

In a Level 2 organization, individual contributors may have meeting skills specifically adapted to their job function, but *this performance is not owned by the organization.* The organization has not established a resilient performance capability specific to the kind of work performed there.

That doesn't mean they're not trying! Take a look at the following Amazon customer review for Cameron Herald's book *Meetings Suck!,* a volume which includes a handful of specific meeting designs but focuses mostly on teaching the basic best practices from the Core Competencies list in Chapter 5.

> *5.0 out of 5 stars*
> **We order *Meetings Suck* a box at a time and you should too.**
> May 2017
> **Verified Purchase**
>   Over the last 6 months my company integrated the learning from this book into every aspect of our day-to-day operations. We ordered a hard copy of this book for every employee. This book is included in welcome packet for all of our new employees. We designed a poster for every conference room in the office that has key principles from the book. We run regular trainings on how to run effective meetings. And we are seeing incredible results. We've effectively eliminated and streamlined a lot of our ongoing meetings and now spend significantly less time per meeting. Our customer and employee satisfaction is at all time highest. As the founder of the company one of the feedback I've gotten is that the team feels that we are doing everything we can to protect their time, to take care of them in the professional area that people often hate the most and make them feel more empowered and better prepared to deliver more value to our clients in shorter meetings, hence scaling the impact of this book outside of our organization. We are now sending it out to all of our new clients as a part of our welcome packet. It is not an exaggeration to say that this has been one of the most influential books for the entire organization
>
> — Amazon Review

This is exactly the kind of transition Pacific Bold is making. The work of this transition is:

1. Establishing basic meeting skills.
2. Efficiency: making sure meetings don't take too much time.

Both of these efforts have a dramatic positive impact on effectiveness.

When Level 2 Works

Level 2 is the typical starting place for new organizations led by experienced founders. It is also the natural transition point for maturing organizations that decide to hire a cohort of managers and focus on operational efficiency.

Level 2 works well for small organizations in transition. The gentleman who left that glowing Amazon review shows how impactful improving meeting performance can be as an organization grows. Groups like this have become too big or too busy to just wing it all the time, but they aren't yet stable enough to worry about specific process repeatability.

Level 2 is also appropriate as a foundational level for extremely large organizations. Intel, for example, is famous for ensuring every meeting adheres to a set of shared best practices across the organization. I've worked quite a bit with teams from Intel, and it's clear that Level 2 performance is expected from everyone there.

Some teams within Intel operate at much higher levels of meeting performance maturity, but because the organization is so big and diverse, it isn't vital for every team or location to achieve these higher levels. Many groups there achieve a solid, but rudimentary, Level 2 proficiency and call it good. Other microfiche to fry and all that!

Level 2 Challenges

I call Level 2 the "Professional" level because meetings here are usually organized, businesslike, and orderly. Participants expect an agenda, and they're comfortable with concepts like assigning action items and tabling a discussion. All the trappings for a functional meeting are in place.

Professional does not mean *effective*, however. Professionalism is a prerequisite for success, not a determinate. I've attended many meetings led by Level 2 professionals that had an agenda but lacked energy, clear outcomes, and any noticeable impact on the rest of our day. Because a Level 2 approach does not guarantee that the person in charge knows specifically what they want to achieve or how to achieve it, these meetings can evolve into little black holes dotted across the calendar. Time and energy go in, but no light emerges.

If they aren't careful, Level 2 organizations can find people going dutifully through the motions during meetings, then immediately shaking off any memories of those conversations as they return to their "real work."

The Level 1 and 2 Trap

Why do so many organizations get stuck at Level 1 or Level 2?

They get stuck because they misunderstand the function of meetings. Consider this 2015 quote from Stuart Butterfield, the CEO of Slack, a company that rocketed from a small group of scrappy technologists to nearly 800 employees in just a few years.

People can go to work every day for a year and not really get anything done because they're just doing the things that they felt they were supposed to be doing. We just went through this process of canceling almost every recurring meeting that we had to see which ones we really needed. We probably do need some of the ones we canceled, and they'll come back—but we'll wait until we actually need them again.

—Stewart Butterfield, Slack CEO

This approach to canceling bad meetings reflects classic Level 1 and 2 thinking. The group at Slack had generic meeting rules, but they still felt that meetings were occupying too much time and that they were attending meetings out of unconscious habit. So they quit them entirely. Sound familiar?

I heartily approve of canceling bad meetings, but I don't advocate this blanket cancel-everything approach. Slack went on a real-world example of the meeting fast, which as you may recall, works like a dietary fast. Yes, a fast will keep you from eating for a while, and you'll probably lose some weight. But waiting to see if you actually need food and then going with whatever you happen to grab in your starving desperation is not the way to successfully change eating habits. Instead of creating a healthy relationship with food, canceling all the meals and daring them to come back just leads to guilty eating and self-loathing.

Organizations that operate with Level 3 meeting performance maturity and above understand that every meeting serves a specific purpose. When a more mature organization has a problem with too many meetings, they evaluate which of these meetings still serves a function, which have outlived their usefulness, and which need to be re-worked. They may cancel lots of meetings, but they won't have to guess which ones need to stay.

Level 3 Organizations
Established teams tend to operate at Level 3 or above.

Meetings in a Level 3 group have an understood function. Where Level 2 leaders work to run better meetings, Level 3 leaders run meetings designed to solve business problems. These folks know the difference between a status update, a Decision Making meeting, and a brainstorming session. They recognize the meetings in the taxonomy, and know which ones they use in their work. Most meetings have either an agenda or a standardized structure of some kind, and people within the organization know what to expect from the different kinds of meetings.

Groups within a Level 3 organization may have adopted their practices wholesale from an established methodology. Project managers, for instance, may be PMI certified, using meetings to formally track risks, issues, and action items. Product groups may adopt Lean or Scrum meeting rituals. Sales representatives will use call scripts and a predefined process for engaging with prospects.

Level 3 is rooted at the team or department level and doesn't always spread to the whole organization. This is because, while functional groups are likely to use an established methodology, internal teams, departments, and leadership teams often do not. These internal discussions may have a regular meeting cadence but don't necessarily follow a purpose-built agenda. This keeps the overall organization at Level 2.

Level 3 groups provide basic meeting training, primarily addressing meeting mechanics. Level 3 organizations have not yet established the facilitation competency that enables them to successfully manage challenging interpersonal dynamics.

Level 3 organizations will have documented meeting outcomes, but they have not necessarily established feedback loops or mechanisms for reviewing meeting performance.

When Level 3 Works

Level 3 works quite well for many groups, especially if they achieve Level 3 across the entire organization.

An organization moving from Level 2 to Level 3 can see enormous productivity benefits and improvements to team morale. Transitioning from the generic soupiness of Level 2 to having "a way" to make decisions, share information, and keep work on track clears roadblocks and reduces uncertainty. Participation typically improves, as does work momentum. Simply knowing how and when a group will meet alleviates a ton of wasteful cognitive overhead and prevents valueless decision fatigue, which happens when people waste their decision-making energy on figuring out how to run each and every conversation instead of saving it for making important business decisions.

Organizations seeking Level 3 performance will find many well-lit paths to follow. There are established practices and methods for every major functional group in the modern organization. Designers, developers, product managers, human resources, customer service, sales, marketing, committees, boards, emergency teams, safety teams, trainers—you name it, there's a meeting prescription for it. Leadership teams? Hooboy—so many options! As they work to achieve Level 3, the group's job is to figure out what they need to achieve in their meetings, then find which of these examples to follow.

Achieving Level 3 across the organization means no more mystery meetings. Because the majority of meetings have a basic clarity of purpose and some kind of documented outcome, you can expect them to provide an adequate PMQ and NPI.

Does that mean Level 3 is good enough?

For many organizations, yes. Certainly this works for my team. We're competent, we don't run meetings that are a waste of time, and we get stuff done. For a small company, we punch above our weight, and I believe a lot of this can be attributed to the effectiveness of our meetings.

Operating at Level 3 can fail, though, when organizations mistake their adopted meeting standards as inflexible mandates. When a team follows a prescribed agenda without understanding the underlying intention behind that design, commitment and performance both suffer. The team begins meeting on autopilot and can lose awareness of why they meet the way they do. Leaders may doggedly "stick to the script" to ensure they've checked off all the boxes and lose sight of important changes in meeting context. Because a Level 3 organization lacks mechanisms for monitoring and adjusting their practice, it becomes especially prone to "going through the motions" in a way that disengages employees and evokes the worst of bureaucracy. Worse still, as the world changes, the organization could find itself sticking to a process that does more harm than good.

This perversion of purpose leads to the kind of tongue-lashing Diana Larsen received at a conference of Agile practitioners. Diana is the co-author of two books about running successful meetings with Agile teams, including the gold standard *Agile Retrospectives*. At this conference, she found herself in a discussion group with a few folks who didn't know this about her—that she is in fact the world's leading authority on how to run retrospectives well—when one fellow complained that people weren't engaging in his retrospectives. Diana suggested that he might try asking his team a different set of questions. He angrily snapped back, "No, that's not how it works. I know what I'm doing. My Agile coach was clear when he taught us that you ask these three questions in retrospectives, so I know

I'm doing it right. The problem is my team!" This guy clearly thought the specific rules he'd been taught were the only way, rather than one example approach.

Level 3 can also fail when it doesn't mature to Level 4. Level 3 begins at the team or functional group level. This can create a ripple through the organization, inspiring other teams to clarify how they meet. But sometimes those ripples can dissipate, leaving the Level 3 team stranded on an isolated island in a sea of Level 2 generic practice. Do the seas recede, putting all the teams on dry land? Or does the island get washed away?

Before coming to Lucid Meetings, I worked at a company that was taking its first steps toward Level 3. I've already talked about how the development team switched to using the Agile methodology for their meetings—a Level 3 progression. In the same company during the same time period, the sales team attended Sandler Sales Training, began documenting their sales funnel, and scripted out the various calls they'd make at each stage. The customer project teams developed a formalized client kickoff, a discovery process, a project retrospective practice, and a weekly all-projects review meeting (called the PORK, an acronym that stuck with me even though I've long since forgotten what it stood for).

There was no coordination regarding meeting practices between these groups. No one (to my knowledge at least) was trying to figure out if the Sandler process and Agile Scrum were compatible. The functional groups were all speaking different languages, so that was a challenge, but on the bright side, people in each group knew why they were meeting and how to get work done in those meetings.

Unfortunately, this Level 3 wave did not wash over the senior management team. They never adopted a predictable or purpose-driven set of meetings, which in the end led to the erosion of many of the Level 3 gains made in other departments. I was there long enough to see the butchery of the PORK meeting and the sales scripts, and I made my exit happily just before the dissolution of the Agile practices in the development group.

Ideally, Level 3 is a stage that teams and organizations transcend. Level 3 serves as an awakening: people learn how and why to meet, and they begin using meetings as handy tools for getting things done. Then, as their skills grow, their awareness changes, and their needs evolve, they progress to Level 4.

Level 4 Organizations

A Level 4 organization maintains both prescriptive meeting standards dictating how certain meetings will work and a developing library of more general-purpose processes and techniques. Prescriptive standards are actively updated and revised, so while the process used may be strict for a given meeting, it remains flexible and adaptive over time so it can be improved for future meetings.

The Level 4 organization has developed systems that make this balance between control and evolution possible. When new groups form, the system ensures they have access to the organizational meeting standards. As individuals and teams across the organization use these standards to run their meetings, the system provides a way for them to track results and report on their experiences so that others can learn from them.

Often a Level 4 organization will have this structure in place because they must. When you work in certain parts of the government; international standards development; or in other regulated, certified, and audited environments, there are rules to be followed and records to keep. There is never a question of whether to prepare an agenda. Instead, the question might be how far in advance that agenda needs to be published.

Training and education in a Level 4 organization includes meeting facilitation skills. Meeting participants learn how to provide constructive criticism, how to respectfully listen and challenge, and how to actively contribute. Meeting processes may be designed to foster teamwork, engagement, and trust as well as execute work deliverables.

Level 4 organizations may not have trained facilitators on staff, but they know what these professionals do, and they make use of their services.

When Level 4 Works

Level 4 organizations integrate meetings into their business workflow. Most meetings achieve a useful result. If people feel a meeting isn't working well in a Level 4 organization, they are likely to look at how to improve or cancel that specific meeting rather than reacting against all the meetings in the organization.

When an organization operates at this level, the conversation changes. We see meetings discussed in context, and we see consultants offering more targeted advice.

For example, instead of talking about *how* developers should meet (a Level 3 basic structure question), the discussion may turn to developing Agile fluency (a Level 4 managed capability discussion).

An example of the power of a Level 4 approach comes from the $30 billion+ annual direct selling industry. Level 4 standardized meeting systems power companies such as Amway™, Herbalife™, Mary Kay®—and who hasn't heard of a Tupperware party? Brownie Wise developed the original Tupperware party for Tupperware in the 1950s, teaching housewives across the U.S. how to sell Tupperware to friends and relatives from home. Over the years, the standard meeting structure for a Tupperware party has evolved. Hosts are no longer required to wear stockings and gloves, for example, but the Tupperware party persists. A comprehensive system of oversight, centralized reporting, and ongoing training help Tupperware sellers follow successful standard approaches across the globe. At its peak, Tupperware sellers hosted parties in over 100 countries. You can't scale a successful meeting approach like this without some kind of systematic support in place.

Tupperware gives us an example of another Level 4 characteristic. Meetings across a Level 4 organization use similar language and follow similar structures, but they are not identical. Tupperware parties in Germany are not exactly like Tupperware parties in Indonesia. In the MPMM, we refer to this diverse-but-aligned approach as "harmonized."

That step—where an organization harmonizes practices across locations and/or teams and creates the systems to support those shared practices—also contributes dramatically to an organization's ability to sustain these practices over time.

Level 4 Challenges

Organizations operating at Level 4 risk becoming stale. Level 4 can break down when groups stop questioning the process, or when the larger environmental conditions make the process obsolete.

Continuing with the example of Tupperware, while there are still parties, they are no longer held in as many countries as they once were. In recent years, Tupperware products have become available from the company directly online, and the company has experimented with selling through more conventional retail outlets. The Tupperware meeting system still drives private sellers everywhere, but it isn't as effective as it once was.

In our practice at Lucid, we see Level 4 organizations that have become very comfortable with their current process. Meetings run smoothly, people know what to expect, and they achieve consistent results. These organizations also tend to have a fairly stable membership.

Much like those heart-stopping moments in a thriller movie, things are quiet. Perhaps *too* quiet.

The problem these groups run into is stagnation. Everything works fine, so they stop looking around them to see what else they might try. And because the process they're using was created at a time and place with an older core membership group, it gets rooted in a way that makes it hard for new people to join in.

If a Level 4 organization runs into problems with a meeting, they're mature enough to change the process and fix the problem. But if they don't have obvious problems, the process gets rigid, increasing the risk that it will break badly in the future.

Level 5 Organizations

Level 5 meeting performance maturity is rare. An organization operating at Level 5 will have an established team of internal facilitators and a continuous improvement mindset regarding meetings. This continuous improvement mindset is essential for Level 5 performance, because that's what prevents the fragile rigidity problem organizations can encounter at Level 4. Level 5 practices are resilient.

I see Level 5 meeting performance maturity in two places: in departments or teams within larger organizations, and in mid-sized organizations led by people who champion meeting maturity—even if they don't call it that.

In the introduction to this section, I mentioned how Ray Dalio and the folks at Bridgewater Associates use meetings to drive performance. I encourage you to watch Dalio's TED Talk, where you'll see him explain the systems Bridgewater has put in place to support their practices with real-time evaluations and feedback. Each participant in their meetings is invited to offer written guidance to every other person and rate them on how well they exhibit the company's stated values. They also make video or audio recordings of nearly every meeting, giving everyone a chance to review the results and comment on ways to improve the process. This commitment to continuous learning and improvement ensures that the organization's meeting approach stays rigorous but not rigid.

Bridgewater Associates provides an extreme and highly successful example of Level 5 meeting performance maturity.

Another Case in Point

For a department-level example, the executive teams within high-performing companies often operate at Level 5. My partner John Keith likes to tell stories about Intel under the leadership of Andy Grove, the author of *High Output Management* and a close collaborator with Peter Drucker, both of whom were strong advocates for effective meetings.

John remembers one especially vivid meeting he attended in his twenties, where he had to present his team's project results to Andy Grove and the executive team. John's boss helped with the presentation, and then John's boss's boss coached them both to get the message right. John was expected to be clear, efficient, on-point, relevant, and ready to engage in the follow-up discussion. What great training for a young engineer!

There was no question about whether a meeting with Andy Grove or anyone at the Senior Vice President level and above would be effective. As we discussed when looking at Level 2, this wasn't true of every group at Intel then and isn't today, but as high-performing meetings were the expected *minimum bar* at the executive level, meeting performance became aspirational and common throughout the organization.

When Level 5 Works

Level 5 works. This is the height of performance maturity, where the organization values meetings, understands how to use them, and continuously improves meeting practices to achieve consistently excellent results.

And really, who doesn't like consistently excellent results? I'm seeing an increase in the number of organizations with an internal facilitation team—a sure sign that the organization recognizes and invests in systematic support for effective meetings.

When Level 5 Fails

Wait, what? This is the peak level of maturity. How could it fail?!

It's certainly possible and easy for Level 5 performance to regress back to a less mature level. Level 5 can fail to be Level 5 when support or investment wanes.

That said, I haven't seen enough organizations operating with Level 5 meeting performance maturity to have encountered one where consistently operating at Level 5 created problems. This is an ideal to which organizations aspire and by definition a stage of continuous improvement.

Allow me to speculate, though. I think a potential risk could be this:

Meetings are a tool. They're a useful, powerful, and important tool, and we need to mind how we use them, because a meeting's impact can be mighty. But the meetings are never the point, and it's possible with Level 5 focus, an organization could be spending just a bit *too much time* paying attention to them. I haven't encountered very many organizations at Level 5, and while I find this level of performance extremely compelling, many people have built very successful organizations without getting there.

A Caution Concerning Questionable Cause

Before I dive into the specific criteria used to evaluate an organization's meeting performance maturity, I want to take a moment to discuss complexity. Have you heard of the logical fallacy called *Questionable Cause* or *False Cause*?

Here's a brief definition from yourfallacyis.com:

> **false cause**
>
> You presumed that a real or perceived relationship between things means that one is the cause of the other.
>
> Many people confuse correlation (things happening together or in sequence) for causation (that one thing actually causes the other to happen). Sometimes correlation is coincidental, or it may be attributable to a common cause.
>
> Example: Pointing to a fancy chart, Roger shows how temperatures have been rising over the past few centuries, whilst at the same time the numbers of pirates have been decreasing; thus pirates cool the world and global warming is a hoax.
>
> — yourlogicalfallacyis.com/false-cause

Social psychologist and author Robert Cialdini has shown how marketers and salespeople can use this fallacy to their advantage by getting buyers to focus attention on something specific just before sellers present their product. Pictures of bikini-clad women drinking draft beer can lead one to believe that draft beer attracts sexy, uninhibited ladies. Marketers know that we often believe that "what's focal is causal," or said another way, that because we're paying attention to a thing, that thing must be important.

In my experience, draft beer attracts wasps and drunken uncles. Bikinis and draft beer? Eh, not so much. (Now margaritas, on the other hand....)

Meeting performance maturity looks at one aspect of how an organization operates in isolation. Hearkening back to my biological analogy of organizations as organisms in Part 1, we're just looking at the circulatory system here.

The Meeting Maturity Performance Model implies that by designing better meetings, you can lead a more successful organization.

Do better meetings make for a healthier organization? Yes. Also, healthy organizations have better meetings.

There's a very tight *correlation* between the quality of meetings and the organization's overall performance, but it's important to recognize that leaders like those I met at Zingerman's do not attribute their organizational performance primarily to how they meet.

At the risk of being overly reductionist, I would say that the high-performing organizations I've studied attribute their success mostly to clarity of vision and transparency in operations. Clarity and transparency certainly provide a common cause for both excellent meetings and excellent organizational health.

Overall, though, this is complex stuff. It's interrelated in surprising ways. As you consider how you'll engage in your journey toward better meetings, keep this in mind and be prepared for the ripples.

CHAPTER 12

Zingerman's:
A Profile of High Performance

I spent four days in Ann Arbor, Michigan, visiting Zingerman's Community of Businesses.

The Zingerman's universe consists of 10 separate-but-connected businesses focused on great food, great service, and great finance. If you like very tasty things, you should check them out. They have a mail-order service, so you can even experience their tasty things without ever braving the Michigan snow.

I had seen Ari Weinzweig, one of the founding partners, speak at a conference and suspected that this organization knew how to do meetings right.

However, this was only a suspicion, so I decided to ask if they'd be open to an interloper observing their meetings. I spent half an hour on the phone with Mara, the coordinator for Zingerman's speaking engagements. Before I asked about a visit, I probed Mara for evidence that the trip would be a worthy investment.

"Mara," I asked. "Can you tell me about the different kind of meetings your team has?"

Sure she could! Mara's team has a weekly meeting, just like the teams across all the related businesses. Many people also serve on committees that meet regularly to tackle things like safety and benefits. The folks at the deli are incorporating Lean—ask them about their Katas (a kind of short, continuous-improvement project review meeting). The managing partners from each business meet every two weeks for three hours and have an offsite once per quarter. There's also... (the list went on).

Zingerman's has a clear cadence of functional meetings. You can ask anyone in their organization this same question, and they don't even blink. They simply rattle off the list.

"Do you have defined roles in your meetings?" I asked Mara. "And who leads the meeting?"

"Well, do you mean the leader or the facilitator?" she replied. "Because the facilitator is in charge of the process, of course, and the leader owns the content. Does that make sense? We also have a time keeper, a note taker, and a monkey minder."

"Did you say 'monkey minder?'"

"Oh, that's what we call the to-dos," Mara said. "You know, for things that come up that people need to do. The monkey minder keeps track of what people said they'd do and when they expect to have it done, and then we report back on our monkeys at the next meeting."

I had planned to ask if they used any special Zingerman's language in their meetings. No need.

"Gotcha," I said. "Okay, what about rituals? Are there any special things your team always does? Maybe at the start or end of a meeting?"

"You mean the bookends? Sure," Mara began. "We start our meetings with an energy meter. Everyone says where their energy is on a scale of zero to 10 (10 is great) and why. That lets us know how everyone's doing and gives people a way to say if there's something going on for them that others should know. Then we always close with appreciations, sharing specific things that someone else did that we really appreciated. It's nice, and Ari says it's also a good way to prevent the 'meeting after the meeting,' because we're all really ready to get back to work after that. Is that the kind of thing you're thinking about?"

Yep, that's precisely what I was looking for! Final question: "Do you have any trained facilitators on staff?" I asked. Remember, the flagship business in the Zingerman's community is a deli.

"Oh, yeah," Mara said. "We actually have a facilitators' training class here that any employee can take. Elnian teaches that one. You should meet her if you come to visit."

I booked the trip to Michigan.

Based on my conversation with Mara, I expected to find a high-performance meeting culture. I expected the meetings to run smoothly, with clear agendas and records distributed afterwards. I expected to see team leads walk the group through business results, keeping the meeting content focused on larger company goals. I expected to watch the leaders model language that reinforced the company values and to hear a handful of token appreciations to close each meeting out.

I wasn't prepared for what I actually saw.

Yes, the meetings covered the key business results, but it wasn't the manager who led this part. I saw line cooks and servers and food runners stand up and report on ticket sales, net promoter scores, and revenue. Appreciations were genuine, not token. Appreciations were specific, abundant, and heartfelt. Nancy, a server who clearly delights her customers, heard compliments about her fabulous service read aloud from the table surveys and was visibly moved by the warm round of applause this inspired.

In a meeting with another team, one person proposed adding the team meeting norms to the top of the agenda and meeting notes, just so they could have them handy for new people and as a reminder for themselves. The people in the room agreed that this could be really useful—without a drop of irony. They all appeared to believe that meeting norms were a genuinely useful tool, and they wanted to have this tool at the ready. I know trained facilitators who get squeamish about ground rules! This one caught me off guard. And while I'm sure everyone had their company manners on, I don't believe my presence had a significant impact on the proceedings.

At dinner one night I asked Rick, one of the managing partners, about how they make decisions.

He replied without hesitation: "We use consensus."

"What does *consensus* mean for you?" I asked. Too often, groups assume consensus is implied by the lack of strong opposition. Consensus fails when it isn't clearly defined. Many groups never learn this and operate for years with false consensus.

Rick immediately replied, "Consensus is when you're 80% on board with the content of a proposal and 100% willing to support it, and we all unanimously agree on this."

I heard this same description from five different people at separate times. They've defined *consensus* and that definition is broadly understood.

"Yes, the partners' group uses consensus." Elph confirmed at lunch the next day. He's an Information Technology (IT) manager who also happens to be a trained facilitator. "Of course, that's the best of the four decision-making methods we have, so we try to use it whenever we can. There are times when Delegation, Consultation, or even Command are necessary too, so it's the leader's job to make that clear."

How many decision-making methods do the IT people in your organization know?

The Meeting Performance Maturity Model defines specific benchmarks that help us determine an organization's performance maturity. I'd been able to check off that Zingerman's had most of these in place myself during the visit, but there were several that I wasn't sure about. I pulled up the list and asked Elph about the last few.

Before I share his reaction, let me give you some context. When I originally put these benchmarks together, I shared them with several expert meeting consultants, business gurus, and academic researchers. The overwhelming feedback I heard was that I'd set the bar too high. I was establishing an unrealistic standard that no organization could meet. They told me I'd be lucky to find more than a handful of organizations that could ever achieve Level 3, much less the highest-end Level 5.

When I shared this same list with Elph, he seemed confused. "What do you mean, 'Do we let people experiment with new technology and techniques?' Why *wouldn't* we? They just do it. If someone has an idea for something that could make our meeting better, we give it a try. Last week one of my guys brought us this new mobile polling app for our meeting, and we tried it out. If it's really expensive, they'd have to lead that change and make the case, but anyone who has an idea can write up a proposal. Why would we get in the way of people trying to make our meetings better?"

I asked about whether they talked about meeting participation when they gave performance reviews. Elph replied, "If someone isn't participating at all, that's going to come up for sure. But for all of the managers, we expect them to participate in meetings. Actually, every manager has to teach at least one class too. It's one of the ways they develop as leaders. So, yes, I'd say meeting performance is built into the job."

For this organization, the benchmarks were not too high. They were assumed—to the degree that it seemed silly to ask the questions.

"What am I missing?" I asked. "I feel like I've come looking for a high-performing organization, and so that's what I see. I'm worried that this is all confirmation bias."

Elph responded, "Well, you're asking, 'Do we do *this or that good meeting practice,*' but you're not asking about what's messed up in our meetings.

You probably *are* getting confirmation bias and should ask a different question."

"You're right. Good point. Okay, Elph, what's not working in your meetings? What could Zingerman's do better?" I asked.

He considered, began to speak, stopped, then laughed. I relished the pause and a handful of sweet potato fries. (Did I mention they have great food?)

Finally, he said, "We don't have a class that teaches people how to be good participants. Especially some of these really young employees and the part-time people who haven't been to many meetings before. A class for meeting participants could help them better understand how to get involved. I'd also like to teach a course on how to take minutes. It's harder than people think, and if you haven't done it before, you may not understand what needs to be written down and how to make it easy for people who weren't at the meeting to pull out the key points. We could be doing better there."

I don't know. When the room for improvement is better training on meeting participation for part-time, frontline staff, I think you're doing pretty darn good.

I also had lunch with Elnian, who teaches the facilitation class. She shared the seven steps to effective Zingerman's meetings, their glossary of meeting terms, the outline for her class, and more. I asked her, "Elnian, now that you've been in this role for a while, what still surprises you? What's turned out to be quite different from what people would expect if they were just reading about all this?"

Elnian answered, "What strikes me now as so important and so *not obvious*—even though it *sounds* obvious—is that doing great work is a choice. It's my job, and it's the organization's job to give people here the opportunity to make that choice. But whether they buy in or not, that's up to them. And it's hard! Making that choice to do the right thing every day—it never stops. Sometimes I'm not sure how I'll actually pull it off and I'm tired, and I realize I have to make that choice again, every time. It can be really, really hard....

"And, yeah, I love it."

CHAPTER 13

The Five Focus Areas of Meeting Performance Maturity

The Meeting Performance Maturity Model (MPMM) provides structure for evaluating meetings across your organization, with the belief that meeting well is a foundational capability that organizations must develop in order to thrive.

In Chapter 5, I introduced a set of core competencies every organization should know and use to establish basic proficiency. Every meeting involves people sharing information and creating shared meaning, and as such, every meeting must address the essential foibles inherent to human communication so that the shared meaning can emerge.

So there are basics: rules that are not universally true, but truly useful.

Pacific Bold is moving from Level 1 to Level 2 with the creation of their Meeting Code. You'll see how this fits into the benchmarks below.

After an organization gets the basics in place, there's a vast array of good practices, novel techniques, and experimental approaches for achieving mastery in a variety of contexts. What works in one meeting does not necessarily work in another.

Organizations that achieve higher levels of meeting performance maturity go beyond the basics and become masters of how they engage with each other and the world around them. Meetings are a tool, and master craftsmanship is achievable.

Now that we've looked at the five levels of performance maturity and some examples of what performance looks like out there in the real world, let's dive into the details behind how you can assess your organization's MPMM level.

There are five major focus areas of meeting performance. They are:

1. Meeting Design

The Meeting Design component looks at how well a group understands and standardizes its approach to the different kinds of meetings it holds. Low-maturity organizations make little distinction between meeting types and no attempt to standardize their approach. High-maturity organizations develop standardized meeting practices specific to each meeting function and tailored for their unique work context and culture.

Note: there are no benchmarks for Level 1 since organizations do not put a focus on meeting capability development at that Level.

Meeting Design Benchmarks
Level 2: Professional
- Expected meeting practices are documented.

Level 3: Effective
- Business units use predictable meeting structures and cadences designed to deliver pre-determined business outcomes.
- Distinct meeting roles are identified and documented.
- Meeting designs clarify the process for making decisions within that business unit.
- Meeting process documentation is maintained, communicated, and accurate for each business unit.

Level 4: Systematized
- Business process definition includes identification and integration of meeting practices across business units.
- Standard organization-wide meeting structures are documented for each distinct type of meeting conducted as part of normal operations.
- Unit-specific meeting practices are evaluated and harmonized when a proven performance benefit can be achieved.
- Standardized decision-making methods are developed and shared across the organization.

Level 5: World Class
- Meeting designs intentionally reflect organizational values and strategic priorities.

- Existing meeting designs evolve based on experimentation and regular critique.
- Proactive initiatives are taken to design new meeting structures based upon gaps identified through self-assessments.
- Meeting process documentation and controls are proactively developed and validated when work on new systems, products, or initiatives begins.

2. Meeting Skills

The Meeting Skills component assesses the ability of people in an organization to schedule, convene, facilitate, design, and effectively participate in meetings. Low-maturity organizations take no special effort to recruit or cultivate these skills. High-maturity organizations develop these skills across the organization and support skill development as part of recognized job functions.

Meeting Skills Benchmarks
Level 2: Professional
- Meeting leaders are expected to follow the documented practices.
- Meeting records provide evidence that the expected meeting practices were followed.

Level 3: Effective
- Training programs for meeting leaders in best-practice methodology and basic facilitation are in place.
- Training and/or mentoring on meeting participation is in place.
- Meeting outcomes are consistently documented and traceable across sequences of related meetings.
- Job descriptions and interviews address meeting conduct.

Level 4: Systematized
- Training programs for meeting facilitation and design are in place.
- Meeting leaders and participants receive ongoing training and have access to mentorship and coaching programs.
- Meeting performance expectations are documented and discussed as part of job performance review.

Level 5: World Class
- Meeting facilitation and design is a recognized job function and core competency within the organization.
- Effective meeting participation enables distributed decision making throughout the organization.
- Individuals take advantage of resources for continuously improving meeting-related skills.

3. Stakeholder Satisfaction

PMQ and NPI! Are meetings in the organization considered enjoyable and useful? Do the people involved both inside the organization and externally feel like the meetings are relevant and productive? Do meeting outcomes serve both the meeting participants and the people affected by those outcomes? The Stakeholder Satisfaction component digs into this aspect of performance maturity. Low-maturity organizations do not ask these questions; high-maturity organizations track this information and use it to improve.

Stakeholder Satisfaction Benchmarks
Level 2: Professional
- Meeting participants are empowered to require meetings adhere to documented practices.

Level 3: Effective
- Key stakeholders are identified, including both meeting participants and those impacted by meeting outcomes.
- Metrics are established and collected for both qualitative and quantitative meeting satisfaction and performance indicators.
- Proactive initiatives are in place to minimize or eliminate ineffective meetings.

Level 4: Systematized
- Stakeholder feedback is consistently collected across the organization.
- Inappropriate meeting structures or behaviors impacting stakeholder expectations receive corrective attention from management.
- Meeting performance metrics are available for audit and regularly

reviewed.

Level 5: World Class
- Stakeholder feedback validates that the meeting structures used meet or exceed stakeholder expectations.
- External stakeholders and observers have qualitatively consistent experiences when meeting with different groups within the organization.

4. Facilities, Technology, and Resources

This component examines the infrastructure in place to support and measure meeting performance, with an emphasis on how easy the organization makes it to plan and lead consistently effective meetings. Low-maturity organizations have little support beyond basic meeting scheduling. High-maturity organizations use systems to streamline meeting tasks and records collection, and provide world-class facilities for conducting meetings.

Facilities, Technology, and Resources Benchmarks
Level 2: Professional
- Support for scheduling, holding, and recording meeting outcomes is in place.

Level 3: Effective
- Centralized meeting records are available for the standard meetings conducted by each unit.
- Meeting facilities and technology support the designed meeting processes.

Level 4: Systematized
- Systems are in place to automate high-frequency meeting tasks.
- Meeting content is centrally available and can be easily reviewed.
- Meeting design and process documentation is available in standardized formats.
- Meeting performance metrics are consistently collected, are readily available, and can be examined on multiple dimensions.
- The organization maintains a well-stocked meeting toolkit,

including appropriate facilities, technology, and supplies for in-person meetings and remote meetings.

- Employees have access to internal resources that support continuous improvement in meeting skills.

Level 5: World Class
- Meeting facilities and technology are consistently updated to support a wide range of meeting practices.
- Individuals throughout the organization receive support for participation in professional development activities outside the organization.
- Individuals can access experimental technologies and resources for evaluation in support of continuous meeting-performance improvement.

5. Cultural Ownership

The Cultural Ownership component addresses integrity in the organization's meeting practice. As many consultants will tell you, the easiest way to determine an organization's true culture is to observe a team meeting. Low-maturity organizations just meet, leaving the way that people treat each other and what they talk about to the discretion of individual managers. High-maturity organizations walk their talk. They have an established code of conduct for meetings that applies equally to everyone, and they adopt rituals that expressly reinforce their stated values and priorities.

Cultural Ownership Benchmarks
Level 2: Professional
- Meeting expectations are consistently communicated across business units.

Level 3: Effective
- Participation from everyone invited to a meeting is expected, encouraged, and supported by the meeting structures in use.
- Updated meeting practices are developed with input from various employee groups.
- Employees feel empowered to raise questions about meeting practices and performance.

Level 4: Systematized

- Meetings incorporate organization-specific language and rituals that harmonize the organizational culture across business units.
- Employees and leaders assume joint ownership for meeting success.
- People are recognized for demonstrating effective meeting skills.

Level 5: World Class

- Meetings embody the organization's declared culture.
- Meeting design efforts optimize for both business outcomes and cultural cohesion.
- Past meeting outcomes are reviewed and evaluated for net positive impact.

What it Takes for Organizations to Change Levels

We like to think that organizations become more mature over time, but as discussed in Chapter 11, it is also possible for organizations to regress to lower levels of maturity as the people and systems in place change.

Some organizations fail to mature at all because they lack the resources required. As this table shows, higher levels of performance maturity require increased investment.

Transition	Individual-Led	Leadership-Led	Systematic Support
Level 1 to 2	Possible	Ideal	Minimal
Level 2 to 3	Possible	Ideal	Ideal, but not required
Level 3 to 4		Required	Required
Level 4 to 5		Required	Required

Achieving meeting performance maturity of Level 3 or above must be supported by those in charge, and with systems that make this performance sustainable.

Stories of Organizations in Transition

Moving from Level 2 to Level 3

I have seen a handful of companies try to move from Level 2 to Level 3. They worked to define approaches for customer calls, for kicking off projects, and for running internal program review meetings. Two of the three companies I watched failed because the CEO didn't support the effort and refused to participate in the new structure. One remained firmly at Level 2, and the other regressed fully back into Level 1.

In the third company, the board fired the CEO and replaced him with someone who was ready to take the company to the next level. That company excelled and was successfully sold within the year, achieving a key business goal.

Regressing from Level 3

The secretary for an advisory board called when they experienced a precipitous fall all the way from Level 3 to Level 1 following a leadership change. This board had an established history of structured meetings, clear roles, and documented results. When the new leader arrived, he declared, "We don't need all this structure!" and threw it all out, much to the confusion of the rest of the group. As an advisory board, they weren't bound by the same legal requirements for documentation that govern a fiduciary board, but it was pretty wild to suggest that their meetings should be structure-free.

It's not clear what the new leader found objectionable about the way the advisory board's meetings worked. Maybe he felt that the structure they were using was too binding, and it kept the group from really engaging. Maybe he didn't like the transparency and accountability the structure provided. Regardless of what the real issue was, his actions caused the group to regress to Level 1—they sometimes use an agenda, but they aren't producing documented results anymore. After this new leader leaves, the board will be whipped around to whatever the next leader wants, and their shared identity will get even weaker. A Level 4 solution would have been to update the meeting structure to address the problems he saw with it, rather than throwing it all away.

Operating at Level 4 and 5

Both Level 4 and Level 5 maturity require some kind of systematic support. Traditionally this takes the form of dedicated personnel to schedule, run, and document meetings. Increasingly, organizations use software to provide this systematic support.

In my work with standards committees, which are composed primarily of volunteers, I have seen organizations slip from Level 4 to Level 3 when they lost funding for their centralized secretariat. In committee work, a secretariat staff ensures that all the meetings run consistently and produce reliable, standardized results regardless of which committee they support.

When the secretariat went away, each volunteer committee chair had to run their own meetings. Each group had some basic guidelines to follow and a long history of documented meeting minutes to learn from, but they didn't get the training or oversight they needed to help them apply these guidelines. Some could, but others flailed. Consistency vanished, and quality suffered at all but the highest levels. The top-level committees and board continued to operate well because their meetings ran according to stricter rules set in the bylaws—a Level 3 enforcement that kept them functional.

By contrast, a decade or so ago the leadership team at ASTM International, one of the largest and most prolific standards-developing associations, determined that they wanted to lead the industry by producing more standards at higher quality more rapidly than anyone else. They dramatically reduced the time it took for a new standard to get approval, in some cases shaving *years* off the total project time, due in a large part to a concerted investment in running better committee meetings. They refined and locked the meeting structure, then put staff and technology in place to support those meetings. Within a year, zoom! New standards were flying out of there like swifts from a chimney.

CHAPTER 14

Seizing Cultural Ownership

> The structure, aliveness, deadness, whisper or shout of a meeting teaches and persuades us more about the culture of our workplace than all the speeches about core values and the new culture we are striving for ...
>
> What we call meetings are critical cultural passages that create an opportunity for employee engagement or disengagement.
>
> -Peter Block, in the foreword to
> *Terms of Engagement: New Ways of Leading and Changing Organizations*

This brings me to a final set of overarching guidelines. In Chapter 5, I talked about training people in the Core Capabilities, like how to structure a meeting and the need to post meeting results. In Chapter 10, I also shared the Game Changers—those practices I've seen organizations adopt in order to dramatically improve their meeting quality quickly.

The final set of guidelines concerns cultural ownership—one of the focus areas for establishing meeting performance maturity. As I looked at the stories of prominent meetings throughout history, across sectors, and from the high-performing organizations I encounter today, two patterns became clear.

First, successful meetings everywhere share a common underlying structure. The Welcome → Discuss → Wrap Up pattern can be found in everything from campfire huddles to the proceedings of a parliament. Techniques like the Go-Around, where everyone takes turns answering a question one at a time, appear in meetings records from Roman times forward. There appear to be master structures humans are wired to understand, and when we ignore these, meetings suffer.

Second, while they share a unifying structure, successful meetings everywhere employ highly specialized language. Ray Dalio's team talks a lot about their "idea meritocracy." Zingerman's has the Monkey Minder. Teams everywhere create their own rituals too. Internal meetings at Starbucks start with a coffee tasting, helping every employee better understand their product. A team at Google used to end meetings by awarding the Whoops Monkey to the person who made the most educational mistake in the previous week, reinforcing their belief that mistakes should be acknowledged, shared, and celebrated so that everyone can learn from them.

When a Level 3 organization adopts a standard meeting methodology, they'll use the language and patterns prescribed by the experts. As the organization matures and begins to "own" the process, that changes. This cultural ownership in meetings creates a sense of shared identity between teammates, helps meetings feel more personalized and special, and often makes the experience way more fun.

1. Adopt intentional language.

This may the most powerful tip in this book.

What you call a meeting changes how people feel about that meeting. I am quite serious when I recommend against the use of the word "meeting" as something you allow on your schedule, because this word is too generic and too overloaded with negative associations.

The language you choose to describe the topics, practices, and results of your time together also changes how people react to these elements.

A simple example: the name Monkey Minder for the person responsible for tracking action items and commitments evokes the sense of a friendly zookeeper working to prevent too much mayhem. The Monkey Minder is a well-meaning Man in the Yellow Hat, trying to keep Curious George out of too much trouble. That same job could have as easily been called the Action Item Tracker (listless, boring), the Accountability Cop (scary, perhaps a little badass) or even the Guardian of Getting Things Done (very Knight's-Quest-meets-hipster-business). The task is the same no matter what name you give it, but your enthusiasm and pride in taking on that task will be very different. Capulet or Montague? Perhaps these names shouldn't matter, but they surely do.

Study after study has shown that the words we use to describe what we do can have a dramatic effect on what happens next. In his books *Influence*

Four Ways to
Design Meeting Experiences
That Embody the Culture
You Want to Live

1. Adopt intentional language.

2. Create culturally meaningful
   ground rules.

3. Develop preferred rituals.

4. Experiment and improve.

and *Pre-Suasion*, Robert Cialdini shares dozens of enlightening examples. In social psychology circles, this phenomenon is called *priming* or *framing*. The way you frame a meeting can set the tone and the boundaries, and shift everyone's approach accordingly.

One of Cialdini's examples that's particularly relevant for us here concerns the use of language at SSM Health, a U.S.-based health care system which in 2017 owned 23 acute care hospitals, one children's hospital, 10 post-acute care facilities, a health maintenance organization, a national pharmacy benefit management company, and a network of physician practice operations. All of SSM Health's businesses share the same mission: to heal. As part of ensuring everything they do is imbued with this mission, they forbid the language of violence in their work. Cialdini was not allowed to share "bullet" points when he addressed them, but he could share "talking" points. SSM Health leaders don't "attack" problems or "hit targets"; they "approach challenges" and "reach goals."

Professional facilitators also pay very close attention to the language they use, and because they each tend to work with similar kinds of organizations over time, they develop strong feelings about what works in their context. The language used by facilitators who work with corporate leadership teams differs from the language used by the facilitators who work with co-ops and social movements. While both can be very formal, the language of the church sounds quite distinct from the language of government. When I publish a generic meeting technique with example wording, I can be sure that I'll hear from a half-dozen facilitators about the "correct" words I should have used. All of them will have a very useful point, and not one of them will agree with the others.

Another example: what you call a meeting matters. It's a common practice for teams from every sector to have a short daily meeting to coordinate on the work of the day. This meeting typically lasts less than 20 minutes and covers a simple list of topics: what happened since yesterday, what's going on today, and what needs extra attention now. This meeting is very similar the world over, and yet it goes by a dozen different names: The Daily Huddle, The Stand-Up, The Shift Change Meeting, The Daily Scrum, The Check-In, The Adrenaline Meeting... to name a few.

My team runs a Check-In, not an Adrenaline Meeting, and I think that tells you something about us. What you choose to call your meetings will tell your team and the world at large about your organization too.

Hold On! Isn't All This Intentional Language Use Facipulation?!

Facipulation is a term describing the sneaky application of facilitation techniques used in an attempt to manipulate a group toward a predetermined outcome. Facipulation is basically tricking people into thinking they had a choice, when you were really cleverly setting it up to make sure you got your way all along.

This is a common concern expressed by non-facilitators. With regard to this concern, I offer this for your consideration: There is a difference between intentional design and an attempt to trick people. Intentional language, meeting design, and ethical facilitation all seek to help a group come to a shared result together. **Everything you do in a meeting is a choice and will have an impact, and conscientious people pay attention to the impact they are having on others.** The only way *not* to have an impact is to cease meeting altogether, which eventually leads to the dissolution of the group. That's a pretty big impact too.

The words and actions used within a meeting create the frame. There is always a frame. The question to consider is *how does that frame get set?*

The example below comes from the academic research world. It's a story related by Dr. Kathleen Blee, a sociologist studying how activist groups form, and shared at the Gothenburg Meeting Science Symposium in 2017.

She was observing the formation of a new group that wanted the U.S. to void the debt burden of poor nations. The group's founder hosted the initial meeting in her home, and like many first meetings, began by asking everyone to introduce themselves. The founder didn't provide any other instructions. The first woman shared her name and then which church she attended. Based on this example, everyone else also shared their names and their church affiliations. There wasn't any obvious reason for this; the group wasn't forming to address a faith-based social issue, but there it was. The frame was set.

> From this small act, meetings reflected a sense that religious faith was the main framework for the group, sidelining other possibilities. Thus, in the next meeting as the group discussed how to recruit additional members, they never raised the possibility of seeking college students or people affiliated with the broad progressive community, even

through the coalition with which the group was formally aligned. Rather, they only discussed how to find new members through Pittsburgh's networks of churches and synagogues....

Not surprisingly, such actions shaped the trajectory of the group's membership as active church members were attracted and stayed while less religiously identified recruits dropped away. It also etched the group's sense of options for action. As they implicitly regarded themselves as a group of religious people, discussions in their meetings were cast in moral terms.... In the religious framework the group had adopted, pressure politics were secular and thereby inappropriate to even discuss in a faith group working on a "moral concern."

—Dr. Kathleen Blee,
Democracy in the Making: How Activist Groups Form

There is always a frame. If it is not set intentionally, it will be set unintentionally.

Pay close attention to the language in your meetings. A mindful approach shows awareness and respect for the people and their work. All the high-performing organizations do it.

Besides, even if you wanted to exploit people through the use of framing language, outright manipulation isn't sustainable. People have strong sensors—they won't fall for the same tricks for long.

2. Create culturally meaningful ground rules.

The Pacific Bold team did this as their first step when moving from Level 1 to Level 2, but there are many Level 2 and 3 organizations that miss this opportunity to explicitly embed the organization's values in practice. Ground rules can be strictly procedural—things like always starting on time or turning off cell phones—but they can also spell out the ways the organization wants people to approach conflict, learning, accountability, decision-making, and more. As you know, an organization's true culture is not what gets put on the poster—it's how people behave and how they treat one another. Ground rules give you an opportunity to clarify what this behavior should be.

When you create or update your group's ground rules, think about the culture the organization espouses. Does your startup believe in "failing fast"? If so, what does that mean for your meetings? What questions do people need to ask, and what courtesies should they adopt for teams to embody that value?

At our company, we're fans of Don Miguel Ruiz's book *The Four Agreements*, and we built his book's high-level values into our organization's values statement. Our meeting ground rules then give us specific ways to live these agreements in practice.

One of Ruiz's Four Agreements asks us to "Always do our best, recognizing that our best is going to change from moment to moment." How does that show up in our meetings? First, it reminds everyone to be present so we can do our best. If something is getting in our way, everyone has permission to point it out so we can stop the meeting, deal with what's keeping us from doing our best, and then get back on track. Another of the agreements—"Don't Make Assumptions"—means that questioning, constructive conflict, and learning are expected from everyone in our company.

3. Develop preferred rituals.

Where the first tip above asked you to be mindful about the specific words you do and do not use to describe the work in your organization, this one asks you to use those words in the creation of meeting rituals that embed your desired culture in practice.

The most common (and often most useful) rituals to craft are the meeting bookends: the check-in and the check-out (or "closing"). As you read in the story above about framing, the check-in sets the tone for everything that follows. The check-out *also* sets the tone for everything that follows it, which in this case means the rest of the workday.

Lucid Meetings clients include several First Nations Boards. For those of you outside the U.S. and Canada, these boards represent the Native American tribes and manage their interests. Some of these groups manage large business operations—casinos are a big income driver for the tribes in the Pacific Northwest—while some focus primarily on concerns of governance and cultural preservation.

Many of these boards run their meetings following a strict interpretation of Robert's Rules of Order, where the standard way to begin is with a roll call and the approval of the minutes from the previous meeting. Not exactly a rich cultural practice, especially for a First Nations Board.

I had coffee with a board member who expressed his frustration with this approach. "We get a lot done eventually, but the meetings are either chaotic as we try to keep everyone on the agenda, or extremely boring. It's also difficult for many of our board members to participate well. Some of these guys went to college, but most of them are fishers or craftsmen. Smart guys, but not too interested in learning all the rules around dealing with motions. All that Robert's Rules stuff is pretty foreign to them," he told me.

"Sure, I can see that," I said. "Have you all talked about maybe backing off on Robert's Rules and finding another way to meet? Lots of boards save the formal rules for big votes, but otherwise run their meetings in more collaborative ways."

"No," he admitted. "I think that could help a lot, but I'm not sure how I'd introduce it."

He needed a story to share that would get the conversation started, so I offered two.

Story 1: The Origin of Robert's Rules of Order (RRONR)
Robert's Rules aren't the first or only set of parliamentary procedures in the world, but they are certainly the most commonly used today. Thousands of copies are sold every year. Countless organizations refer to RRONR as the authority for how decisions get made. When in doubt, refer to the (Robert's) rulebook!

Part of this popularity is now traditional. It's what people do by default, and it's always easiest to do what other people do when you don't have a better plan. The other reason has to do with how the rules got created.

Henry Martyn Robert was an officer in the Army Corps of Engineers before and during the U.S. Civil War. Prior to the war, he agreed to chair a meeting at his church where the group would discuss issues of slavery and abolition that were fueling tensions within the congregation. The meeting went badly awry, and Robert was deeply embarrassed.

He later wrote:

> One can scarcely have had much experience in deliberative meetings of Christians without realizing that the best of men, having wills of their own, are liable to attempt to carry out their own views without paying sufficient respect to the rights of their opponents.
>
> — Henry M. Robert

In other words, these were a bunch of pushy folks! Over the next 50 years, Robert worked to create and refine his *Pocket Manual of Rules of Order for Deliberative Assemblies* (later becoming RRONR), which he used to make sure the meetings he led *never again* erupted into open conflict.

There are two things the modern organization may want to keep in mind about Mr. Robert's story.

1. He wrote these rules based on the parliamentary meeting rulebooks available at the time, all of which reflected the practices of government. As the name suggests, parliamentary rules originate with early Western European parliaments. That's a very particular perspective that may not align with your modern-day board's values.

2. He wrote these rules so that chairs had a way to *control* the conversation, prevent abuse, and defuse conflict. These rules were written to clamp things down (literally, bring "order") at a time when the people at a meeting might physically come to blows.

Since then, society has evolved. Most boards can reasonably assume that no one at their meeting will resort to fisticuffs if they don't get their way. We also have collaborative techniques now that ensure everyone can participate, preventing some of the dominance problems addressed by rules in RRONR. Perhaps most importantly, RRONR has become weaponized by those who use it to block out their opponents. A canny board member can use RRONR procedural rules to stymie opposition and make sure their favorite proposals are the only ones that get approved, turning what was once a way of preventing unruly behavior into a vehicle for creating an unfair advantage.

The point of this history lesson is this: If your board isn't fighting, you don't have to treat them like they are. Instead, consider running board meetings in a way that makes it easier for board members to work together collaboratively. Save the formal rules for those items requiring a legal vote, and make the rest of the time more human.

This leads to the second story I shared over coffee.

Story 2: Embracing Existing Rituals

The Canadian government has been working to improve relations with First Nations people living in Canada. The government convened a series of meetings between First Nations representatives and government ministers. The first few meetings were rough. The issues involved go way back, everyone had a vested interest they needed to protect, and the discussion was largely acrimonious and nonproductive.

Then, they changed how they began the meeting. Instead of just running a call to order (standard-issue RRONR), they invited a First Nations elder to open meetings with a smudging. Smudging is a traditional ceremony used to clear negative energy and bless a space. The smudging had a transformative effect on subsequent meetings. Ministers who had previously adopted a defensive posture began to listen, ask questions, and offer solutions. As one witness related, "It was amazing. Such a small thing, but it made a huge difference. I wish we had something like that for our team meetings."

Of course, you *can* have something like this for your team meetings. Go for it! Perhaps your building isn't set up for regular smudging ceremonies, but you can add a moment of silence at the beginning of your team meetings. Or a prayer. Or a quick jog around the room. Or a chat about your favorite moment in the past week. Or a coffee tasting.

You get to create the environment you need for success, and culturally appropriate rituals like these provide simple, effective ways to go about it.

4. Experiment and improve.

> We do not learn from experience… we learn from reflecting on experience.
>
> —John Dewey, Philosopher and Psychologist

Small changes can create big ripple effects. When you change how you run your meetings—and especially if you follow the three tips above—you will change the culture in your team. A behavior change is a culture change, and your new approach to meeting will place a stone in the stream that all the other work will run up against.

Think of the stream of work in your team like a stream of water. A stone in one place can calm the flow of work, but placed in another spot, it could cause the stream to overflow its banks and damage the surrounding landscape. Only you and your team know which spot creates the change you're seeking.

When you experiment with new language and new techniques, two practices can help protect you and your team from any unintentionally aggressive ripples.

First, Be Transparent about the Experiment and the Goal

Let your team in on what you're trying to achieve and enlist their support. That way, you can try new techniques without freaking everyone out ("Um, why is Phil waving that stuffed monkey around?") and you can get their input on how it's going. When you ask people to experiment with you and to give it a try a few times before you all decide whether it works, you may all be surprised at what happens.

Here's an example that comes from RSF Social Finance, another group of investment bankers (not Bridgewater Associates, mentioned earlier).

A young banker had a stellar first year at RSF. He'd done well, and as was the tradition, the boss called him in and granted him a favor. "Great year! What would you like?"

"I'd like for us to start our team meetings with a minute of silence," the young banker said.

His boss reacted immediately: "No."

The young banker persisted. "Well, hang on. Think about it a minute. Imagine what I could have asked."

"No. Pick something else," his boss replied.

"Look," the young banker said as he stood up to leave, "just think about it overnight. Don't answer me right now."

The next day, his boss came to him and acquiesced. "All right. We'll try it, but just for one month. If it doesn't work, we stop. Deal?"

So at the next meeting, this group of high-powered investment professionals begrudgingly powered off their devices, shut their eyes, and spent one minute in silence. At the end of the month, the boss asked the group if they should continue with the practice or go back to how they started meetings before.

The group unanimously agreed to keep the practice, suggesting that it might be even better if they spent more minutes in silence beyond the prescribed one.

Over the course of the next several months, the team found that they did make better decisions when they were centered, and the company's performance improved. Equally important to them, they became a better team.

They began spending time together outside of work. They began practices centered in gratitude and random acts of kindness. They shared stories about their families. They became more cooperative and less competitive, and their job satisfaction soared.

It was a small experiment that the team agreed to try, and agreed to alter when they saw a way to improve, that had a big positive ripple effect.

Second, Measure and Review Your Results

If you approach the changes you make to your meetings as an experiment, the second half of that equation involves testing your hypothesis.

This implies that you've formulated your hypothesis—not a difficult thing to do, but an easy step to miss. I recommend writing down the impact you expect your change to create. This will make it easier for you to share your ideas with your team and to revisit them when you evaluate your results later.

In the story above, the young banker's hypothesis was that a minute of silence would help them make better decisions. The metric for this hypothesis was decision outcome: did they indeed make better decisions? In their case, the answer was a clear yes. The other benefits to camaraderie and work satisfaction were just a big, fat cherry on top.

Data-driven decision making is all the rage. Lots of people want hard evidence that what they tried worked, and by "hard" they mean "measurable in numbers." If you fall into that camp, here are some things you could measure and that your experiment might change.

- Work velocity.
- Time spent in meetings.
- Money spent in meetings (calculated as: (employee burdened rate * meeting hours) + meeting-specific expenses).
- Number of decisions made.
- Percentage of action items completed (at all and/or on time).
- Number of people actively participating in meetings.
- Meeting satisfaction ratings.
- Work quality: defect rates, production levels, error rates.
- Customer satisfaction.
- Employee engagement.
- Employee retention rate.
- And so on....

Other times, the change you seek isn't so neatly quantifiable. To review these kinds of changes, I recommend running an Action Review meeting about how you run meetings. (Sounds logical, right?)

An Action Review meeting—in this case specifically an After Action Review or a Retrospective—gives teams a way to look at what happened, notice how it was or was not what they expected, and then decide what they're going to do next. Read more about Action Reviews in Chapter 20.

CHAPTER 15

Assessing Meeting
Performance Maturity

Congratulations! You've made it through all the research, theory, and general meeting advice in this book. The next Part gets specific, diving into details about each of the 16 Types of Business Meetings, then wrapping up with a look at how to use different meetings together in Meeting Flow Models designed to solve specific business problems. Before we do, let's take a moment to move past theory into practice.

At this point, you now understand why people meet, how meetings can be used as a tool to get work done, and the characteristics of an effective meeting. (Say it with me: "High Perceived Meeting Quality + Net Positive Impact = an effective meeting!") You also understand the different levels of meeting performance maturity an organization can achieve and why it might be useful to aspire to a higher level of performance. Finally, you've gained a sense of how all this works for other organizations in the many stories embedded throughout.

Now what?

At Lucid Meetings, we have a service called the Effective Meeting Results Program that we offer to clients who need help going from "Yikes! We need better meetings!" to "Our meetings are powerhouses of organizational awesomeness!" This program starts with an assessment, in which we figure out where to begin the improvement journey.

For those of you who aren't ready to spend a year in consultation with me and my team, here's a self-guided approach you can use.

Tool: Meeting Performance Self Assessment

What It Is
This process involves conducting a bit of research on your meetings and then evaluating them against high-level performance criteria.

How It Works
Step 1: List all your meetings.
You're going to make this list because solving a "meetings problem" means solving the problems found in specific meetings. Generic meeting rules help set the stage for improvement, but they don't get to the root problem. So, start by listing all your meetings. This is easiest to do when you're looking at the calendar. I like to make this list in a spreadsheet.

Step 2: Rate your meetings.
I gave you several metrics you can use at the end of the previous chapter, and you can also refer to the maturity criteria. In Lucid's program, we look at all these kinds of details and more—but then, we get paid to do that!

If all of that is too overwhelming or just too much, use this simplified evaluation criteria. In your spreadsheet, create four new columns and label them:

- Time
- People
- Effectiveness
- Importance

For the Time column, enter the number of minutes this meeting takes every two weeks. So, if it's a daily meeting that takes 15 minutes, you'd enter *15 minutes * 5 days * 2 weeks*, which equals 150 minutes. If it's a meeting you have every once in a while, just enter how long that meeting typically lasts.

For the People column, enter the number of people who typically attend that meeting.

These two columns let you see the relative cost of each of your meetings. Time * People = cost in cumulative meeting minutes.

Next, rate each meeting's effectiveness. You pick whatever scale works for you. Great → Good → Okay → Lousy? 1 to 10? It doesn't matter, just as long as it helps you see differences between the meetings.

Finally, rate each meeting's importance. Which ones do you know matter to your team's success? Which ones don't?

If you're tackling this project on your own, go ahead and move to the next step. Alternatively, ask a team member to do this exercise too. That way, you'll be able to compare notes for the next step.

Step 3: Find the patterns.
You may now have a list that screams answers at you. If you find a meeting that involves a lot of people but isn't effective, that's where you start.

Or not. You could now have a nifty spreadsheet, but not a lot more insight than when you began. In that case, look for patterns. Did you rate all the meetings Okay or Good? What do you think made that slight difference? Are all the meetings basically fine, but the total time adds up to far more than it should? Are none of the meetings registering as particularly important?

To reiterate: there is no such thing as a generic meeting problem that has a singular solution. You can only solve problems with specific meetings, so it's your task to figure out which of your meetings deserves your attention first.

Step 4: Cancel the crap.
Look at your list, and refer to the checkpoint at the end of Chapter 10 if in doubt. Anything that isn't important or effective does not deserve the investment of anyone's time. Be bold, be heroic, and cancel any meeting that doesn't measure up. Lousy meetings have to go!

Step 5: Fix the top three meetings on your list.
Finally, pick the three most important and/or time-consuming meetings on your list, and change how they work.

Start by getting crystal clear about exactly what *kind* of meeting each one is, then writing out the meeting's *purpose* and *desired outcomes*. Next, answer these questions for each of the top three meetings on your list:

- Do we as a team know what those outcomes look like specifically? How are they documented?

- Do we know how to get those outcomes? Does the meeting process walk the group through creating those outcomes?
- Are we doing anything in these meetings that isn't relevant to the purpose and outcomes?
- Are there people in these meetings who aren't necessary for achieving these outcomes?
- Do we typically have the information we need in advance so we can spend our time in the meeting getting to these outcomes?
- Do we have enough time in the meeting to achieve all the desired outcomes?
- When we fail to get the outcomes, what's getting in our way?

The answers to these questions will show you where to start making changes.

When I run through this process with clients, I can quickly see lots of ways to experiment with improving specific meetings. Beware, though! I also usually find that meetings fail due to larger organizational failures.

For example, one organization was having trouble getting its clients to open up during interviews. It turned out that each person conducted interviews using a different process, no one addressed confidentiality up front, and they didn't explain to their clients how the organization was going to use what it learned. Beyond working on a standard agenda approach to the interview process, fixing these meetings also involved crafting a non-disclosure statement, creating a password-protected place to store the notes from these interviews, and training all the people conducting interviews on how to avoid the kinds of questions that freaked their clients out.

This is why I never try to fix all of the meetings at once. Changes to meetings ripple through the organization. Start with three meetings, learn from those, and build from there.

PACIFIC BOLD

This brings us back to our friends at Pacific Bold. When we last saw them, Craig and Nelson had just put up their new poster of meeting rules in the conference room and enjoyed Charla's congratulatory hug.

The new rules had an impact. In fact, they had many impacts, but none of them were as dramatic as Craig had hoped. It was like what happens when a meteor breaks up in the atmosphere: lots of little flame bursts but no big, impressive crater on the ground.

In general, meetings were better, and when they weren't, everyone in the company now had a way to talk about it—a big win! People began regularly holding each other accountable for sending an agenda and sticking to the scheduled time, often with a bit more finger-pointing than strictly necessary.

The leadership team met to discuss how the rules were working out, and they concluded that they hadn't produced a big enough win. That's when they called my team. As you might remember when we first met Pacific Bold, I said, "Here's your challenge: Make sure there are no meetings on your calendar for the next two weeks."

A pause.

"But we told you," Charla said. "We already tried canceling all our meetings. It didn't work. You think we should try it again?"

"Sorry, no," I said. "I don't want you to cancel anything, necessarily. This challenge is different. I'm asking you to get specific in how you use language. You should have no 'meetings' on your schedule, but you might have a 'One-on-One,' or a 'Working Session,' or a 'Project Kickoff.' I'm literally talking about *removing the word 'meeting' from how you invest your team's time.* Saying you'll have a 'meeting' is not clear enough. And if you can't figure out a more specific name for that event, then, yes, you should cancel it."

The rest of this book is all about how to get more specific using the Taxonomy of Business Meetings to solve business problems, improve organizational health, and accelerate performance.

Part 4

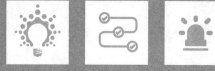

The 16 Types of Meetings That Work

A Meeting is Not a Meeting

When you ask enough people what they feel makes a meeting a good use of their time, clarity emerges.

(Surprised? I dearly hope not!)

I mean that literally—people ask for clarity. The Lucid Meetings team asked this question in a recent survey, and while a few people requested free beer, most asked for the meeting to be clear and relevant: A clear reason for the meeting, clear outcomes, and a defined agenda. If you think I sound like a broken record on this point, you should spend time reading our survey results! Talk about repetitive....

What was striking was that no one asked for simplicity—folks are willing to wade into troublesome water when they understand the necessity. Nor did anyone request brevity—people are equally willing to roll up their shirt sleeves, pour a second cup of coffee, and see a job through to the end.

It's utterly clear: People want clarity.

Clarity of purpose, process, and outcomes is also a requirement for achieving organizational meeting performance maturity of Level 3 or above.

Knowing the 16 types of business meetings makes it much easier to achieve clarity. Each type of meeting has a specific work function, a pre-defined set of possible outcomes, and a handful of reference structures you can build on when crafting your agenda.

Also, no meeting works on its own. The outcomes from one meeting are used to start the discussion in another meeting. When you understand each type of meeting and how to use them together to accomplish your goals, it becomes possible to use meetings as tools for streamlining your business operations.

Here's an example from my own experience. During one of Lucid's regular weekly team meetings in January 2018, the Lucid marketing team decided we needed to review 2017 performance. Seems like a good idea, right? The team lead scheduled a meeting on everyone's calendar: one hour reserved for the 2017 Marketing Review.

What are the desired outcomes for a meeting called 2017 Marketing Review? And how do we know it will take one hour to achieve them?

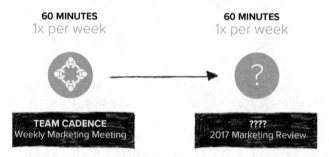

A few days before the review, a colleague asked how to best prepare. It quickly became evident that we didn't have clarity about what this meeting was meant to accomplish, because we couldn't answer her question. So we all turned to the taxonomy list of possible meeting types. We eliminated most of the meeting types—this wasn't a regular Team Cadence meeting, nor was it an Issue Resolution, or a Training, or a Problem Solving meeting—and narrowed the options to Sensemaking or Action Review.

Sensemaking meetings are designed to generate new learning and insights that can be put to use in the future, but they don't necessarily lead to any decisions or follow-up assignments. Action Reviews, on the other hand, walk a team through learning and insights straight to a set of agreements, often in the form of experiments the group wants to try in order to improve future work.

Both options were valid choices. The Sensemaking meeting would fit within the hour, but it would also be less conclusive. If we were mystified by our 2017 performance or considering a wildly different approach, this type of meeting would have been the right call. We would then have scheduled a Planning meeting, after everyone had an opportunity to digest what we'd learned.

We chose instead to make our meeting an Action Review. We didn't expect to ponder epiphanies; we simply wanted to look at the big picture and tease out any successful patterns we could expand on in the coming year. We also didn't want to come up with a whole new plan. We just wanted to refine the plans we already had in motion.

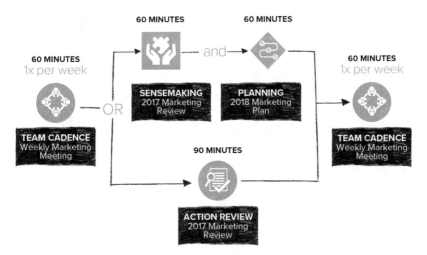

Once we clarified the meeting type, we knew what to do.

First, we increased the scheduled meeting time. Action Reviews take longer, especially when they cover a whole year's worth of work. Second, we updated the agenda to follow a popular structure that works well for Action Reviews, asking the group first *What?* (in which we review what happened), then *So what?* (in which we list our insights and conclusions), and finally *Now What?* (in which we define the experiments we want to try to in order to test these insights). Third, we gave everyone reporting assignments, making sure we had all the information ready beforehand.

The meeting went well, and we came away with some nifty ideas, but that's not the point here. The point is this: we were about to have a crappy soupy mess of a meeting, but we didn't because we used the taxonomy to fix it.

The chapters in this section cover each of the 16 types in more detail. You'll learn how to identify each type of meeting, tips for making or breaking that kind meeting, and how that meeting works in conjunction with other types of meetings.

If you find all this riveting, I invite you to continue reading straight through. Don't you let anyone tell you it's not cool to like a book about meetings—you do you!

That said, **each chapter can stand on its own. If you'd prefer to flip between chapters or skip this whole bit and save it for reference at a later time, that works too.** For those of you who can't decide, I've got good news! We're starting with the Cadence meetings, and those are relevant for everyone.

Questions Answered by Each Type of Meeting

Not sure what kind of meeting you've got? Confused by the names we've used to describe each type? Here's a tip. Think about your meeting and ask yourself: what are the questions you and your group need to answer during this meeting? Each type of meeting is a tool that works well to answer some questions but doesn't help you answer others. When you know what questions you need answered, you'll know what type of meeting you need to run.

Cadence Meetings

Team Cadence
Since our last team meeting: What's been done? What still needs doing? What's changed? What do we need to focus on next?

Progress Check
Since our last project/program meeting: What's been done? What still needs doing? What's changed? What do we need to focus on next? *Note:* Team Cadence and Progress Check meetings answer the same questions for *different kinds of groups.*

One-on-Ones
What's happening with you? What's going on with your work? How can I help?

Action Reviews
What was our plan? What did we learn? What should we change in our approach going forward?

Governance Cadence
How did we perform? What's changed? What needs our intervention? How does this change our strategy going forward?

Catalyst Meetings

Idea Generation
What are all the ideas we can think of in this situation?

Planning
Given this new goal and what we know now, what's our plan? Who will be responsible for what, by when?

Workshop
We have lots of questions to answer and will devote two or more hours to answering them.

Problem Solving
What do we know about the problem? What are our options? What are we going to do to address it?

Decision Making
Given the options before us, which one do we choose and why? Who is responsible for the next step?

Learn and Influence Meetings

Sensemaking
What can we learn from each other about this topic? How can we make sense of this situation?

Introductions
How might we work together in the future? Are we interested in meeting again sometime?

Issue Resolution
Given that we do not agree on what to do next, can we find a mutually satisfactory way to move forward?

Community of Practice
What can we teach each other that may help us improve our individual practice in this area? How can we advance this topic together?

Training
What do I know that you need to learn? How can we be sure you've learned that successfully?

Broadcast
What do we know that we feel should be shared with our larger group? With the outside world?

CHAPTER 16

The Cadence Meetings

I call this category the Cadence meetings because their primary purpose is driving work momentum. They work much like a heartbeat, often repeating more rapidly for fast-moving teams than they do for their more sedate counterparts. "Cadence" is another word for "rhythm," and Cadence meetings sound out the rhythmic heartbeat of your organization.

As we do the work of our organizations, we learn. The plans we made on day one may work out the way we expected, but maybe not. New stuff comes up, and before too long it becomes obvious that we need to adjust course.

Cadence meetings include meetings like day-to-day team check-ins, weekly project status meetings, One-on-Ones, and board meetings—all the regularly repeated meetings that make up the vast majority of the meetings held in modern workplaces. These meetings involve existing groups executing on known work. They maintain and shape the organization's current state.

Most involve some form of information sharing, problem solving, and decision making—the traditional breakdown of meeting types. But these are *not* dedicated Decision Making meetings (those fit into the Catalyst meetings section, coming up next).

Organizations that implement successful Cadence meetings use them to **review performance, renew team connections, and refine their approach** based on what they've learned.

Success eludes most teams. Complaints about "too many pointless meetings" often refer to Cadence meetings, whether the person complaining knows it or not. These are the meetings everyone has and no one seems to love. They're necessary, but they can feel "necessary" like an overdue trip to the bathroom. People often dread attending these meetings and then leave worn, shaken, and relieved to be done with it.

Why are Cadence meetings so unpleasant for so many people? Partly it's because they aren't special. When someone has to lead a Workshop, or give a demo to a big, new client, they're going to take the time to figure out how to structure that meeting well. Cadence meetings don't get the same kind of attention. It's more common for a team leader to pull the group into a room and simply start talking or for a project manager to march a team dutifully through a giant spreadsheet. Cadence meetings don't get the love they deserve.

It's a serious mistake to confuse *common* with *unimportant*. Leaders who don't take the time to critically examine and design their Cadence meetings have left one of their largest business investments to chance. These are the meetings where your team sees you live your values (or not), where great ideas get shared (or not), where you learn about tricky problems on the horizon (or not), and where your team members renew their commitment to each other and your organization's mission (...or not). Most groups spend *at least* one hour of every employee's time per week on these meetings. That's an expensive investment made in pursuit of important outcomes, but an astounding number of leaders just show up and wing it—badly.

> If someone offered me a single piece of evidence to assess the health of an organization, I would want to observe the executive team during a meeting.
>
> —Patrick Lencioni,
> author and organizational health expert

Another real challenge with Cadence meetings is that they're often over-loaded. A lot of people don't understand how these types of meetings work and what they can and cannot achieve, so they use that reserved time on the calendar to tackle whatever comes up. One week, the team members can find themselves enduring a tongue-lashing over a missed deadline, only to show up the following week to hear an open-ended directive to be more innovative! Take risks! Meetings like that don't merely fail to set and meet a consistent set of expectations; they give teams emotional whiplash.

When run well, Cadence meetings follow a regularized pattern; each meeting works basically like the last one, and teams know what to expect.

Because the participants and the format are all known, these meetings often require less up-front planning and less specialized facilitation expertise to succeed—**once you get a really good structure in place first**.

Finding and perfecting the structure of your team's Cadence meetings has a radical impact on how well you work together.

I'll discuss what works best for each of the different types of Cadence meetings in turn, as there are practices uniquely suited for each of them. That said, there are a few considerations you should keep in mind that apply to all of the Cadence meetings.

1. Work to balance accountability with camaraderie.

The Cadence meetings drive work momentum. In order to do that well, they have to make sure teams stay accountable to meeting their commitments. Questions to ask in Cadence meetings include:

- Did we hit our deadline?
- Did we stay within our budget?
- Did you complete that action item?
- Did our company hit our quarterly targets?

In other words, did the team do what it said was going to do? Many leaders have no problem raising accountability questions during Cadence meetings. This is good. That's one of the reasons to have these meetings—they help everyone stay on track. Others find it deeply uncomfortable, so they avoid anything they consider might feel like "calling someone out." Then there's a hefty cohort that fail to write down any commitments in the first place, which makes it impossible to consistently follow up on them at all.

If you don't have any targets or goals or commitments to check in on, you aren't ready to schedule a successful Cadence meeting. If you do have commitments in place, then you need to check in on them.

Then there's that other driver of momentum: *will*. Does your team have the will to do what needs to be done?

Very few people get enthusiastic about a pure monetary reward. Real motivation comes when people are doing something they believe matters with people to whom they feel connected. Good Cadence meetings work to grow and strengthen positive relationships between colleagues. Camaraderie is what makes it possible for people to help each other out when the work gets tough. Strong relationships create the trust a team needs in order to take risks. If you run a Cadence meeting, you must make sure to consider how the interactions within that meeting contribute to the sense of camaraderie in the group.

This is tricky stuff! Accountability is all about holding people accountable—not a particularly friendly thing to do! Camaraderie is all about friendship. How can you be "friendly" with someone with whom you also need to communicate that you are "dissatisfied with poor performance"?

Successful Cadence meetings work to balance these competing objectives. The chart below shows some of the signs you can monitor to help you do that. When you notice that your group is exhibiting behavior from the lower half of the grid, it's time to figure out what you can change that will bring your meetings back into balance.

Qualities to Balance

	A Focus on Accountability...	A Focus on Camaraderie...
Signs You're Getting It Right	• Drives execution. • Provides clarity. • Makes progress visible.	• Builds relationships. • Invites cooperation. • Deepens shared learning.
Signs You've Overdone It	• Makes people intolerant of failures. • Discourages risk-taking. • Creates a command-and-control dynamic, reducing participation.	• Avoids talking openly about performance. • Inhibits healthy conflict. • Assumes consensus.

2. Move the big stuff to a different type of meeting.

Cadence meetings include just five of the 16 meeting types. There are two other categories with another 11 types of meetings, all of which work to achieve more definite outcomes than your typical Cadence meeting.

For example, the Catalyst meetings category includes dedicated meeting types for Idea Generation, Planning, Problem Solving, and Decision Making. These are all things that you might reasonably expect a team to do in a Cadence meeting, yes? Certainly boards make decisions in board meetings, and teams solve problems in project status meetings.

That's all fine and works well—if the decision or problem can be safely and quickly tackled as a routine matter.

The decisions made in a regular board meeting are often a legal formality;

much of the legwork happens before the official voting in a series of separate Planning, Problem Solving, and Idea Generation meetings. With all the options explored and evaluated in advance, it becomes possible for the board to vote on several large decisions in the same session. When a board is facing a contentious decision with multiple viable options that have yet to be debated, then an effective board turns their "board meeting" into a Decision Making meeting that happens to have all the board members in it. And that's all they do that day—complex decision making does not leave time for other business.

I said *"safely and quickly* tackled" above. These words are deliberate, and here's why.

Safely: Cadence meetings work best when they create a psychological feeling of togetherness—of being part of the group. When you are part of a group, you care about the needs of the group and doing your part to help the group succeed. Trust is built when people make a commitment to the group, and then follow through on that commitment over and over. This is a great environment for accountability and camaraderie, but a terrible environment for risk-taking, standing out in the crowd, and thinking outside the box.

Consider how masterful teams operate in sports or the arts. When they're in the middle of executing a committed play, do the other players like it when one of them decides to try something new and creative? Does the orchestra appreciate it when one of the players asks everyone to stop so they can work out a tricky rhythm? No! Teams crush individuality if it comes out too strongly when they're in the middle of getting things done.

Decision making, idea generation, and problem solving conducted during a Cadence meeting will be restricted. Because these meetings intentionally ask participants to execute to a plan and minimize risk, the options considered will be limited to what feels safe within those limits. "Safe" is *not* innovative. "Safe" does not stand out, break new ground, or confront the uncomfortable truths. When you need to really dig into something challenging, take it to a meeting framed for courage, creativity, or candor, and get it out of your risk-averse Cadence meeting.

Quickly: The time it takes to work through a challenge is an easier clue. If it takes more than 10 minutes, it probably needs to be broken out into a separate activity. Clarify this by creating an action item assigning someone to schedule the right kind of meeting. This keeps your Cadence meeting on time and ensures the challenges that are important or difficult get the focus they need. Otherwise, you'll be tempted to rush to a premature and inferior conclusion just to keep your Cadence meeting from going long— not the reason you want to see for making a lousy decision when the consequences come due.

Cadence meetings can be tricky. Let's make things a little easier by looking at tips for each of the specific types.

CHAPTER 17

Team Cadence

Answering the Questions

Since our last team meeting:

What's been done?

What still needs doing?

What's changed?

What do we need to focus on next?

Examples

The Weekly Team Meeting

The Daily Huddle

The Shift-Change Meeting

A Regular Committee Meeting

A Working Session

Purpose
- Ensure group cohesion.
- Drive execution.
- Clarify immediate next steps.

Work Outcomes
- Clarity about what everyone is doing.
- Help solve anything preventing work completion.
- Information about circumstances affecting the planned work.
- Visibility into significant victories or setbacks.
- Documented decisions and action items.

Human Outcomes
- Increased trust.
- Connection to the group's shared mission.
- A sense of belonging and of being valued by other team members.
- An appropriate sense of urgency to get work done.

Common Challenges
Team Cadence meetings can suffer from all the classic "meetings are a waste of time" problems, including:
- Lackluster energy.
- Multitasking.
- Tardiness and absenteeism.
- Failure to participate.
- Failure to prepare.
- Failure to generate meaningful results.
- Rambling discussion and tangents.
- General dissatisfaction with "wasted time."

What to Expect in a Team Cadence Meeting

Expected Participation
Team Cadence meetings are typically led by the "boss" or manager, but they can also be effectively led by any team member. The best results happen when everyone invited engages collaboratively, and the right structure will make this automatic. Healthy relationships are important to meeting success.

Cadence Frequency
Daily and/or weekly

Required Preparation
Leadership teams may spend 15 to 20 minutes prepping for weekly meetings. Most other Team Cadence meetings should require little to no preparation time.

During the Meeting
Team Cadence meetings start with a check-in, followed by a round of quick updates. Daily meetings then end with a quick run-down of any new actions identified.

Weekly meetings and working sessions last longer and spend more time on task clarification. Teams may spend time solving small problems and adjusting near-term plans in the meeting, as well as identifying topics that should be tackled in separate meetings.

These meetings include a review of new action items at the end.

After the Meeting
The meeting report should be created collaboratively during the meeting and made available instantly afterwards. This record provides the starting material for the next meeting.

Top Tips for Successful Team Cadence Meetings

Team Cadence meetings are the most common, most poorly planned, and most frequently abused meetings in organizations today. They are also essential to organizational success. Happily, you'll find many examples and templates for excellent Team Cadence meetings on our online resource page linked at the end of this chapter. Remember: **well stolen is half done!**

Most Team Cadence transgressions can be counteracted or prevented by following these guidelines.

1. Combine structure and cadence to achieve success.
Think of the Team Cadence meeting as how you nourish your team. These meetings provide a regular infusion of information and connection—the necessary fuel teams need in order to keep their work healthy. The *structure* sets what kind of information you provide: it's what's on the plate.

The *cadence* determines how often the team shares. Just as some people thrive on six small meals a day where others prefer one large meal and a snack (and spiders can go months without a meal!), the structure and cadence your team needs will depend on the nature of your work.

2. Structure the meeting to require engagement.
Most effective Team Cadence meetings either start with a check-in, or in the case of the Daily Huddle, consist primarily of a go-around. A go-around as the first thing in the meeting makes sure everyone participates within the first few minutes; there's no chance anyone gets to sit this one out! Then, everyone invited should have a job to do in the meeting—a deadline they need to report on, feedback they're expected to give, or even responsibility for taking notes.

When you find the right structure for your team, make sure to use the same structure for each meeting. The NPI (Net Positive Impact) for this meeting will come in part from how much time it occupies in the work week. A consistent structure makes it easier and faster for people to prepare for the meeting and decreases your total time investment.

3. Stick to a regular cadence.
Most teams meet at least once per week. Some meet every day. Some do both. Stick to the same time and day for every meeting. This creates a predictable time for teams to coordinate and minimizes interruptions to other work, since team members can plan accordingly.

Then, review and update the meeting structure and cadence every 90 days. Team Cadence meetings should feel comfortable but never boring. Every quarter (or sooner if there are obvious problems), take time to review your Team Cadence meetings to make sure they continue to serve your team well.

4. Embed a focus on your core priorities and values.
When you select a Team Cadence meeting structure, you have an opportunity to live your organization's values and hone the focus of the work. What you talk about first and how much time you spend talking about it clarifies your work priorities. For example, if your strategic plan says your team's goal is to raise a certain metric by 50% in 30 days, then that metric should be one of the first topics of discussion. You have the same opportunity with how you open and close the meeting. The best close to a

Team Cadence meeting will recap next steps—confirming priorities—and restate your values with an expression of gratitude, a rallying cry, or whatever fits your need.

5. Don't blow scope!

The remaining problems I see in Team Cadence meetings start with blowing scope: the team is having the wrong meeting. Team Cadence meetings bring together existing teams executing on planned work. During the meeting, the team keeps each other updated and refines the plan, but—because life happens—team members also bring up new ideas and problems. If these new things can be addressed very quickly (in 10 minutes or less), go ahead and do it. Otherwise, resist the temptation! Problem Solving meetings work differently than Team Cadence meetings. Idea Generation meetings work differently than Team Cadence meetings. Meetings for making big Decisions work differently... you get the idea.

If you hear the group begin to go around in circles, if blame or finger-pointing become part of the discussion, if people are trying to make a decision or solve a significant problem they just learned about minutes ago, *stop*! Recognize what's happening and stop the discussion. Then, schedule the meeting you really need to have. If it's urgent, you don't need to wait for another day, but you do need to finish the meeting you're in and take a break so people can prepare for the kind of meeting they need in order to get a quality result.

The Time I Enjoyed Lunch with Two Managers Who Hated the Team Meetings They Were Running

As I mentioned, Team Cadence meetings go awry often. I met two managers at a conference recently that illustrated how this can happen.

During the conference lunch break, I chose an empty spot between two friendly bespectacled types at a table of six who looked like they might be open to a chat. And they were! The dark-haired fellow in the polo shirt on the left turned out to be a high-level information officer at an aerospace firm. His group creates the software that keeps airplanes on course and ensures the safety systems work. The red-headed stranger in the button-down was the CIO for a National Football League team famous for its rabid fan base and iconic hats. Very nice people doing pretty cool stuff.

Team Cadence or Progress Check?

How is a Team Cadence meeting different from a Progress Check meeting?

Team Cadence meetings involve standing teams that persist over the course of multiple initiatives—a department or a standing committee, for example. The team is working toward a common goal or serves a common function, but its work is never "finished" while the team still exists. These teams may be involved in several different projects at once.

Progress Checks, on the other hand, involve teams assembled for a specific project or program. When the work is finished, the team dissolves. The Progress Check meeting content addresses specifically what's going on with that singular project, and nothing else.

What about Agile Rituals? What type of meetings are those? Part of the brilliance of the standard Agile meetings is that they formalize the separation of meetings by type, creating a pattern that includes Team Cadence meetings, Progress Checks, Planning meetings, Idea Generation meetings, Work Sessions, and Action Reviews. Larger teams also include Workshops and Decision Making meetings in their pattern. Agile Rituals are not a type of meeting; they're elements in a Meeting Flow Model (see chapter 35) defining all the different types of meetings Agile developers need in order to get their work done.

Then I shared what I do and pulled out a postcard with the Meeting Taxonomy chart on it to explain. That chart is nowhere near as cool as airplanes or football, so imagine my surprise when everyone at the table lit up.

"My team meetings are terrible!" exclaimed the airplane executive.

"Why is that?" I asked. "Does your manager know?"

"I am the manager!" he exclaimed. "These are my meetings, and I hate them! Everyone hates them. We all get in a room and try to go around and talk about what we're doing, but it's just pulling teeth. I sit there watching the clock, and I can literally feel time slowing to a crawl. I know everyone else is thinking the same thing. The meeting is so bad I changed it from every week to every other week. I think if anything, that made it worse, but there's no way I'm going to put more of these dreadful meetings on my team's schedule. Nothing seems to work. Meetings are such a waste."

After a round of murmured sympathies from others at the table, I offered some unsolicited advice. (This is a bad habit shared by most authors.) "It sounds to me like the cadence might be a problem," I said. "Have you considered meeting more often rather than less? Maybe run a few 15-minute check-ins every week instead of the one big meeting every two weeks?"

"Oh," the airplane executive replied. "I meet at least once a week with every group that's working on a project together, and that works fine. It's just the team meeting that I can't get right."

Aha! There was my clue. His "team" that he met with every two weeks didn't have any shared work! This was a group of people with similar job descriptions and a shared reporting structure, but they didn't have anything they were building together. There were no shared projects they needed to keep running, no common cadence, and no reason for mutual accountability. In other words, they were a team in name only, so they had no need for a Team Cadence meeting.

If we had more time, I would have suggested he cancel that useless biweekly meeting and instead set up a monthly Community of Practice meeting where all these people could network, share things they'd learned on their separate projects, and use the time to refine their skills instead of reporting out to a group who couldn't care less.

But before I could pipe up, my new friend from the NFL said, "My team meetings are terrible too! My problem is my co-manager. If it were up to me, we'd have an agenda for every meeting and a report afterwards. I'm an orderly type of guy. Like, you should see my sock drawer. It's amazing. But my partner thinks that's all too formal and stuffy, so whenever I bring an agenda, he just ignores it. Then of course the meetings always go long, we never get through what we wanted to talk about, and we just end up having more meetings to hash it out again. I guess I should put my foot down and start forcing him to use an agenda."

He sighed.

There are easily five things you could pick out of the statement above as problems worth addressing, but the big one is the conflicting beliefs between the managers. One wants to follow rules; the other sees rules as needless constraints.

"Have you heard of a Real-Time Agenda? Or Lean Coffee?" I asked. He hadn't, so I explained how it works. (See chapter 7 for a reminder.)

Team Cadence meetings don't necessarily need an agenda *per se*, but they do need to be run in a consistent way that everyone understands and that leads to a recognizable result. For this group, the Real-Time Agenda technique provides the structure and clarity of results my new friend needs and the priority-of-the-moment flexibility his partner values. Everyone wins!

At first blush, these two managers had the same problem: They both led internal team meetings they hated. (And for all I know, they still do! Someone please hand them a copy of this book!) Digging just a tiny bit below the surface, however, it's easy to see that the solution for the airplane team was not a fix that would have helped the football team.

The best approach to your own Team Cadence meeting may look very different from what works for another team—even other teams within the same company.

We all have unique styles when it comes to decorating our workspace, and we benefit from taking a personalized approach to designing how we work together too. Embrace that, and you can start to have some fun.

Meeting design is the process of designing the meeting experience for a specific team working in a specific setting. Why not encourage each group to design meetings that make them happy?

Additional Resources for Team Cadence Meetings

Visit the Team Cadence Meetings Resource Center on Lucid Meetings. lucidmeetings.com/meeting-types/team-cadence-meetings

Progress Checks

Answering the Questions

Since our last project/program meeting:

What's been done?

What still needs doing?

What's changed?

What do we need to focus on next?

Note: Team Cadence and Progress Check meetings answer the same

questions for different kinds of groups.

Examples

The Project Status Meeting

The Client Check-In

The Sprint Demo

Purpose
- Maintain project momentum.
- Ensure mutual accountability.

Work Outcomes
- Clarity about work progress.
- Information about circumstances impacting the planned work.
- Visibility into significant victories or setbacks.
- Decisions on how to address potential changes to the project plan.
- Documented decisions and action items.

Human Outcomes
- Reassurance about the project.
- Renewed project momentum.

Common Challenges
The problems that arise during Progress Checks are very similar to the challenges faced in Team Cadence meetings, but more extreme. Because the individuals in Progress Checks don't necessarily share a common team history, these meetings do not benefit from the mutual bonds that team members in Team Cadence meetings have formed over time. This lack of established relationships makes any meeting problems here feel more acute.
- One person (usually a project manager) doing all the work.
- Lackluster energy.
- Multitasking.
- Tardiness and absenteeism.
- Failure to participate.
- Failure to prepare.
- Rambling discussion and tangents.
- General dissatisfaction with "wasted time."
- Accusations, frustration, and even personal attacks.

Chapter 18: Progress Checks › 217

What to Expect in a Progress Check Meeting

Expected Participation

Project managers and account managers lead these meetings, and everyone else participates in a fairly structured way. In many ways, these meetings are designed to inform and reassure people that everyone else on the team is doing what they said they'd do, or if not, to figure out what needs to happen to get back on track.

Functional relationships matter, but it's not as important to the overall result that these people enjoy each other's company. Because these meetings are mostly designed to "make sure everything is still working," which matters to project success and the organization's ability to plan, these meetings can often be very boring for individual contributors who already know what's going on with their work.

Cadence Frequency

Weekly, biweekly, or even monthly

(The frequency of progress checks depends on the project.)

Required Preparation

Fifteen to 20 minutes for biweekly or less frequent meetings. Information for weekly meetings should already be available in the central project records. Progress Checks with clients may warrant more preparation time, especially if the meeting will include a demonstration of completed work.

During the Meeting

Progress Checks follow a regular pattern. Some are very strict about following a pre-defined agenda, others less so; this varies by the team and the kind of work they do. Regardless of whether there's an agenda, surprises are entirely unwelcome. Any major surprise will cause a meeting failure by derailing the planned discussion. Teams may spend time solving small problems and adjusting near-term plans in the meeting, as well as identifying topics that should be tackled in separate meetings.

These meetings include a review of new action items at the end.

After the Meeting

The meeting report may be created collaboratively during the meeting or may be the responsibility of an assigned note taker. It should be made available as soon as feasible and always within 24 hours. This record provides the starting material for the next meeting.

Top Tips for Successful Progress Check Meetings

The Progress Check is the meeting Angie at Pacific Bold and her team of project managers struggle with. I've participated in and led many Progress Checks myself, and I know the struggle is real.

First, you need to get a group of people together who all report to different bosses and all have more going on than just your project. Second, you may or may not have anything to discuss that they care about. Third, if you don't hold a Progress Check fairly regularly, you can be quite certain that your project will fall by the wayside as louder, more urgent priorities drown it out.

For project teams the world over, Progress Checks feel like a necessary evil. Frankly, while I hate to admit this, I believe that may often be true. But just because these aren't always the most exciting meetings, that doesn't mean they must also be long, boring, or frustrating.

More importantly, these meetings make work get done. In my experience, many people treat the task deadlines written in the project plan as advisory. The real deadline for any task is "just before I have to prove to someone else that it's done." Progress Check meetings put those "prove it" deadlines on the team's calendar.

Many of the tips for Team Cadence meetings also work well in Progress Checks. In addition, I recommend:

1. Keep internal Progress Checks as short as possible.

Tammy Adams Spann is the coauthor of two books on the topic of facilitating project meetings, and she believes that the best possible Progress Check structure looks just like a Huddle. Everyone in the meeting quickly answers:

- What's been done?
- What's in progress?
- What else does everyone here need to know about? (This can include new issues, blocks, key learnings—whatever.)

Why keep it so quick? Because Progress Checks interrupt other work. If you must interrupt, keep it short.

That said, this structure may be too brief and informal for your organization. If that's the case:

- **Start with the mandates of your organization.** Does your group need to provide detailed records for compliance or regulatory reasons? Do you need clear audit trails for your work? If so, structure the meeting to help the team create or confirm these records quickly.
- **Adjust the meeting duration and structure to match the work cadence.** If you meet often, make meetings shorter. The three-question Huddle pattern above takes 15 minutes or less, but it works best for Progress Checks run at least twice per week. Progress Checks run once per month or less frequently will typically take an hour, because there's always something that comes up when meetings are spaced farther apart, and you need to plan time to deal with it.
- **Make the work ruthlessly efficient.** You may have seen advice that says meeting leaders should ask big, open questions to encourage engagement. You may have read recommendations about spending meeting time on developing team relationships. Perhaps you've learned to incorporate big silences in your meetings to give the introverts and slow processors time to think. Usually, this is excellent advice.

  Not for Progress Checks. The best Progress Checks are lean, mean performance machines. When you design your Progress Checks, figure out the information you absolutely must share during your meetings and figure out the fastest way to get it.

Note: the people who lead Progress Checks know that most people would rather be doing something else, and this is one reason they *hate it* when surprises emerge during the meeting. A big project surprise makes it impossible to keep the meeting focused and efficient, because everyone has to stop and deal with this new information. A really masterful meeting leader can manage surprises in the moment by acknowledging them, assigning a subgroup to deal with it outside the meeting, and then moving on. This requires a rare and magical combination of meeting-savvy, team leadership skills, and calm under pressure in the meeting leader. You're better off doing your homework in advance to get ahead of any big surprises before the meeting starts.

2. Focus external meetings on answering questions and establishing trust.

Where internal Progress Checks need to fly fast, Progress Checks with external stakeholders can stroll at a more leisurely pace. Your job in these meetings is to make sure the client feels comfortable with how your team is handling the project. Often, this includes starting with a demonstration of completed work. It can also mean engaging your client in a discussion about challenges the team faces, enlisting their help in finding solutions (and making them your ally rather than your adversary).

3. Know when to zoom in and when to zoom out.

I am not a very good project manager, and I'm not even embarrassed to admit it. I'm far too conceptual and approximate to really excel at that kind of detail-oriented work. And yet, I often take on this role for our team when we meet with clients—and we get lots of positive reviews! Lucid Meetings has had government agencies ask if we can come in and train their project teams (we declined). Our commercial clients want to know what software we use to keep everything so nicely organized.

The truth is that we don't keep things as nicely organized as a good project manager would. But we are excellent communicators, and that makes all the difference. When I run a Progress Check with a client, I know that my client hired us because they aren't experts in what we do—otherwise, they'd do it themselves a lot cheaper! They've entrusted us to complete this work, and as long as we don't do anything to violate this trust, they're not going spend a lot of extra time thinking about it.

Knowing this, I created a simplified graphic that I use to show project status. I update this graphic before meetings, and I start there—super high-level, zoomed out. This lets everyone see the current project status in relationship to the overall scope and where we're heading next. For some clients, this quick visual is all they need. I then end the meeting with a recap of what they can expect in the next few weeks and confirm the next meeting date.

Other clients want to know more. They want to know about all the technical implementation details and how their project compares to any similar project I've ever done with other clients. They want to tell me their stories—all the internal politics they're wrangling or about their experiences working with other vendors. In those cases I start at a high level but come prepared to go deep. I make sure to have spreadsheets, specifications, and demo sites ready to go. We zoom way in. This ability to quickly zoom in or out in a Progress Check gives our clients confidence in our team, even when we miss a deadline or struggle to live up to their original vision.

While my examples refer to external clients, the same principles hold true for internal clients as well. A colleague who used to work in a very large corporation confirmed this: "When you're making your presentation, the rule is the higher-up the executive, the fewer words you put on the slide. We used to joke that when we made slides for the CEO, they should only include the project name and a big thumbs up."

My colleague deeply admired his CEO, but he knew that someone who looked across so many different projects didn't have time to "get into the weeds." Thumbs up!

4. Schedule to minimize interruption.

Progress Checks always interrupt someone. To keep this interruption to a minimum, consider one or all of the following.

- **Use time blocking to schedule all Progress Checks on the same day.** For more on what this is and why it helps, see chapter 9.
- **Keep the group as small as possible.** If your project involves lots of people from multiple teams, only include team leads in Progress Checks. If you'll be covering multiple projects during the same meeting, schedule each topic for a specific time so that people can attend for just those projects that involve them.
- **When working with a team that's all in the same time zone, schedule Progress Checks just before the midday break.** This puts the meeting at a natural work stopping point and encourages your hungry colleagues to end the meeting on time.
- **Find a way to make Progress Checks optional.** If someone is deep in the flow, allow them to opt out of Progress Checks. You may need to establish guidelines for this one, and it works best when people who miss a meeting commit to communicating progress with the group in some other way.

What Makes for a Compelling Action Item?

"I want to know if you do tasking right," he said without so much as a hello. "I see you have meeting software and that you say you track action items, but do you *really*?"

I was immediately taken aback and suddenly unsure. The Lucid Meetings platform does indeed capture action items assigned in meetings, and as far as I knew, these were the real deal. But here at our conference booth, this personage-of-the-strong-opinion caused me to doubt.

"Yes, we track action items from meetings," I replied. "Tell me more about what you mean when you say, 'doing tasking right.'"

To make a long story short: We were not, in his opinion, doing tasking right.

The Lucid Meetings platform captures the core Who, What, and When of the classic action item. In my experience, this is about the limit of what you can expect people to capture during a meeting. Frankly, many people become squeamish when it comes to setting the "Who" and "When" (they see this as pushy or overly prescriptive), so they just write down the "What" and hope it will all work out magically. My new conference friend found our simple format woefully inadequate.

He started the lecture: "Now see, if you've ever managed a project or a group of people," (I had.) "then you'd know that no one actually completes assignments written that way. You have to get more detailed. Every task needs to be broken into its subtasks. You can't ask people to file a report—that's too big! You've got to spell it out. Step 1: Get the data. Step 2: Write the report. Step 3: Send the report to a colleague for proofreading, and so on. Each step needs its own status. And even—ha, look there—all you've got is 'Complete' or 'Incomplete!' No! You need to track *at a minimum* whether the status is Not Started, In Progress, Complete, or Paused. At a minimum! Then, what you're calling an 'action item' here would get updated to show the progress made on all the individual subtasks, and only get checked off when all those steps are complete. You've got to break it down, or there's just no point. Otherwise these 'action items' are just useless. No one will ever do them!"

Aha! Now I understood where he was coming from. He had a point, because it's true, many action items don't get marked "complete" by the people assigned to them. This leads to one of the more painfully common activities in Progress Checks: the drudgery of, "let's all watch as the project manager tries to get all these tasks updated in real time because no one bothered to do their own updates in advance."

That bulldog-with-a-spreadsheet determination gets the required information up to date, but it's painful to sit through and a terrible waste of a team's time.

I believe the tasking wizard I met at the conference was probably right.

People probably are better able to complete tasks when they're broken into subtasks. Yet even though this could clearly make completing the task easier, I also believe I would lose my cool if a project manager tried that with me. I personally would find it both insulting and a frustrating waste of the project manager's time. There has to be another way.

I don't have a miracle answer here, but I do know of a handful of studies that provide useful clues.

First, meeting experts already consider it a best practice to start all action items with a verb. Verbs makes it clear that the owner needs to take some action. So, rather than, "The report for the board needs to be completed this week, Jane," you write, "Jane: Complete the report for the board this week." The first can be mistaken as information only (Great, Bob! Good to know!), but the second cannot.

Second, research also shows that people are more likely to follow through on tasks to which they've publicly committed and which they've written themselves. To use this in meetings, ask everyone to write the tasks they own into the meeting record themselves. This means that each person gets to word these tasks in a way that makes sense to them and set their own due date. More importantly, they've literally put in writing that they will do a specific task by a specific date. This strongly invokes the self-consistency principle, which says that people are very reluctant to do things which make them appear unreliable or inconsistent.

> Equally important is what "writing it down" symbolizes... the act implies a commitment, like a handshake, that something will be done.
> —Andy Grove, former CEO at Intel

I have used this technique in my meetings, and it does improve action item completion rates. This is one reason I'm not a big fan of delegating all the note taking to a single individual, or even worse, an automated bot. The farther removed we are from the act of writing down our commitments, the weaker the claim they have on our future selves.

Beyond the basic self-consistency considerations, I think the other reason this works so well is that some people will "accept" tasks during a meeting that they never intend to complete, just to seem polite. I find that when a participant must write down their own tasks in a shared document, they'll hesitate before signing up for something they don't actually intend to do. This gives us a chance to have a more honest dialogue about what to expect from each other and prevents meaningless tasks from getting on the list in the first place.

Additional Resources for Progress Check Meetings

Visit the Progress Check Meetings Resource Center on Lucid Meetings.
lucidmeetings.com/meeting-types/progress-check-meetings

CHAPTER 19

One-on-Ones

Answering the Questions

What's happening with you?

What's going on with your work?

What do I need to understand?

How can I help?

Examples

The Manager/Employee One-on-One

Coaching Sessions

Mentorship Meetings

The "Check In" with an Important Stakeholder

Performance Reviews

Purpose
- Career and personal development.
- Individual accountability.
- Relationship maintenance.

Work Outcomes
- Clarity about progress made.
- Clarity of expectations.
- Clarity about the other person's intentions.
- Actionable advice.

Human Outcomes
- Support and/or reassurance.
- "Clearing": getting things off one's chest.
- New ideas and opportunities to consider (learning).

Common Challenges
The biggest challenge with One-on-Ones is regularity. One-on-Ones get canceled a lot; it's the easiest meeting to bump because it affects the fewest number of people. Other challenges include:
- Pulling teeth: one or both participants aren't actively engaged.
- Unhealthy conflict.
- Missed opportunities: one or both participants don't realize how they might benefit from the meeting.
- Unintended side effects as others on the team speculate about that private conversation.
- Failure to get a productive result.

What to Expect in a One-on-One Meeting

Expected Participation
These meetings involve two people with an established relationship. The quality of that relationship is essential to success in these meetings, and leadership may alternate between the participants based on their individual goals. While these meetings may follow an agenda, the style is entirely conversational. In some instances, the only distinction between a One-on-One and a plain old conversation is the fact that the meeting was scheduled in advance to address a specific topic.

Cadence Frequency
Weekly, biweekly, or even monthly

Required Preparation
Varies.

During the Meeting
This too, varies. Ideally, you'll aim for an equal exchange of questions, ideas, and advice. These meetings work best when they conclude with a quick review confirming any decisions and action items identified in the meeting.

After the Meeting
One-on-Ones don't necessarily get documented like other meetings, as these are often considered private "anything goes" conversations. The people involved may send each other a thank-you and follow-up email.

Top Tips for Successful One-on-One Meetings

One-on-Ones are the least-structured meetings in this taxonomy. Experienced and dedicated leaders will develop an approach to One-on-Ones that they use often, but the intimate nature of these meetings defies rigid structure. The One-on-One provides time and space for talking through those things that don't fit neatly into the other meetings, that may not yet be ready for the full light of day, and that impact our work but aren't topics we're going to discuss in front of a group.

No one likes to hear an unpleasant surprise in a One-on-One, but they definitely prefer to learn such news in a two-person meeting rather than in a Team Cadence or Governance Cadence meeting. If you're going to quit the organization, planning to fly to the moon, or you've just invented the cure to aging, you're way better off telling your manager privately before you share that with the board. Here are some other tips for designing successful One-on-One meetings.

1. Be consistent and fair.
One-on-Ones serve an important function in your team's overall communication infrastructure that only works when you hold them consistently. This means picking a cadence and sticking to it for at least 90 days.

It also means that you need to be consistent with every team member. If a manager meets 30 minutes every week with three out of five team members, but frequently reschedules or cuts short meetings with the other two, that's a recipe for hurt feelings and misunderstandings.

2. Focus on the opportunity.
Here are things you might get out of a One-on-One as a manager:
- Visibility into things that are inhibiting your team's progress.
- Feedback on how your team feels about the organization's strategy, policies, and processes.
- Early warning of any trouble brewing in the team.
- Honest assessments of team progress.
- Insight into the personal motivations and outside factors that impact your team's work.
- Awareness of the interpersonal dynamics between team members that you can factor in to future work plans.
- Information you can use to make performance and salary recommendations.

For employees, you have the opportunity to get:
- The specific actions your manager thinks you should take to advance.
- Insights into the rationale behind decisions made in higher levels of the organization.
- Help dealing with a challenging colleague.
- Ideas and tips to refine a proposal you're working on before you present it more widely.
- Assistance managing personal issues that may impact your work.
- A sounding board for concerns, worries, theories, and hopes.
- Time to highlight your accomplishments and advocate for yourself.

Meeting with a colleague or a mentor? You can get:
- Insight into how other companies or people have solved the problems you're facing.
- Introductions to new people who can help you succeed.
- Recommended resources for tackling your next project.
- Someone you can bounce ideas off of who's not going to mistake them for decisions or orders.

Remember, for every meeting there is both a work outcome and a human outcome. No matter what your role, when you hold regular One-on-Ones focused on creating real opportunity for each other, you might also get yourself a friend.

3. Always wrap with next steps and a next meeting date.

Because One-on-Ones don't typically have a strict structure, it can be easy to treat these like a conversation that simply ends when time runs out. Instead, every One-on-One should end with a few minutes spent clarifying outcomes and confirming the next meeting date. This makes sure both parties know what they got out of the time, reinforcing the value of this meeting.

4. Express appreciation for take-aways.

This is good practice for many meetings but vital here, where the people involved may have unequal social status or lack any other form of mutual accountability. Paul Axtell, author and trainer, advises leaders to call out the specific value they picked up on in a conversation by making a list. The leader says: "Thank you for the conversation today. Here's what I'm taking away from this." Then the leader specifically lists two or more key points from the conversation.

One-on-Ones in the Wild

I didn't understand the value of One-on-Ones when I first began my career. I found One-on-Ones with my manager a waste of time—he already knew what I was doing! Why did I have to tell him again every week? It felt like bureaucratic nonsense to me, so I always tried to duck out or cut them short.

Not only did I fail to understand the opportunity these meetings gave me to improve my career—an opportunity I missed—I failed to understand how my disdain for the One-on-Ones hurt the team. My teammates could see that I got unequal treatment because I had fewer private meetings with the manager, and some of them worried for me. I also made my manager's job harder. When he tried to advocate on my behalf for raises and promotions with the larger organization, I hadn't given him a list of my accomplishments or any input into where I wanted the job to go in the future. He had nothing from me to work with.

Appreciations Force You to Meet Better

Forcing function #1: When you know you will end a meeting by expressing your appreciation for the specific value you got out of the discussion, it means you *must actually listen* while the other person speaks. You can't pull out any key takeaways from them if you're doing all the talking or if you are just thinking about what you'll say when they're talking instead of listening.

Forcing function #2: Making a specific list of take-aways helps you clarify that value in your own mind. When you list the take-aways, the likelihood that you'll retain and act on them goes up dramatically. After all, it's pretty hard to follow through on the good ideas you heard weeks ago if you can't remember them!

Forcing function #3: Explicit appreciations invoke the reciprocity principle. When I say, "Thank you for sharing your concerns about the upcoming release. Here's what I'm going to do about that," to a colleague, the natural social response is, "Thank you for...," which forces them to think about the value they've received from you. Bonus!

We ended up with an inconsistent pattern because I didn't understand the value of these meetings, even though my teammates did. And my manager didn't realize how clueless I was, so he never explained it in a way I understood. As a result, my teammates worried, and I got passed over for promotion. These were not the desired outcomes for any of us!

This wasn't a problem for my partner early in his career. When he started a new job at the research lab for Intel, his supervisor soon called him in for his first One-on-One.

"I need to explain to you the difference between activities and results," the supervisor began. "Here, we don't expect you to simply keep busy. When it comes time to report on your progress, I am not interested in all the ways you've filled your time. I am interested in what you've achieved—specifically in what you've learned and what you've created that brings us all closer to hitting our goals. A working prototype is a result. Troubleshooting a prototype is activity. Does this make sense?"

My partner is one of the most results-oriented guys out there; for him, this was so obvious it was almost insulting, which he told his new supervisor.

The supervisor continued, "Look, it sounds obvious. But as you know, many of us came from academia. I myself was a university professor before coming here, and when I was there, I knew a man who'd been there longer than most of us but who never got tenure. There were many reasons for that, but the biggest one I saw was that *he never asked what he needed to do to get tenure.* I know he was frustrated that he kept getting passed over, and I know he could have progressed if he'd been focused on the right kind of results. But this professor got caught up in the activities and never stopped to ask anyone if these activities were leading to the kind of results that would get him tenure. That's why I always talk to every new person about the difference between activities and results—none of us will make that mistake here."

My partner's supervisor shared that story to educate his direct reports about this distinction between activities and results. There is a second lesson in his story: if you aren't getting the recognition you think you deserve, or if you aren't sure how to be successful in your role, *you should ask.*

Ben Horowitz, a noted founder, venture capitalist, and business advisor writes extensively about the importance of One-on-Ones as part of a well-architected communication infrastructure.

> This is the free-form meeting for all the pressing issues, brilliant ideas and chronic frustrations that do not fit neatly into status reports, email and other less personal and intimate mechanisms.
>
> If you are an employee, how do you get feedback from your manager on an exciting, but only 20% formed idea that you're not sure is relevant without sounding like a fool? How do you point out that a colleague that you do not know how to work with is blocking your progress without throwing her under the bus? How do you get help when you love your job, but your personal life is melting down? Through a status report? On email? Yammer? Asana? Really? For these and other important areas of discussions, one-on-ones can be essential.
>
> —Ben Horowitz, "A good place to work"

Horowitz sees One-on-Ones as so important to employee well-being that he famously threatened to fire a manager and his supervising Vice

President when he discovered the manager had failed to hold One-on-Ones with his team for over six months.

At the top of the first page in this section, I listed these as the underlying questions for a One-on-One:

What's happening with you? What's going on with your work?

What do I need to understand? How can I help?

When you first read these questions, you may have assumed that these are questions that managers ask employees. The Intel labs supervisor and Horowitz make it clear that while that could be true, it's more important that employees have an opportunity to ask these questions of their managers.

I love Horowitz's emphasis on the "well-architected communication infrastructure" here too, because it's a reminder that the One-on-One does not work when it's the only regular meeting. Teams must also have regular Team Cadence meetings and Progress Checks in which they get through all the work status issues, in order for the One-on-One to have a chance of doing its job. Otherwise, One-on-Ones become a time for employees to report status to their manager—not an optimal use of this opportunity for a private discussion.

It's easier to see how to make the One-on-One exchange more equal and not simply a status update when you meet with a colleague or an external advisor. For example, I meet about once a month with Diana Larsen. She's the author of several books about running meetings for Agile teams, she's a female small business owner like me, and she works like I do to bring out deeper meaning in a space that's heavily weighted in favor of people promising miracle quick-wins. In other words, we have a lot to talk about. Larsen and I don't prescribe what we'll discuss in advance, but we always cover the core One-on-One questions above and we always walk away with copious notes. Before we leave, we compare our calendars and schedule the next meeting. Finally, we each send each other an email with our key takeaways and follow-up items the next day.

These meetings would be easy to skip. Larsen and I don't owe each other anything, and neither of our businesses are directly dependent on the other to make progress. And yet, every month we both have plenty to put into our takeaways email.

Horowitz expects his managers to run One-on-Ones every week. That's a pretty common cadence in the startup world. Paul Axtell, who's written two One-on-One meeting templates for the Lucid Meetings template gallery, works with clients in manufacturing, chemicals, and other large-scale environments. He's seen people succeed with meetings held weekly, every other week, and even monthly.

For a final twist, let's look at the story shared by Jennifer Garvey Berger and Keith Johnston in their book *Simple Habits for Complex Times*. It's the tale of an engineering team plagued by infighting. These engineers had tried team-building Workshops, they'd tried coaching, and still, they found themselves working against each other rather than cooperating. They were failing to pull together, which was causing them to fail to reach their goals.

So they decided to try again, this time asking a different question. What in their workplace environment was attracting, or drawing out and encouraging, this competitive, distrustful behavior? Since this is a chapter on One-on-Ones, I bet you can guess the answer.

> Each engineer had weekly meetings one-on-one with the CIO and forged excellent relationships with him. As they looked across their experience, though, they noticed that there was a way of relating to the CIO that the engineers didn't even know they were engaged in until they saw the pattern. They saw, in fact, that perhaps they were all competing in one way or another for the CIO's attention and they had a guess that the competition was fueled in part by their one-on-one meetings. They asked to change that attractor by simply shifting to weekly meetings of the whole group with the CIO and all the engineers and de-emphasizing their one-on-one meeting by having them monthly. Suddenly, the interactions among the engineers changed. They began to see the overlaps in their work. They reduced their sense of competition and increased their sense of cooperation. Rather than trying to make their own projects work, even at the expense of the others, they began to try to make the whole engineering department work.
>
> —Jennifer Garvey Berger and Keith Johnston,
> *Simple Habits for Complex Times*

As each example in this chapter shows, One-on-Ones can have a powerful impact. To make sure that impact is a positive one, it's important that these meetings are part of a larger system of well-designed meetings and a well-architected communications infrastructure.

ONE-ON-ONES

Additional Resources for One-on-One Meetings

Visit the One-on-One Meetings Resource Center on Lucid Meetings.
lucidmeetings.com/meeting-types/one-on-one-meetings

CHAPTER 20

Action Reviews

Answering the Questions

What was our plan?

What did we learn?

What should we change in our approach going forward?

Examples

Project and Agile Retrospectives

After Action Reviews and Before Action Reviews (Military)

Pre-Surgery Meetings (Healthcare)

Win/Loss Review (Sales)

Purpose

- Learning: gain insight.
- Develop confidence.
- Generate recommendations for change.

Work Outcomes

- Process improvement.
- Increased team efficiency.
- Improved operational performance.

Human Outcomes

- Shared commitment to quality.
- Continuous learning and individual skill improvement.
- Deepened connection to the shared mission.

Common Challenges

Action Reviews run into these challenges:

- Inappropriate scope: the Action Review tries to cover too much, or the suggested action plan requires commitment from departments or people over which the team has no authority.
- Non-constructive dialogue: teams devolve into blame and recrimination.
- Failure to define experiments or actions that can be implemented.
- Failure to implement the recommended changes, discouraging participation in future reviews.
- Stagnation: people begin giving rote answers to the same old review questions.
- Failure to follow up on results: the recommended action plan may or may not have been tried, but the team doesn't learn whether these recommendations produced the desired results.

What to Expect in an Action Review

Expected Participation

These meetings are led by a designated person from the team. When run well, Action Reviews demand highly engaged and structured participation from everyone present. Because Action Reviews are so structured, they don't require the individuals involved to form great interpersonal relationships. They do, however, require professionalism, focus, and strong engagement. Action Reviews that happen too infrequently or too far away in time from the action tend to become more conversational and less powerful.

Cadence Frequency
Varies based on the pace of action and the value the team places on continuous improvement.

Required Preparation
Minutes to hours, dependent on the scope of action under review. More frequent Action Reviews that go over smaller actions take little to no preparation. Big Action Reviews covering multi-month or year-long projects can take a full week or more of preparation.

During the Meeting
The basic Action Review structure begins with a review of the facts. Then, the team discusses their observations and learnings and the implications of those facts. Finally, based on what they now believe, the team defines a set of new actions or experiments that will refine how they take on their work going forward.

After the Meeting
Action Reviews result in an action plan report.

Top Tips for Successful Action Review Meetings

Action Reviews are my personal favorite type of meeting. They're amazingly powerful when run well. When run poorly, however, they're a great way to waste time and disempower your team. Let's work to avoid that, okay?

Action Reviews are highly ritualistic; these are the kind of meetings that inspire the use of the word "ritual." The Action Review is a tool for continuous learning; the more frequently these are run and the tighter the team gets, the faster the team learns and improves. Teams can and will change how they run these meetings over time based on what they've learned, and this avid pursuit of change for the better is itself part of the ritual.

I mentioned that when run poorly, an Action Review causes frustration.

These meetings are meant to help a group learn and change. If the meeting does *not* result in change, the group feels cheated—like they were asked for their ideas not because leadership planned to listen to them, but instead as an attempt to pacify the group.

1. Fast and frequent works best.

Action Reviews need to be held right before or right after the action under review. This makes it possible to reflect while the details are fresh. More importantly, it means you can apply that learning sooner.

2. Establish and enforce psychological safety.

Have you heard of "blameless" retrospectives? In the software community, I see widespread emphasis on ensuring that retrospective meetings (also known as Action Reviews) are about sharing insights and learning, and not about placing blame, venting, or working out your interpersonal issues. **This is because scapegoating shuts down learning.** People who are under attack are not learning how to improve their work—they're learning who their enemies are. People focused on blaming others are not focusing on the lessons they can learn, the actions to change, and how they can take responsibility for improving results going forward.

3. Focus first on what you know to be true.

Humans are naturally wired to spot flaws, which leads many teams to launch directly into criticism. We are not, however, wired to actually notice all the details; we have very selective reality filters that help us navigate our busy world without getting overwhelmed. This means, though, that our knowledge of what actually happened will always be incomplete—a deficit that can be counteracted when we review and compare our facts with other people's facts.

We also tend to overestimate our own skills and underestimate the influence of luck when it comes time to review successes. Perhaps you won a contract because yours was the best proposal, or maybe it was because your competitors had too much business and had to back out at the last minute. Winning a contract is a success, but learning what actually happened to get you there is vital to making that success repeatable.

4. Choose your questions with care.

The questions you ask will frame what you learn. Beyond the kind of learning you want to pull out, think also about what's going on with your team.

The U.S. National Wildland Fire Leadership council, for example, provides several different formats for running Action Reviews. There's a standard format, plus a format for teams that just worked for 16 hours without eating, and a format for a group that hasn't worked together before and doesn't know how to run a review, and even one that breaks experienced teams out of a rut. The Wildland Fire Leadership council knows that Action Reviews are a vital tool for teams fighting large, unpredictable fires—they have to communicate and learn and adjust their strategy fast if they're going to save lives. But this doesn't mean they need to stick to one strict script regardless of the circumstances.

5. Create viable experiments that will actually happen.

Action Reviews only have value when they result in new actions. At the end of the meeting, you need to walk out with some concrete actions to take: new experiments to try. For a meaningful result, make sure the planned experiments coming out of the Action Review are realistic and implementable by the people involved.

Why do I call these "experiments"? Because until you try out a new approach and then review what actually happens, you're just hypothesizing that your idea will make things better. In practice, you may find that your Action Review identified supposed safety measures that slowed down projects but didn't increase safety, for example. Treating Action Review recommendations as experiments also helps accelerate the learning, because you can state in advance what you expect (hypothesize) will happen, develop a theory, and then compare this against what actually happens (testing the theory). The Scientific Method isn't just for Chemistry class.

Create a Culture in Which It Is Okay to Make Mistakes and Unacceptable Not to Learn from Them

This is Work Principle number three in Ray Dalio's book *Principles*. It resonates deeply with me and with the people I've met who strive to operate at high performance levels.

I don't know how this topic came up, but it did. Tom, the tall, confident gentleman sitting next to me as we waited for the presentation to begin, may have seen my bright Lucid Meetings bag. Perhaps I had the Taxonomy of Business Meetings postcard out to show someone else and he noticed it. However it started, it wasn't long before we found ourselves happily gushing about the wonders of Action Reviews.

"Action Reviews are my favorite," I enthused. "And they're just so under-appreciated! I don't think people understand how transformative it can be when you build Action Reviews into your regular practice! Except maybe the military. Have you read about how OPFOR uses Action Reviews to win most of their battles and educate officers? Or any of the books by Generals McChrystal or Marquet?"

"Oh, I can do better than that," Tom said. "Before I joined the private sector, I was a general in the U.S. Army Reserves. I worked with the OPFOR group, and the teams under my command ran a lot of Action Reviews, especially when we mounted simulated grid attacks with the guys we pulled from DEF CON®. But that wasn't the case for every military group. Some of them get it; others are clueless. One of my most nerve-wracking experiences came when I had to tell the admirals just how clueless they were before they walked in to brief the Secretary of Defense. Not an easy thing to do, let me tell you. Admirals don't like to be told that their people are incompetent."

Before I relate more of Retired General Tom's story, let me provide some context for everyone who doesn't spend their time reading novels about hackers and terrorists and covert operations.

OPFOR is the Opposing Forces unit stationed at a U.S. military training base. OPFOR's job is to wage mock war on all the folks who come to the base to learn and practice, and despite the fact that OPFOR is always a smaller, under-supplied group, they almost always win. One reason they win so often has to do with their rigorous use of Action Reviews. Each unit goes over all the details for every operation in a Before Action Review and then evaluates what happened in an After Action Review. The learnings from all these meetings at the unit level flow quickly up and down the command chain, making the group incredibly nimble, adaptable, and informed. You can read more about this in the article "Learning in the Thick of It" by Marilyn Darling, Charles Parry, and Joseph Moore in Harvard Business Review.

DEF CON in General Tom's comment above refers to the competitive hacking conference. Computer hackers from around the world get together and compete to see who can crack codes and breach secure computer networks fastest. General Tom led a military group that staged simulated attacks on the U.S. electrical grid and communications infrastructure, demonstrating how terrorists might try to take out all the power on the East Coast, for example. He liked to recruit the DEF CON winners for his team.

Back to General Tom's story: "I tell you, it was hard to do, but I knew this admiral was getting ready to walk in there and tell the Secretary that we were ready for an attack, and we just weren't. He'd been led to believe that everything was in order by the advisors from the intelligence community, but our team knew that they weren't anywhere near as prepared as they thought they were. Frankly, those guys were all amateur hour, but that's not something they wanted to hear from a reservist like me. So I went in and, as respectfully as I could, I told the Admiral what I knew.

"'With respect,' I started, 'these teams are not ready, and if you go in there with that message, you will embarrass yourself and these units. I know I'm a reservist and that I don't rank here, but we are all on the same team. I thought you'd rather hear this from me than fail in public in front of the president and the cabinet. I'm on your same side here, and I can tell you that you're making a mistake.'

"Of course, no good deed goes unpunished. My speech got me put in charge of training up all these units I just said weren't prepared. They cleared out the FBI Academy, and we filled it with all these hackers. We scheduled 48 hours to stage a major attack on the East Coast grid that these guys would need to defend against.

"When we got started that first day, it became really clear that things were worse than I thought. They were terrible. I mean really, truly bad. My team already had a practice of running AARs [that's After Action Reviews] at the end of every day, but with these new guys, we bumped it up to *every two hours*. Every two hours we shut the whole simulation down and drilled them on what they'd learned—what worked, what didn't, what caught them by surprise, and what they were going to try next. But even then, we were getting into the afternoon and they were still making tons of mistakes. Thank heavens it was a simulation, because they just weren't learning fast enough! So we brought it in even tighter and started running the AARs *every 30 minutes*.

"That worked. It was grueling, and I know we didn't endear ourselves to any of those guys. But you know what? By the end of that second day, they were pretty damn good. I was able to go back to the admiral and say, 'Okay, sir. Now you can go tell the Secretary we're ready, because we are.'"

There's a lot to learn from that story (beyond just how cool some people's jobs sound!). First, *the cadence for Action Reviews sets the pace of shared learning*. Action Reviews are the way that teams reflect, learn, and improve together; they focus learning and ensure it gets shared. Second, *Action Reviews help teams discover the most promising reality-based experiments*. Instead of speculating and talking about possible actions in Planning meetings, teams take action and use what they learn to quickly adjust their tactics based on what actually happens.

Teams that build Action Reviews into their regular operations will still make lots of mistakes, but they won't be repeating preventable mistakes. As Bob Sutton, Professor of Management Science and Engineering at the Stanford Engineering School, said:

> After event reviews—whether focused on failure alone or both successes and failures—spark learning. Sure, you already knew that—but it amazes me how many companies don't have time to stop and think about what they learned, but seem to have the time to keep making the same mistakes over and over and over again.
>
> — Bob Sutton

Additional Resources for Action Review Meetings

Visit the Action Review Meetings Resource Center on Lucid Meetings.
lucidmeetings.com/meeting-types/action-review-meetings

CHAPTER 21

Governance Cadence

Answering these Questions

How did we perform?

What's changed?

What needs our intervention?

Examples

Board Meetings

Quarterly Strategic Reviews

QBRs (Quarterly Business Reviews between a vendor and client)

Purpose
- Strategic definition and oversight.
- Regulatory compliance and monitoring.
- Maintenance of relationships and organizational identity.

Work Outcomes
- Finalized decisions.
- Confirmation of strategic priorities.
- Legal oversight.
- Operational advice.
- Access to external resources.

Human Outcomes
- Clarity of direction.
- Mutual accountability and support.
- Improved situational awareness and contextual understanding.

Common Challenges
Governance Cadence Meetings run into these challenges:
- Procedural failures: not following the rules for that kind of meeting.
- Process rigidity: following an overly formal format that stifles discussion.
- Inadequate preparation, leading to harried participants and unproductive meetings.
- Lack of role clarity, when people don't understand what's expected of them and fail to contribute appropriately.
- Insufficient participation—absent participants can prevent the meeting from moving forward.

What to Expect in a Governance Cadence Meeting

Expected Participation
The teams involved in Governance Cadence meetings are known in advance, but don't necessarily work together often. Nor do they need to; these aren't the kind of meetings where everyone has to be pals to get good results. These meetings are led by a chair or official company representative, and participation is structured. This means that while there are often times for free conversation during a governance meeting, much of

the participation falls into prescribed patterns. These are often the kind of meetings that warrant wearing nicer shoes.

Cadence Frequency
Monthly to annually.

Boards for newly formed or highly active groups may meet monthly. Established groups tend to meet quarterly. Finally, some groups meet just once per year, the minimum requirement by law.

Required Preparation
Governance Cadence meetings are highly structured. When run professionally, there is always an agenda, it is always shared in advance, and minutes are recorded. Preparation can take anywhere from many hours to several days. Organizers must prepare the agenda and any supplemental reports, and participants are expected to review all material in advance.

Many Governance Cadence meetings have advance notice requirements (stated in bylaws or other governing documents), stating how far in advance the meeting schedule must be posted and how far in advance the agenda and materials need to be shared. These requirements mean that preparation often needs to be done well in advance of the actual meeting date.

Governance Cadence meetings are *not* the time for surprises. In fact, best practice for important Governance Cadence meetings includes making sure everyone coming to that meeting gets a personal briefing in advance (see Sensemaking or One-on-Ones) to ensure no one is surprised in the meeting. A surprise in a Governance Cadence meeting means someone screwed up.

During the Meeting
Governance Cadence meetings all have formal attendance requirements, so they begin by making sure all the required people showed up. Then, there's often a formal beginning such as an official welcome, a benediction, or a call to order.

After that, the meeting proceedings vary to fit the needs of the group. Many groups begin by reviewing the agenda and moving things around if needed; this is sometimes called "agenda bashing." Then the leader works through the agenda items in the planned order.

Governance Cadence meetings can run anywhere between an hour and a full day or more, which means many often include several planned breaks.

Once all the business concludes, Governance Cadence meetings close with a review confirming any decisions that were made and the assignment of any new action items.

After the Meeting

Most Governance Cadence meetings are documented by formal minutes. Minutes aren't the same as meeting notes; they are legal documents that may be published (meaning, to the actual public) and used in legal proceedings. Because official minutes carry so much more legal weight than your garden-variety meeting notes, the person responsible for them may take several days to get them ready for review. Even then, the minutes aren't usually considered official until the group approves them in their next meeting.

Even though minutes take longer to prepare than other types of meeting records, you should still hope to see the first version within a week of the meeting. Any longer than that and the group risks losing important details that the minutes writer forgets as time passes.

Top Tips for Successful
Governance Cadence Meetings

Before we get into guidelines for Governance Cadence meetings, I'll address a common misconception: Not all meetings attended by board members are Governance Cadence meetings. Official board meetings that result in legally documented meeting minutes are Governance Cadence meetings, but a team-building offsite, a strategic brainstorm, or a board Training event are not.

Governance Cadence meetings are designed to provide oversight and guidance for contracted relationships. Many Governance Cadence meetings are literally prescribed in the organization's legal formation documents.

For example, in the U.S. there are over 40,000 Special Districts (SDs)— local organizations which qualify for about $100 billion in annual federal government spending. Many of these SDs are tiny, consisting of a handful of citizens working together to control the local mosquito population, for example. Others are huge. Where I live, one SD controls our public transit system and another coordinates emergency services across multiple cities.

Yet regardless of the SD's size or scope, each one must hold publicly accessible board meetings every year. Open board meetings are part of their legal charter.

In other cases, there's no legal mandate, but there is an implied contractual obligation. For example, the Quarterly Business Review (QBR) meeting between a vendor and a client exists to ensure both parties regularly review performance against their contract. Once per quarter, the vendor looks at what they promised to deliver and reports on results. They also talk through challenges and any opportunities they see to improve results going forward. While many people think of the QBR as an opportunity to sell the client additional services, that's only possible when the client is satisfied with the results they're getting already. Yet this meeting happens regardless of whether the client is happy or not, which means it may actually focus more on corrective action than on new sales opportunities. The QBR happens every quarter regardless of the state of the contract because its primary function is contractual oversight.

Given that context, our first guideline should be no surprise.

1. Follow the rules, but don't fear the rules.

It's important to know the rules that apply to your Governance Cadence meeting. There are three reasons you need to learn the rules:

First, if you don't follow them, you can run into trouble later on. Unwinding problems caused by a sloppy process is far more painful than preventing these issues in the first place.

Second, what you don't know can and will be used against you. If your group is tackling anything contentious, there will be people in the room who know the rules and will use any misstep on your part to block progress. The rules are intended to enforce order, and if you don't know the rules, you are the one upon whom this order will be enforced.

Finally, once you know what the rules strictly require, you can confidently shift your focus to the real issues at hand.

You should think of the legal requirements that apply to Governance Cadence meetings like you do the rules of the road. It is absolutely required that you stop at red lights, drive on the correct side of the street, and maintain a reasonable speed. But when you are trying to get somewhere, you don't focus on the rules of the road—you focus on getting to your destination. The rules exist to help you get there without causing undue mayhem.

Learn your rules so you can follow them unconsciously, freeing up the headspace needed to achieve a quality result. The most effective boards I've seen check off the legal requirements quickly and painlessly, then give the majority of their time to engaging dialogue.

2. Learn how to use the meeting before the meeting.

Did I mention that Governance Cadence meetings are not the time for surprises? It is both appropriate and advisable to hold quick One-on-Ones and small team working sessions with others in advance of a Governance Cadence meeting. If you are facing a Governance Cadence meeting and you're not confident about how it will proceed, figure out which other meetings you need to fit in first.

3. Make the highest and best use of everyone's time.

The time an organization gets with the people in the Governance Cadence meeting can be one of the organization's most valuable assets. These are people who can make great things happen for your organization. When you use this time to slowly track attendance, to read reports out loud, or to discuss basic facts that could have been shared in advance, you have squandered that precious resource.

Instead, high-performing Governance Cadence meetings optimize the time of those present by:

- Minimizing time spent on legalities.
- Ensuring everyone arrives prepared.
- Asking everyone to take on an appropriate task.

This last is the power tip. High-performing leaders know the strengths of the people participating in their Governance Cadence meetings and plan in advance to ask each of these people to help in a way that maximizes the value that person can offer.

Jeff Bonforte, CEO of Xobni, discovered that his company's success was contingent on his board doing their best to help—so he put them to work. He said:

Once I realized the board was there to help and not just to judge, I became much better at asking for and getting that help. I found that the harder the board worked for Xobni, the better it functioned at all levels.

— Jeff Bonforte

Boards are People Too

As a young professional, I found The Board intimidating. It really didn't matter what The Board was a board of—it was always clear that The Board included many Very Important People who made Important Decisions. I think a lot of people feel this way about their boards, and it creates some unique challenges to board work. Boards already operate with more requirements and constraints than other groups, which reinforces this idea that every board must operate as The Board does.

Boards are responsible. They influence strategy, provide fiduciary oversight, oversee management, and guard against undue risks or compliance violations. They may direct programs, lead fundraising, and champion the organization. In the smallest organizations, the board *is* the organization. These are big responsibilities and important tasks to get right, requiring the careful attention of well-informed, intelligent, and conscientious board members.

You know, Very Important People.

Who's really on the board?

My alma mater just reminded me that I'm nearly 20 years into my career. Over that time, I've served on and worked with many kinds of boards, and seen lots of board members in action.

I know now that my early impressions were both entirely correct and also dead wrong.

I know The Board is indeed made up of Very Important People. These people are important because the work they do is important. And the best board members really are intelligent, thoughtful, energetic, conscientious, pragmatic, and involved. So in that sense, I was right. Very Important, Impressive People!

But more important is that, whether in the boardroom or not, every board member is also very much just another person. These folks may or may not be "important" in any special way that you'd recognize outside the board meeting. They may not be particularly intelligent, thoughtful, energetic, or pragmatic. Board members can be self-serving, petty, and negligent. They might be shy, anxious, and intimidated. And even with best intentions, they can be wrong.

Basically, they're people. Even the superstars.

My "Aha Moment" about Board Members as People

I once attended a board committee meeting full of honest-to-goodness Very Important People: high-powered directors from Microsoft, the FDA, major professional organizations, judges, and one particularly impressive gentleman who helped develop nuclear submarines for the U.S. Department of Defense. At the time, I was (in my eyes) a trumped-up web designer who could barely walk straight in my business heels. Simply being in the room was very intimidating.

At the first meeting break, the very scary U.S. Department of Defense representative approached me. I began to sweat—surely he wondered how I'd even got into the room, and I was about to be grilled! Instead, he offered to split the last oatmeal raisin cookie with me. Turns out we both were trying to watch our weight but also really needed a sugar boost after the deadly-boring presentation we'd all just suffered.

As the meeting went on, it became clear that these Very Important People were all just *people*. One important person whined a lot. One kept getting confused about what we were discussing. An important person attending by phone fell asleep before hitting the mute button, and snored loudly throughout the next hour (delightfully, the session was recorded!). The chairwoman was professional, calm, reasonable, and clearly irritated more than once. By the end of the meeting, vital issues had come to light, and important decisions were made; then everyone rushed out for badly needed drinks.

This meeting was enlightening for me—one of those moments that helped inspire the work I do at Lucid today. From this meeting and many that have followed, our team has learned some important lessons about how to approach board meetings.

1. The biggest constraints aren't what you think.

When I showed up at that meeting, I wasn't entirely sure what I could and could not do. Was I allowed to comment on the discussion as a newbie? I didn't have full voting rights and didn't have an agenda item to present. I was mostly there to learn. Did I have to sit somewhere special?

The first time someone has to create the agenda for a Governance Cadence meeting can be even more nerve-wracking. Many of us know that there are rules about when and how these groups meet, but we're not quite sure what those rules might be. Really, though, figuring out the rules turns out to be pretty easy. This is why I advise you to "Follow the rules, but don't fear the rules."

The confusion about the rules governing these meetings is understandable, because in reality, the rules are different depending on the kind of group. For example, with boards the rules vary based on whether it's a board for a nonprofit organization, a government agency, a partnership, a corporation, and so on.

Happily, it's usually pretty easy to find out which rules apply to you. First, you should take a look at your organization's bylaws, articles of incorporation, or contracts. Often you'll find everything you need in there to cover your legal bases: things like how far in advance you need to send out the meeting notice, how many people have to show up in order for the meeting to count, and so on.

Sometimes, though, you won't find anything in your organization's documents about the meeting you need to lead. This probably means your organization isn't too formal, but you should look next at any rules governing your kind of group in your state or jurisdiction.

In my experience, those groups with lots of rules and legal constraints are *very* aware of those rules. The chances that a) you're in charge of a Governance Cadence meeting where there are lots of strict rules about how you need to set up the agenda, and b) no one told you exactly what to do, are essentially zero.

So, yes, there are always at least a few things you do need to take care of, and these are generally pretty easy to figure out once you know where to look. Even then, most rules concerning these meetings have very little effect on the meeting agenda.

The more challenging constraint is *you can't pick whom to invite!*

While Governance Cadence meetings are special, they're still meetings. When you strip away the formal language about contracts, motions, quorum, and whatnot, what you have is a group of people working together to unblock issues, get to the root of big questions, and make decisions that move the organization forward. In essence, you have the kind of thing going on that you get in most meetings, and all the same opportunities for dysfunction.

People who are good at running meetings in the business world work hard to focus the agenda down to only the most important topics and only invite those people vital to the discussion at hand. You can't do that as easily with a Governance Cadence meeting. Each official member is invited every time, whether you think they have anything relevant to add or not. When you run a QBR with a client, you don't get to pick the decision-maker representing the client's interests. To make it even more challenging, many decisions require most or all of these people to agree. For the meeting to succeed, figuring out how to design and facilitate the discussion to get that agreement is far harder than figuring out any legal wording requirements.

2. Personality comes across larger in Governance Cadence meetings.

I mentioned the whiner in my "aha moment" meeting above. In the half-day we spent together, I got a really good sense of that personality. There was an issue under discussion, and he really cared about it. As his stress level rose, and his need to have his point heard and accepted became more acute, all this unpleasant wheedling and shaming and strident demanding came pouring out. The seemingly reasonable requests he had previously made in writing before the meeting now felt petty, because of the attitude he brought to the discussion.

Governance Cadence meetings bring together people who may not know each other well (or at all) in a situation where they are expected to behave impressively. When I was younger, this was intimidating for me—I rarely spoke up during the meeting. I watched as some others, also clearly uncomfortable, overcompensated by working hard to say something declarative during every exchange. I doubt any of us left a good impression with the seasoned board members.

When under stress, most people revert to their "backup stress behavior." Usually this isn't their most charming self. In a meeting where people often have to make stressful decisions, and where constructive conflict is required for an effective result, these backup personalities can start to take center stage. I really doubt the whiner achieved his level of professional success by annoying his way up the ladder, but that board meeting created a situation that made this dark side of his personality gratingly obvious.

3. Responsibility creates risk-aversion, sometimes for the wrong reasons.

Olivier Sibony, a director in McKinsey's Paris office and researcher looking at decision making in organizations, observed that "the further up the hierarchy you go, the harder it becomes to say, 'My judgment is fallible.'"

The members involved in Governance Cadence meetings are ultimately responsible for the consequences of their decisions, but individual members may not always understand the ramifications of the decisions they face. Yet we expect and value Governance Cadence teams full of confident decision-makers, encouraging them to sometimes act with a confidence they don't actually feel. As a result, the team may make what they feel to be the "safest" decision available.

When I served on my son's PTA board, the "safest" decision was usually the one that made the angriest person in the room happy. Like many nonprofit boards, the PTA was full of well-intentioned volunteers just trying to help out. Without better information about the legal and practical implications of a request, the PTA board deferred to whatever decision made the scary parents chill out.

On the corporate side, I once worked with a board chairman who liked to say, "Sometimes the best decision is no decision," whenever confronted with a complicated or controversial subject. When the board lacks the information with which to make a good decision, this could be the case. Usually, though, issues brought to the board for decision *need* to be resolved, as all other avenues short of the governing team's intervention have already been exhausted. Eventually, we had to stop working with this group as the board became stalemated and ineffective, and their company stagnated.

If participants are not careful, Governance Cadence meetings can generate lots of decisions that are "safer" and easier, but not better.

4. Boring is boring.

Governance Cadence meetings put participants in a tricky position. These participants must make important decisions that have big impact on what the organization they serve will do—but paying attention to the organization at this level usually isn't their full-time job. They don't know the day-to-day details. They don't have the nuanced understanding that comes from living with a problem.

The people bringing information to the meeting know this, and may try to compensate by preparing super-detailed presentations and exhaustive reports to get everyone up to speed. Too often, this results in that poor guy who called in and snored through the call, which in turn results in everyone else in the room giggling quietly through your presentation because, while we're all sure this must be mission-critical data, um, he's snoring really loud!

5. If it's too easy, be afraid.

Sometimes you start to prepare for a Governance Cadence meeting, and it feels like a chore. There aren't big decisions coming up, you don't expect any particular controversy, and you're mostly planning a meeting because, legally, you have to. You fully expect to go through the motions of reviewing reports, asking and answering a few softball questions, and securing the official sign-off you need in order to make your records look good should an auditor ever come calling.

A business-as-usual Governance Cadence meeting signals one of two big problems:

First, boring meetings may be a sign that the organization or your contract relationship is dying. When this happens, your organization has lost its spark. If you're entirely happy with the status quo and have no interest in growing or achieving anything new of note, then fine. If not, a Governance Cadence meeting without something to either be excited or anxious about is a sign of stagnation. Growth, by definition, requires change, and change brings controversy, big decisions, and meaningful meetings. It is the nature and purpose of these meetings to help oversee and guide change. As such, Governance Cadence meetings should always be at least interesting and at best incredibly stimulating events.

Another case in point: at Lucid Meetings, we use one very expensive piece of software that requires a large annual commitment. For the first two years of our contract, our account manager met with us every quarter to review our product usage, make sure we were getting good value, and let us know about new features coming out that could help us.

Then, about 18 months in, I did a case study with them. They got their testimonial—hooray for them!—and the quarterly reviews ceased. They no longer call to see how we're doing, and they don't waste any time trying to optimize our relationship. I assume they've either changed their practice or decided we're too small to worry about; either way, this is no longer a relationship for me. It's just software now, and if something better or cheaper comes along, I'll switch in a heartbeat.

GOVERNANCE CADENCE

The other possible cause of boring Governance Cadence meetings is unwarranted complacency. In the 2011 preface to *The Board Book*, William Bowen cites board complacency as one of the factors leading to the U.S. subprime mortgage crisis and subsequent economic implosion of 2008. Leading up to that time, the boards of too many financial services firms simply accepted the assurances of management, not ever truly understanding the complicated machinations they were approving. Many other boards spent little to no time addressing risk, leaving their organizations dangerously vulnerable to collapse.

Clearly, no board can fully protect an organization from the malicious intent of management, or the manifold threats they'll face in their future—but they can at least make an effort. A complacent board that rubber-stamps whatever management puts on the agenda isn't doing its job, which puts the organization at undue risk.

So Governance Cadence meetings are special, but more importantly, they're meetings. Everything you've learned in this book about how to run an engaging and effective meeting applies. Adequate preparation, a well-designed meeting plan, and considerate facilitation matter in every meeting and become even more important for Governance Cadence meetings given the high stakes and high-pressure nature of the work.

In that way, a Governance Cadence meeting isn't that different from a big sales meeting or an important client kickoff. The key to success is a shift of perspective—learning to worry less about the formalities and more about making it easy for everyone involved to participate effectively.

Do I still get nervous about Governance Cadence meetings? Sure, but usually only when I'm new to the group. Even then it's the kind of nervousness you feel anytime you need to go be *Important* in front of a group you've never met—and nowhere near as nerve-wracking as public speaking.

Really, though, once I figured out that Governance Cadence meetings are basically just meetings with a few extra rules, attended by a bunch of real people who may or may not be any more prepared than I am, that took a lot of the stress out of it.

I recommend starting with a useful template. Then, remember that everyone in the meeting is a real person, and focus on helping them perform like the Very Important Person they strive to be.

Additional Resources for Governance Cadence Meetings

Visit the Governance Cadence Meetings Resource Center on Lucid Meetings.

lucidmeetings.com/meeting-types/governance-cadence-meetings

CHAPTER 22

The Catalyst Meetings

Where the Cadence Meetings support continuity and momentum along a previously-agreed path, the Catalyst Meetings change that path. New ideas, new plans, projects to start, problems to solve, and decisions to make—these meetings redefine an organization's work. If there is a time when your organization takes a moment and joins together to ask, "What if?", it's in a Catalyst meeting. **These meetings reveal what the organization thinks it should be.**

Catalyst meetings are scheduled as needed, and include the people the organizers feel to be best suited for achieving the meeting goals. That could be an established team, like it is with product Planning or marketing Planning meetings, or the group could be a surprise, like it is with a community outreach Workshop.

Catalyst meetings succeed when following a thoughtful meeting design and regularly fail when people "wing it."

I hear different complaints about Catalyst meetings than about Cadence meetings. Attendees describe a bad Catalyst meeting using language like:

- "Sham," "boondoggle," "bait-and-switch": When they expected one kind of engagement but got something very different. For example, when someone goes to a community engagement Workshop put on by their city, then watches as city representatives spend just five minutes taking questions they don't even bother to write down. (That's not a Workshop—it's a Broadcast!) Or when the leadership team spends three days offsite at a nice resort to create a "strategic plan" that no one else ever sees and that doesn't change anything back in the office.

- **"Love-fest," "pandering," "fluffy," "touchy-feely"**: When participants are asked to engage in a way that doesn't feel authentic. For example, in the Workshop introductions where engineers are asked to share which kind of animal they might be if they were an animal at the zoo. Or in Idea Generation, when the customer success team is asked to come up with all kinds of wonderful ideas about how to delight customers, but are given no new resources and nothing changes in how they're evaluated when taking support calls.
- **"Bullshit"**: When participants' contributions are ignored or overridden by someone higher up the chain. For all those Problem Solving and Decision Making meetings that people work hard to prepare for, only to have the boss cut conversation short then dictate an answer. That's BS!

The clarity needed for a successful Catalyst meeting extends beyond the Purpose and Desired Outcomes. When you run one of these meetings, you must also be clear about the change you expect it to make in the organization. **Participants need to know what to expect not just *in* the meeting but also *as a result of* the meeting.**

Because these meetings are scheduled as needed with whoever is needed, there is a lot more variation in format between meetings. This is the realm of participatory engagement, decision- and sense-making activities, and, when the group gets larger, trained facilitation. A meeting dedicated entirely to solving a problem or making a decision elevates the importance of those decisions. Because these are special events, it becomes possible to use techniques that lead to better outcomes but might feel awkward in a Cadence meeting.

It's *possible* to use more advanced techniques in these meetings but sadly rare that anyone does. Few organizations provide the training and resources needed for their people to use Catalyst meetings as well as they could. The structures that lead to success for these meetings are not difficult to learn, but they aren't obvious or natural either.

To succeed, Catalyst meetings need the right structure.

Just as I did with the Cadence meetings, I'll discuss what works best for each of the five types of Catalyst meetings in turn. But where I focused on the Cadence Frequency and Required Preparation Time for those meetings, factors which determine how those meetings both drive work momentum and impact productivity, here we'll focus instead on the meeting structure.

Each Catalyst meeting has a core structure you can learn and build on to improve results.

In Catalyst meetings, groups struggle to balance "Good" and "Done"—the tension is between getting the best result and reaching a result quickly enough for it to be put to use.

In their book *Momentum*, the team at Meeteor talks about how they use the acronym GETGO to guide them through this tension. They aim for results that are Good Enough To GO (GETGO). Keep this acronym in mind when designing and running your Catalyst meetings. You're not aiming for perfection—you're aiming for GETGO.

The chart below shows some of the signs you can monitor to help you balance these tensions. When you notice that your group is exhibiting behavior from the lower half of the grid, it's time to figure out what you can change that will bring your meetings back into balance.

Qualities to Balance

	A Focus on Good...	A Focus on Done...
Signs You're Getting It Right	• Champions logic. • Incorporates many perspectives. • Creates better long-term results.	• Gets results quickly. • Makes it possible to move on. • Prevents paralysis and stagnation.
Signs You've Overdone It	• Slows the process down. • Misses the opportunity to act. • Wears people out and decreases participation.	• Shortcuts dialogue. • Fails to build buy-in. • Risks taking wrong actions based on hasty assumptions.

Catalyst meetings can be fun and exciting! This is where organizations get their cool, new ideas. This is where change for the better begins! Of course, that's when they work *well*. What are the consequences for botched Catalyst Meetings? Mediocrity at best, and if the pattern persists, organizational demise. Organizations cannot survive without new ideas, without solving problems, nor when they repeatedly make bad decisions.

Let's get into what it takes to successfully design Catalyst meetings that will keep your organization vibrant.

CHAPTER 23

Idea Generation

Answering the Question

What are all the ideas we can think of in this situation?

Examples

Ad Campaign Brainstorming Session

User Story Brainstorming

Fundraiser Brainstorming

New Product Ideas

Party Theme Ideas

Purpose
- Create a whole bunch of ideas.

Work Outcomes
- Lots of new ideas that can be used to seed a new effort.
- Information about what the organization considers possible—the ideas provided reveal the group's accepted boundaries.

Human Outcomes
- Excitement about the chance to be a part of something new.
- A break from the day-to-day routine.
- New perspectives; broadened thinking.
- Inspiration.

Common Challenges
There are a lot of social and cognitive challenges you must overcome to run a worthwhile Idea Generation meeting, including:

- Unclear purpose: participants may not understand how the ideas will be used.
- Distrust: when the purpose is unclear, or based on past experiences where a participant's ideas got a bad reception.
- Groupthink: where thinking becomes limited by what's already been said.
- Overly limiting risk aversion: people can be limited both by fear of looking silly and by a belief that they need to seem practical.
- Unequal processing speeds: some people don't just generate loads of ideas on command.

What to Expect in an Idea Generation Meeting

Expected Participation
Idea Generation meetings often include participants from an established team (typically, the team that's stuck) but not always and not exclusively. That's because while it's always nice to meet with people you know and like, established relationships don't necessarily improve outcomes for these meetings. Instead, leaders who want to get the widest variety of ideas

IDEA GENERATION

possible are better off including participants with diverse perspectives and identities. Relationships are not central here; ideas are.

Like all the Catalyst meetings, Idea Generation works best when led by a dedicated facilitator using a structured process.

Typical Duration
Thirty to 90 minutes.

Note: Often Idea Generation sessions are conducted as one part of a longer Workshop.

Core Structure
1. Introduction
2. Ground Rules and Warm Up
3. Idea Generation
4. Review and Close

These meetings start with the presentation of a central premise or challenge (the *Introduction*) followed by an explanation of the idea generation technique the group will use (the *Ground Rules and Warm Up*). The whole meeting is an entreaty to serendipity: muses and creative forces are welcome. As such, there are few governing principles beyond the rule to never interfere with anyone else's enthusiasm.

After the Warm Up, everyone jumps into some form of *Idea Generation*. There are loads of idea generation techniques, all of which involve a way for participants to respond to a central challenge with as many individual ideas as possible.

The end result of an Idea Generation meeting is simply a big list of ideas—not a solution, not a direction, not even a concise set of options. This is why dedicated Idea Generation meetings are so rare. More often, idea generation is just one step in a Problem Solving meeting or a Workshop.

Here, idea *volume* matters more than anything else. These meetings end with a quick Review of the group's work and a statement about how the ideas will be used going forward.

After the Meeting
The results from an Idea Generation meeting frequently feed into either a Planning Meeting, where people will use the ideas to guide their plans,

or a Sensemaking meeting where people will work to evaluate and make sense of any deeper meaning emerging from all these ideas.

Top Tips for Successful Idea Generation Meetings

It's not every day that you'll see a full-grown Idea Generation meeting in the wild. Brainstorming, sure—meetings are swarming with little brainstorms. But the fully mature Idea Generation meeting is a rare beast. Teams resort to a dedicated Idea Generation meeting when they're stuck. When your team really has no clear next steps and needs to scout a range of territories before picking a path, plan an Idea Generation meeting.

Teams may also use an Idea Generation meeting as a kind of publicity event. You see this when companies invite customers to come share all their feature ideas, or when governments run open public input sessions. The message is, "Look, we're listening to all of your ideas! See? We care!" This is not a bad idea, by the way. This openness to input from "the common person" is believed to be one of the reasons the Netherlands avoided the series of violent revolts that plagued the rest of Europe during the Reformation.

Happily, the tips for success in standalone Idea Generation meetings apply to these activities in Workshops too, so this section does double duty.

1. Maximize diversity to increase divergence.

Idea Generation meetings are all about divergence; about getting as many different ideas that diverge from other ideas as possible. Invite as many different kinds of people as possible. This might include people representing different departments, customers, community members, people from different generations or backgrounds, and people with differing levels of experience. Everyone has a unique vantage point on reality, which means they can each see answers that others can't.

2. Clearly state the meeting goal and how the ideas will be used up front.

For some, sharing new ideas can be scary. They worry they'll be judged, especially if they don't know what to expect. Take this head-on by clearly stating up front why you're asking for all these ideas and what you'll do with them later.

At the beginning of the meeting, make sure to answer:

- What problem are you trying to solve? Do you need new product ideas, solutions to a community challenge, or design guidance?
- What will you do with all the ideas after the meeting? Will there be a report? If so, who will see it? Will names be attached to ideas?
- Who decides which ideas move on to the next phase? What is the next phase?

3. Start with a creativity-sparking warm-up exercise.

There are many techniques for warming up a group. As an example, recent research published in *Harvard Business Review* suggested that having people share an embarrassing story from their past before brainstorming led to a significant increase in the quantity and quality of ideas created by the group.

Another simple technique asks people to create as many sentences as possible containing words that start with the letters in a four letter word. For example, if the word is PIGS, the sentences might be:

- Pretty ingenious geese smile.
- Poop igloos go smooshy.
- Protect innocent gullible soloists.
- Politely ignore green sandwiches.

There are a lot more warm up techniques where these came from. All of these techniques help the group engage the fun, experimental side of their brain before they turn their attention to the work at hand.

4. Provide clear instructions and sensible boundaries for ideas.

Explain how you want people to share ideas and the kind of ideas you need, and then give an example. In most cases, you'll want each idea written down separately and in a specific format. Then, set sensible boundaries. Sometimes you want every wild idea anyone can dream up. In that case, set a deliberately absurd boundary such as: "Your idea doesn't have to be limited to things we know how to do, but it should be at least theoretically possible. For example, any idea that requires an alien invasion is out of bounds. Ideas that rely on access to a helicopter, though, or endorsement from a major celebrity, are fair game. What's the craziest idea you have that *just might work*?"

Other times, the boundaries are much clearer. When brainstorming features for an upcoming point-of-sale system release, for example, the boundaries might be that all the ideas must be ways to improve the payment system that don't require any changes to the hardware being sold.

5. Time the work.

Every part of this meeting should use a timer. In these meetings, the timer plays an active role as the guardian of the process and the keeper of momentum. When the group is creating ideas, that's all they're allowed to do until the timer goes off. Then if the process calls for grouping ideas into clusters, that too should be timed.

For example, you might tell the group to create as many ideas as they can in five minutes. For some groups, this will be a mad dash to get all the ideas out there. For others, they'll finish in the first minute then sit awkwardly for a minute before the second batch of ideas occurs to them. In both situations, this short-but-not-too-short time creates positive creative pressure and focuses the group's energy.

In Praise of Asynchronous Idea Generation

I don't run a lot of stand-alone Idea Generation meetings. I do run lots of idea generation *activities* in the course of other meetings. The Real-Time Agenda, a structure we use as part of our Team Cadence meetings, includes an idea generation step. We generate ideas like a teenager generates text messages!

Recently, I ran a series of Idea Generation meetings while developing Lucid's online coursework. In one meeting, a group of friends and family members listed all kinds of possibilities for an upcoming anniversary party. In another, they worked through ways we might renovate the playground at our neighborhood park. We had a good time, and we ended up with a lot of great ideas—too many ideas, really—but that's how these things work.

This brings me to my current dilemma. I am now the owner of several long sheets of flip chart paper covered in colored marker and sticky notes that I'm supposed to turn into something useful. I know what I need to do and how to do it, but I'm not looking forward to the hours it will take me to type up all these scribbles. This is the kind of task that procrastination was invented for, and I'm using all the procrastination skills in my possession.

In 2015, I conducted a review of several online software platforms that support Idea Generation. I gave detailed reviews for 25 products at the time and have updated the list every few months. There are 28 platforms on that list today.

Each and every one of those tools makes it possible for team members to type in their own ideas. Brilliant! Most then spit out a beautiful little report. You can get all the ideas in a spreadsheet. You can get them in a chart. You can take digital pictures of them clustered together in happy clumps to paste into your reports. The tedious hours of typing go away; you get to skip right to doing something interesting with those ideas!

Perhaps more importantly, when you collect ideas electronically, you don't have to do it all together in real time. People can enter their ideas asynchronously, letting each individual add ideas when they are most inspired. It means each person can also come back repeatedly, adding more ideas as they come up.

Asynchronous idea generation combats several of the social pitfalls that plague traditional brainstorming sessions. First, it gives slower processors time to think. When you use software that allows you to collect ideas anonymously, you help introverts and those lower in the organization's hierarchy open up without fear of consequences or other social barriers. Asynchronous sessions can eliminate groupthink when you keep everyone's ideas hidden until the end. Finally, this can also encourage greater diversity, since you don't have to rely on just those people who had the time and ability to physically show up at your session.

Yes, asynchronous idea generation means you miss out on some fun. Also yes, there's something powerful about getting a group to come together to share their hopes and visions that creates great allies for change. But these benefits are lost if the ideas don't get used, and they are always limited by the time and people available to you at the moment.

For most situations calling for a pure Idea Generation meeting—including public involvement—I advocate for anonymous asynchronous sessions using online software. Then, when you do get the group together in rea time, you can start from the ideas and focus on turning these raw inspirations into concrete plans. That can be a lot of fun too!

You'll also save some poor person many hours of mind-numbing transcription. On behalf of all these long-suffering souls, I thank you.

Additional Resources for Idea Generation Meetings

Visit the Idea Generation Meetings Resource Center on Lucid Meetings.
lucidmeetings.com/meeting-types/idea-generation-meetings

IDEA GENERATION

CHAPTER 24

Planning

Answering the Questions

Given this new goal and what we know now, what's our plan?

Who will be responsible for what by when?

Examples

Project Planning

Campaign Planning (Marketing)

Product Roadmap Planning

Sprint Planning

Event Planning

...and so on

Every group that makes things has a Planning meeting.

Purpose
- Create plans.
- Secure commitment to implementing the plans.

Work Outcomes
- A documented rough plan that can be quickly formalized after the meeting.
- Clarity about who will do what by when.
- Visibility into dependencies, missing resources, and known problems to solve.
- Awareness of the known unknowns; those areas in need of further investigation.

Human Outcomes
- Understanding of the plan's scope.
- Clarity about how one's work will be coordinated with others.
- New knowledge about the possible ways to approach this work.

Common Challenges
More than any other meeting, Planning meetings struggle with the balance between *creating the most perfect result* and *just completing the task*. This challenge gets worse when:
- The goals and objectives aren't sufficiently clear in advance.
- The resource boundaries aren't clear in advance.
- People arrive unprepared.
- Participants don't understand who is in charge of which parts of the plan or how decisions will be made.
- People don't agree on how detailed the planning should be.
- As one or two people work to hash out one detail, everyone else disengages, creating an uneven stop/start pace.
- Participants have different beliefs about how seriously they need to take the plan created in the meeting.
- Everyone becomes so glad to be done that they fail to confirm next steps at the end of the meeting.

What to Expect in a Planning Meeting

Expected Participation
Planning meetings often involve an existing team but may also involve other people as needed. Depending on the size and scope of the plans under development, these meetings are led by the project owner or by an outside facilitator.

Participants are expected to actively collaborate on the work product. They may or may not have established relationships; if not, some time needs to be spent helping people get to know each other and learn what each of them can contribute. That said, these meetings are about getting a job done, so relationships don't get central focus.

Typical Duration
Thirty minutes to 3 hours, depending on the scope of the project.

Note: Planning may also be conducted as one part of a longer Workshop.

Core Structure
1. Introduction
2. Confirm Goal, Scope, and Deliverables
3. Establish Known Plan Elements
4. Plan Creation
5. Plan Review
6. Confirm Next Steps

Planning meetings vary depending on the kind of plan they're creating, but they generally start with an explanation of the overall goal and an analysis of the current situation, and then go on to work through planning details. Planning meetings end with a review and confirmation of the plan created.

Most Planning meetings aren't governed by rules, nor do they follow specific rituals. The meeting format is dictated more by the format of the plan document than anything else. A meeting to block out a new business plan, for example, feels very different from a conference Planning meeting, but those differences are due to the nature of the plan rather than any significant deviations in the meeting process.

Because Planning meetings happen very early in an endeavor's life cycle, successful meetings design for serendipity. Anything you can learn during this meeting that makes the plan better is a good thing!

After the Meeting

The results from a Planning meeting frequently feed into either a Team Cadence meeting or a Progress Check, where the team will manage execution on the plan.

Top Tips for Successful Planning Meetings

Of all the meeting types, Planning meetings may be the most straightforward. The purpose and desired outcome are pretty obvious to everyone involved, everyone invited can usually understand how to prepare, and if you keep the meeting running on schedule, you'll rarely have to field complaints about wasting anyone's time.

How do you keep Planning meetings on schedule?

1. Only invite relevant people.

Who will be responsible for what by when? Anyone who isn't directly involved in creating the plan will start a side conversation, introduce tangents, and get distracted on other tasks, slowing the group down and draining energy. Keep the invite list as small as possible to prevent these problems. When you're working on a large multi-part plan, this means you should break the Planning meeting up so that participants only need to attend when you're forming the portion of the plan that applies to them.

2. Show up with the plan half done.

Have you ever seen an action movie? Of course you have. Nearly every action movie includes at least one Planning meeting. The ace team convenes to go over their plan for how they'll steal the cars, or rescue the town, or invade the castle. The team leader starts by outlining the scenario, the goal, the available resources, and the bones of a plan.

"We need to get the treasure out of the fortress before nightfall," the leader says. "We have a key to the front gate and a contact inside who can open the vault once we're in. I've got a private jet waiting for us at the airport. Now we just need a figure out how to get past the security."

Then the members of the elite squad pipe up:

"I can take half a dozen men around the back wall as a diversion," the commando grunts.

"I've got the towers. We can target them from that ridge," the sharpshooter says.

"I'll take out their communication system from here, so they can't call for backup," the tech geek chimes in.

"That still leaves the zombies," the leader says, shaking his head. "How are we going to get around them?"

"Leave the zombies to me," our hero says. And there you have a plan!

Action-movie Planning meetings clearly illustrate these first two tips: elite squads never invite extra people to the Planning meeting; and they always start the meeting with a clear objective, clear boundaries, and a rough plan in mind. Planning meetings are for solidifying plans and filling in gaps, not for making up ideas about what you could do out of thin air.

If you don't know enough about the task ahead to get the plan half-formed before the meeting, then you aren't ready for a Planning meeting. Consider an Idea Generation meeting or a Sensemaking meeting instead.

3. Close by reviewing next steps and the communication plan.

Are you an elite team of action heroes? Then you know to always confirm the rendezvous point and synchronize your watches. For the rest of us, here's a reminder: I'm surprised by how many Planning meetings end without anyone clarifying where this brilliant new plan can be found after the meeting. I'm surprised mostly because this is something I personally forget to do in the meetings I lead! As the person in charge, I already have an idea of where I'll post the plan we just worked on, so I often forget that not everyone in the room has the same expectations I do.

Like most businesses, we have all kinds of communication tools and all kinds of ways to document our decisions. This makes it vital to explicitly state where each plan will be recorded, how we'll review it going forward, and what the strategy we'll use to track any changes to the plan at the close of each Planning meeting.

Plans are Worthless, But Planning is Everything

I enjoy Planning meetings. I also enjoy large, easy jigsaw puzzles. When you know the basic shape you're going for, and you have a bunch of the pieces handy, it can be quite satisfying to get them to all fit together into a nice, coherent picture. With a jigsaw puzzle, it's very clear that the value is in the activity itself. People who puzzle do so because they enjoy spending their time figuring it out—not because they're genuinely curious about what the end picture might be.

Is Strategic Planning a Planning Meeting?

No. Strategic Planning is an organizational activity comprising several meetings, research, introspection, writing, review, and lots of communication. There will be many Planning meetings throughout the strategic planning process, such as:

- Offsite planning
- Workshop planning
- Communication planning
- Community engagement planning
- Research planning

The creation of the formal plan often takes place in a one- or two-day Strategy Workshop. (That's a Workshop, not a Planning meeting—I'll cover those soon.)

It doesn't have to work that way, though. At Lucid Meetings, we worked with Anna O'Byrne, a facilitator from Canada, to break that traditional Workshop into a series of smaller, dedicated Planning Meetings. Each Planning meeting in that series results in a single part of the plan (just the mission statement, for example) and none of these Planning meetings lasts longer than 90 minutes.

A shorter session designed to create a singular kind of plan is a Planning meeting. A multi-day session designed to walk a group through past performance, team building, and the creation of a multi-part strategic artifact overflows the definition for a Planning meeting. Anything big, long, and with a bunch of outcomes like this is a Workshop.

Like the picture you see when you finish a jigsaw puzzles, most of the plans you get at the end of a Planning meeting aren't really meant to be permanent or binding forever.

That's because the details of a plan often prove incorrect once the work gets underway. Dwight Eisenhower understood this, leading him to use the quote above about plans being worthless in multiple interviews. But he also understood that the planning process made a team dive into the details, explore their options, and consider alternatives. The knowledge gained during this process is what made it possible for them to quickly adapt as the work unfolded.

That's useful, because:

> No battle plan survives first contact with the enemy.
> —Helmuth von Moltke the Elder,
> Chief of Staff of the Prussian army before World War I

Moltke is widely recognized as a brilliant military organization expert and strategist. This rough translation of one of Moltke's theses came from hard lessons learned, as warfare in the 1880s rapidly evolved in response to inventions such as the machine gun. He found it was no longer possible to sit back and plan out a full battle. He could plan the opening moves, and after that he'd need a "system of expedients"—meaning good alternatives—from which his commanders could choose as the battle progressed.

One hundred and thirty years later, Steve Blank, guru of Lean startups and entrepreneurship, rephrased Moltke's quote like so:

> No (business) plan survives first contact with customers.
> —Steve Blank

This has certainly been true in Lucid's business and in every company where I've ever worked. Plans that involve more than five people working together over more than a few days need some midstream adjustment at best, and more commonly, regular and thorough re-jiggering. In the startup world, this even has a name—it's called the "Pivot." It sounds like a clever mid-court tennis move, but really it's a nice way of saying that the original plans were garbage and the company has decided to try something different.

Why am I taking up space with all this pontification about the true value of plans? Because when we go into Planning meetings, we often think that *the plan* is the point. I mean, that's what we're creating and it's the name of meeting itself, so obviously making a plan is part of the point. Yet as so many others who have gone before us discovered, the deeper value comes from all the learning your team does as they work on that plan. The plan itself may well end up proving worthless, but *the learning* is indispensable. Keep this in mind for your next Planning meeting, and watch for opportunities to enhance learning.

Additional Resources for Planning Meetings

Visit the Planning Meetings Resource Center on Lucid Meetings.
lucidmeetings.com/meeting-types/planning-meetings

CHAPTER 25

Problem Solving

Answering the Questions

What do we know about the problem?

What are our options?

What are we going to do to address it?

Examples

Incident Response

Strategic Issue Resolution

Major Project Change Resolution

Purpose
- Find a solution to a problem.
- Secure commitment to enact the solution.

Work Outcomes
- A solution or possible solution options.
- Clarity about who will do what by when.
- A scheduled check-in time.

Human Outcomes
- Understanding of the problem's scope.
- A path forward—getting unstuck.
- Support for tackling the problem.

Common Challenges
If there weren't big challenges here, there'd be no need for the Problem Solving meeting in the first place. These challenges include:
- Lack of information about the problem.
- Disagreements about what a solution needs to achieve.
- Fear, blame, and remorse that interferes with people's ability to participate.
- Urgency leading people to skip steps and make bad decisions.

What to Expect in a Problem Solving Meeting

Expected Participation
Problem Solving meetings involve anyone who may have information that helps the group find a solution and anyone who will need to implement the solution. Depending on the urgency of the situation, the meeting will be led by the person in charge (the responsible leader) or a facilitator. Everyone present is expected to collaborate actively, answering all questions and diligently offering assistance. Tight working relationships can help these meetings go more easily, and participants who establish trust can put more energy into finding solutions since they worry less about blame and personal repercussions. That said, these meetings need the participation of the people with the best expertise, and these people may not know each other well. When this happens, the meeting leader should put extra effort into creating safety in the group if they want everyone's best effort.

Typical Duration

Thirty to 90 minutes, depending on the scope and urgency of the problem.

Note: Problem Solving meetings may also be broken into several shorter sessions.

Core Structure

1. Situation Analysis
2. Discuss Options
3. Select Option
4. Create Action Plan
5. Confirm and Go!

Problem Solving meetings begin with a situation analysis—what happened, what resources do we have—and then a review of options. After the team discusses and selects an option, the team creates an action plan. We've all seen the shortest version of this meeting in movies when the police gather outside of the building full of hostages and collaborate to create their plan. Problem Solving meetings follow this basic structure, which can be heavily ritualized in first responder and other teams devoted to quickly solving problems. These strict governing procedures get looser when problems aren't so urgent, but the basic pattern remains.

In a Problem Solving meeting, the ugly surprise already happened. Now the team welcomes serendipity, hoping a brilliant solution will emerge.

After the Meeting

A Problem Solving meeting results in a possible solution. After the meeting, the responsible parties will try that solution and later report back. Did it work? How well did it work? Now what?

Top Tips for Successful Problem Solving Meetings

Only sufficiently gnarly problems warrant a Problem Solving meeting. Minor problems get solved in the regular course of business, but tricky ones get the focus of a dedicated meeting. This makes every Problem Solving meeting a special occasion. In a perfect world, we don't have gnarly problems, so we don't schedule these meetings as a routine event. But a gnarly problem is by definition *unexpected* (if we had expected it, we would have planned around it!), so that can make these meetings *stressful* too.

To get the best result when dealing with an unexpected and stressful event, I believe every team should have a Problem Solving protocol on hand. These protocols give the team a predefined set of steps to follow that make sure they cover the basics and get to a reasonable solution, giving the team a clear path forward at an otherwise frustrating and confusing time.

When you develop your Problem Solving approach, incorporate these best practices.

1. Explicitly establish psychological safety.

The circumstances that inspire a Problem Solving meeting justify a bit of freaking out, but freaking out isn't a useful approach to solving problems. Open the meeting with a statement designed to help everyone keep calm and focused on finding a solution. You may ask everyone to refrain from blame or personal accusations and just discuss facts. You may want to state that there will be a time for holding transgressors accountable, but that this is not that time. Rally the team around working together as allies in the face of adversity. See "Meeting in the Red Zone" (coming up in the next few pages) for more on this.

2. Define the problem that needs to be solved before discussing solutions.

Begin by restating the known facts. A Problem Solving meeting isn't a Root Cause Analysis—first responders don't need to understand the historical and cultural factors that may have driven a terrorist to act—but they do need to know all the available details about the situation as it exists at the moment. The problem they're solving is not how to eliminate extremism; their problem is how to save the hostages.

Here's a more common business example: it is not necessary to understand why the budget fell short when the problem is that you can't make payroll this week. You *do* need to know exactly how much money you need to write those payroll checks and when you can expect more money to arrive. The problem in this case is how to pay people. You might later have a separate Sensemaking meeting where you work to figure out why there isn't any money, which would then be the time to talk about how you encountered the problem in the first place.

3. Clarify the solution criteria.

This step prevents bad assumptions. Once you get clarity on the problem, answer these questions:

- **What does a solution need to achieve specifically?** Sometimes people believe a solution must provide a perfect answer, when in reality you may just need to stabilize a bad situation.
- **What hard constraints do you have to work within (time, resources, other commitments, etc.)?** Without this clarity, people can spend time discussing solutions you can't use because they'll take too long or require resources you can't access.

4. Keep the discussion focused on finding solutions.

Important: do not use this meeting to discuss who or what is *to blame* for the problem.

There is a time and a place for root cause analysis. There are occasions when a problem really is someone's "fault" and they need to be held accountable. But that's not what a Problem Solving meeting is about. This meeting is about finding solutions. Describe the problem briefly, factually, and as it exists right now so you can focus the group's attention and energy on finding the best solution they can, right now. Too much attention on how and why the problem arose takes up valuable time and shifts the group's energy to fault-finding and away from creating solutions.

5. Ensure commitment from all participants to the action plan.

Once you've settled on an approach, get specific. Who will do what, and by when? Then, review everything. Does your plan address the problem? Do you know exactly what will happen next? Is everyone clear and committed to what they need to do?

Then, set a time to meet again and check progress.

6. Schedule the follow-up while you're still in the meeting.

Your plan will include actions that will either solve the problem or fail to do so. Schedule the follow-up meeting for as soon as you can reasonably expect to know whether the plan is working or not. A brief Action Review works well here, where you'll discuss: What did we expect to happen, what actually happened, what did we learn, and what next?

What's the Difference Between a Problem Solving Meeting and an Issue Resolution Meeting?

At first glance, these two meeting types look very similar. In both cases, there's a problem that needs a resolution, and you're planning a meeting to work through it. The difference between these meeting types comes from what your group has to overcome in order to reach a solution.

In Problem Solving Meetings, the group is aligned on the definition of the problem and agrees on the goals that a successful solution must achieve. In the meeting, they work together to discover the best available option for achieving the goals. In other words, everyone agrees on what needs to happen, and the meeting helps them figure out how to get it done.

For example, when the Pacific Bold team had a problem that was going to force them to lay people off, they met to discuss what to do. This was a Problem Solving meeting. The team was aligned on what a solution needed to achieve—increased revenue—but didn't know how to make that happen. They tasked people to get more information—which was handy because understanding the problem is the first step in a Problem Solving Meeting—and then worked through the possible ways they could address it.

In Issue Resolution Meetings, the people involved agree that there's a problem but not on what a successful solution looks like. These people fall on opposing sides of an issue. They've independently formed strong ideas of what the solution needs to be, but these ideas do not agree. The Issue Resolution Meeting works to help these separate camps find common ground and work toward a mutually acceptable solution.

The Israeli-Palestinian conflict provides a very serious example. The two sides of this conflict have proposed and discussed many possible solutions—they don't lack for options. They do not agree, however, on what these options need to achieve. They do not share the same values with regard to the problem.

Issue Resolution Meetings work to sort through competing interpretations of the facts and different values to reach a new agreement (or appeasement).

Meeting in the Red Zone

At the very beginning of this book, I introduced the team at Pacific Bold in the middle of a Problem Solving meeting where they didn't understand the problem. They had a productivity crisis that was eroding profits, but they didn't know the facts behind the productivity problem so they were flailing, blaming Facebook, and getting frustrated.

When we print it in full color, the 16 Types of Meetings on the Meeting Taxonomy chart are color-coded. Some meeting types are light blue, indicating that these are typically congenial meetings. Team Cadence meetings and Idea Generation meetings are usually very friendly and fall into this category. Some are dark blue to signify their more serious tone—Governance Cadence meetings tend to be more formal that way. Problem Solving meetings are the first type marked in red, indicating intensity.

Intense meetings make it hard to establish *psychological safety*. Psychological safety is a term used to describe whether a person feels it is safe to take a personal risk around their team members. Meetings provide one of the most powerful, repeatable, and focused opportunities for developing psychological safety. Well-run meetings foster psychological safety between team members. Poorly-run meetings erode psychological safety.

In intense meetings such as a Problem Solving meeting, we can all unwittingly slip into blame, anger, and frustration before we realize what's happening. Conflict- and risk-averse people will simply shut down if the team doesn't actively work to reinstate psychological safety.

When someone isn't clear how their contribution will be received or receives a negative reaction to that contribution, this triggers anxiety in the brain. Dr. Amy Edmondson coined the phrase "psychological safety" while she was conducting research into successful teams. She points out that we all know how to avoid these negative reactions from others; we just need to keep our mouths shut.

> It turns out that no one wakes up in the morning and jumps out of bed because they can't wait to get to work today to look ignorant, incompetent, intrusive, or negative.
>
> —Dr. Amy Edmondson

Dr. Edmondson began her research by looking at how different hospital teams performed. She expected to find that the highest-performing teams had the fewest reported errors—that they didn't create as many problem situations as other teams.

Instead, she found the opposite. The better teams reported and talked about *more* problems. They had created a culture in which it was *safe* to raise issues and concerns and safe to discuss mistakes that were made *without fear of reprisal*. So, if a nurse suspected that the doctor's prescription seemed wrong, the nurse in a high-performing team would speak up. This created a chance to find and solve problems before they affected patients. Nurses working in teams where errors were punished and doctors snapped at questions kept their mouths shut when they were unsure. They just did what the doctor said to do, missing the opportunity to prevent an error.

When you think about the example with the nurses, how do you think the Problem Solving meeting went in each team when there was a medication error? When the nurse from the psychologically unsafe team was asked why the patient received an incorrect medication, do you think they admitted they were unsure about the dose but they went ahead and administered it anyway? There is so much at risk in this situation that it becomes very difficult for the people involved to set aside their personal fears and work together openly to solve problems.

Dr. Edmondson found that psychological safety was one of the key determinants of workplace performance. This finding was later echoed by the research into high-performing teams conducted by Google's People Analytics group. They too had believed that the best teams were made up of the most accomplished individuals, but they found instead that:

"Who is on a team matters less than how the team members interact, structure their work, and view their contributions."

Insufficient psychological safety has other implications for meetings beyond a failure to speak up. People who feel threatened can lash out. Dr. Daniel Siegel developed a model of explaining how our brain reacts to threats called the Hand Model that I find useful when trying to understand why someone might be reacting emotionally in a meeting.

He teaches children to imagine that our brain is like a fist with the thumb tucked inside. The wrist and the thumb represent the brain stem and the limbic system—what you may have heard called our primitive "lizard brains" that operate on instinct and raw emotion. The fingers wrapped in a lid over the thumb represent the cortex, the thinking and reasoning part of the brain. When we are stressed, or tired, or we feel threatened, Dr.

Siegel explains that we can "Flip our Lid"—losing access to the higher reasoning and logical thinking parts of our brain. Instead, when we flip our lid, we react based on the fight, flight, or freeze instincts coming from the primitive parts of our brain in the limbic system and brain stem.

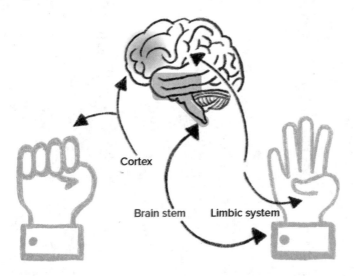

People who've flipped their lid aren't fun to talk to, and they're lousy problem solvers.

I wish I knew a magic formula that would establish psychological safety any time a team found itself in one of the Red Zone meetings like the Problem Solving meeting. The truth is that you can't just declare that an environment is safe now when it hasn't been in the past. Safety must be developed over time and reinforced in everyday practice.

You can, however, destroy this safety in times of heightened stress. I often recall a metaphor comparing trust to a garden: what takes months to nurture and grow, you can burn down in an hour. To make sure your garden stays protected during a Problem Solving meeting, rely on a predefined structure that you've created in advance. The structure can remind you and the team how to stay calm and productive, and it will help you all keep your lids on.

Additional Resources for Problem Solving Meetings

Visit the Problem Solving Meetings Resource Center on Lucid Meetings.
lucidmeetings.com/meeting-types/problem-solving-meetings

Decision Making

Answering the Question

Given the options before us, which one do we choose and why?

Who is responsible for the next step?

Examples

New Hire Decision

Go/No-Go Decision

Logo Selection

Final Approval of a Publication

Purpose
- To decide between two or more options.
- Secure commitment to enact the decision.

Work Outcomes
- A documented decision.
- Clarity about who will take the next steps.
- Documented messages to share with others about the decision.

Human Outcomes
- Understanding of the possible options and decision criteria.
- Awareness of how the rest of the team feels about the decision.
- A feeling that opinions and concerns were considered fairly (or not).

Common Challenges
When a Decision Making meeting goes awry, it's usually because the team wasn't ready for that kind of meeting. Other challenges include:
- The decision-making method isn't clear, creating confusion and bad assumptions.
- The options aren't well understood.
- There aren't enough options: the team is facing a false dichotomy.
- The decision-making criteria aren't defined.
- The process is rushed or, conversely, drags out.

What to Expect in a Decision Making Meeting

Expected Participation
Often a Decision Making meeting involves a standing team, but like Problem Solving meetings, this is not always the case. These meetings may also include people who will be affected by the decision or have expertise to share, even if they aren't directly responsible for implementing the decision. Decision Making meetings may be led by a designated facilitator, but more often the team leader or chair runs them.

People participate in Decision Making meetings as either advisers or decision makers. If the decision under discussion is largely a formality, this participation will be highly structured. If, on the other hand, the group is truly weighing multiple options, the participation style will be much more collaborative. Established relationships are not central to Decision

Making meetings, but the perceived fairness and equanimity of the discussion is. When the group behaves in a way that makes it unsafe to voice concerns, these concerns go unaddressed, which then weakens commitment to the decision. These meetings can be intense.

Typical Duration
One to two hours or more.

Core Structure
1. Confirm Meeting Purpose and Decision Making Process
2. Present the Decision Challenge
3. Debate and Discuss Options
4. Decide and Commit
5. Define Next Steps

Decision Making meetings begin with a description of the decision to be made and a confirmation of how the team will go about deciding. Then, they examine the options. Every Decision Making Meeting has at least two options: yes or no, innocent or guilty, go or no-go. When the meeting concerns binary options like this, the proceedings may be largely a formality and the discussion will go quickly. If the team really is weighing multiple options, this discussion will take quite a bit longer.

When the discussion concludes, the decision is finalized and documented.

Then the group defines who will carry out the next steps, including communication about the decision to the people affected by it who were not present for the meeting.

After the Meeting
A Decision Making meeting results in a documented decision to take some action. After the meeting, the responsible parties will begin the work to execute that decision. The results from a Decision Making meeting may be communicated in a Broadcast meeting. Teams will begin figuring out how to enact the decision in a Planning meeting.

Top Tips for Successful Decision Making Meetings

We make decisions in lots of meetings, but that does not necessarily mean that people run lots of Decision Making meetings. A Decision Making meeting is a special occasion dedicated specifically to formalizing a decision, and nothing else.

Decision Making meetings involve the consideration of options and the selection of a final option. Unlike Problem Solving meetings that include a search for good options, all that work to figure out the possible options happens *before* a Decision Making meeting.

In many cases, Decision Making meetings are a formality, intended to finalize and secure commitment to a decision that's already been made. Ritual is high, and surprises unwelcome. In other situations, the group is weighing multiple options and seeking to make a selection in the meeting. There still shouldn't be any big surprises, but there's a whole lot more flexibility. For example, corporate leadership teams run Decision Making meetings when faced with unexpected strategic challenges. Many of these teams revert to a structure-free conversational approach—just "talking it out" until they reach a decision. Unfortunately for them, teams make the best decisions when their meetings follow a formal decision-making methodology. I've written extensively about this elsewhere, as have many others, so here I'll stick to the tips unique to Decision Making meetings.

To plan a successful Decision Making meeting:

1. Make the Meta Decision

How will the decision get made? Who specifically decides, and if this is a group of people, how will they determine when they're in agreement? If a decision is important enough to warrant a Decision Making meeting, start by clarifying the decision-making process in use. I recommend this step even for groups that always use the same process because it creates a moment for those present to agree to abide by the process and be bound by the outcome. Plus, it's vital for the new team members.

2. Know your options in advance.

A decision important enough to warrant a dedicated Decision Making meeting requires preparation.

Information about the options under consideration should be shared in advance of the meeting. This gives everyone time to consider the ramifications of each option and do their own homework—the due diligence we all wish went into the decisions that affect our futures.

It's worth getting decisions right. At the conclusion of their 2010 study into decision-making, Bain & Company stated:

> We found that decision effectiveness and financial results correlated at a 95% confidence level or higher for every country, industry, and company size in our sample. Ultimately, a company's value is no more (and no less) than the sum of the decisions it makes and executes.
> — Bain & Company

Need to make a decision quickly but you don't have any great options outlined yet? Sounds like you've got a problem! Run a Problem Solving meeting instead.

3. Write out the final decision in the meeting.

The Supreme Court never forgets this step when they finalize a decision, but lots of corporate teams do. It's bizarre. What specifically did the group decide? Make sure this is written during the meeting where everyone involved can read it, mull over the wording, and confirm that, yes, *that specific statement* is what we decided. If you're involved with a documentation-free group that skips this step, prepare yourself for some fascinating discussions. The minute you try to nail a decision down in writing, you'll often learn that the group wasn't quite as aligned as they thought. While the effort involved in getting the wording just right can be tedious, it's an effective way to flush out any lingering misunderstandings.

4. Document next steps for each decision.

In the introduction to his book *The Effective Executive*, Peter Drucker instructs executives to "Take responsibility for decisions!"

> A decision has not been made until people know:
> - the name of the person accountable for carrying it out;
> - the deadline;
> - the names of the people who will be affected by the decision and therefore have to know about, understand, and approve it—or at

DECISION MAKING

least not be strongly opposed to it—and

- the names of the people who have to be informed of the decision even if they are not directly affected by it"

—Peter F. Drucker, *The Effective Executive*

It's a good list! Make sure you get all that covered before you leave the meeting.

Three or More Viable Options and the Meta-Decision

I spend a disproportionate share of my life reading about meetings. I've noticed some interesting patterns related to the authors of books about meetings. Their first book usually tackles a discrete topic: marketing, or facilitation, or perhaps group engagement techniques. But before you know it, they've written a book on one of what I've come to consider the big three topics: relationships, principled/visionary leadership, and decision making. Some authors—Dave Gray and the Heath Brothers come to mind—write about all of these.

I understand the appeal! Meeting research is a kind of gateway drug. You think maybe you'll just dabble in facilitation. Perhaps you might play around with some ideas on productivity, but you're not going to get too involved with the whole business thing. Next thing you know, you're hooked. When you start to take a serious look at what's going on in meetings, you'll see that the meetings are just a setting for the real drama. You start to crave the good stuff: positive psychology, accelerated business performance, decision velocity. Before you realize what's happened, you find yourself curled in a corner, cradling a book discussing the implications of the meeting regimen on the development of civilization. What's more, that book will blow your mind.

So, yes, I can give you a list of steps to follow if you're trying to run a Decision Making meeting, but what can I share that will help you know that the decision made in that meeting is a good one? Now *that's* a worthy challenge!

The truth is, every decision is a gamble—a best guess. My partner and I have an entrepreneurial friend who claims that he never makes bets; he only invests in "sure wins." I think he's partly overplaying his level of certainty, but I also know that he's studied the research on decision making.

He applies techniques that tip the odds of each decision-making gamble firmly in his favor. Barring acts of God, he really does seem to always win.

Originally, I planned to devote an entire Part of this book to decision making in meetings and Decision Making meetings. I am not immune to the addicting lure of that topic. In the end, I decided against that approach, using two of the most consistently useful techniques I've learned about decision making.

1. Seek three or more viable options for every major decision.

> "Write down at least three, but ideally four or more, realistic alternatives. It might take a little effort and creativity, but no other practice improves decisions more than expanding your choices."
> —Eric Larson, founder of the Cloverpop decision-making platform

When I first looked at how to approach this chapter, I felt like I had two options: include the complete text I had drafted (some 40+ pages), or cut it out and just stick with a few tips. With just two options, I'd created a false dichotomy—I perpetrated a logical fallacy!

> You presented two alternative states as the only possibilities, when in fact more possibilities exist.
>
> Also known as the false dilemma, this insidious tactic has the appearance of forming a logical argument, but under closer scrutiny it becomes evident that there are more possibilities than the either/or choice that is presented. Binary, black-or-white thinking doesn't allow for the many different variables, conditions, and contexts in which there would exist more than just the two possibilities put forth. It frames the argument misleadingly and obscures rational, honest debate.
>
> Example: Whilst rallying support for his plan to fundamentally undermine citizens' rights, the Supreme Leader told the people they were either on his side, or they were on the side of the enemy.
>
> — yourlogicalfallacyis.com/black-or-white

Thank goodness I'd read the research on how to improve the odds of making a good decision in a meeting, because my alarm bells went off. I realized I needed more options, so I put together four different treatments for this material, all of which could work nicely. Then, I shared these with my team so we could meet and decide on an approach.

2. Make the meta-decision.

When it came time to decide how much or how little of the text to include, I had the final word. But I'm far from impartial here, so I sought the advice of my team. We ran a short Decision Making meeting using the Consult decision-making process, where everyone present shares their preference and rationale with the decision maker.

At the meeting start, we agreed to use the Consult process. Now everyone could focus on the relative merits of each option without worrying that they had to take responsibility for the final decision. Making the meta-decision up front by selecting a process and communicating that with the group prevents confusion and hurt feelings, because no one goes in expecting to have more influence that they'll get. Getting clear about the meta decision also saves time, because the selected process tells everyone what *done* looks like, eliminating the endless, swirling discussions that can drag an uncertain group's energy down the drain.

What are the options for the meta-decision? There are *way* more than three! You can cast colored stones into bowls, read tea leaves, or listen for the loudest cheer. Hand-to-hand combat was once popular. You can take turns deciding, draw straws, or defer to the eldest team member. So many options!

That said, the four most common decision-making approaches used in a business context are:

1. Command
2. Consult
3. Counting Votes
4. Consensus

Let's examine each.

Command

How it works:

A decision is made. In the meeting, people are told what the decision is and what they are expected to do next.

Pros:

- Fast and simple.

Cons:

- Most of the time, people really hate being told what to do.
- Doesn't build commitment to action.
- Excludes potentially important perspectives from the decision-making process.

Command sounds harsh, and it can certainly feel that way sometimes. It's also an entirely appropriate decision-making approach for many situations. And, as an organization grows, what may have been a very involved and inclusive process for the leadership team will eventually devolve into commands delivered to the front line. Command is unavoidable at some point.

Happily, my review of the scientific and business perspectives on decision-making give me guidance about when a command-style process can be appropriate.

- If you can decide and execute safely all by yourself, use command.
  "Okay, self, put on yellow socks! Yes, ma'am, yellow socks it is!"
- If the decision is appropriate for your role in the organization, and you don't need a lot of cooperation to execute, use command.
  "Get that subscription to Lucid Meetings. Here's my department credit card."
- If you are in a chaotic situation or facing crisis, use command.
  "Bolt the doors and get out the sunlamps! The vampires are coming!"

Consult

How it works:
One person makes a decision after seeking input from others. Ideally, the person making the decision commits to remaining persuadable.

Pros:

- Efficient, but not careless.
- Keeps lines of responsibility and accountability clear.
- Can increase buy-in to the decision.

Cons:

- Tricky. It's hard to stay truly persuadable.
- Can shortcut the opportunities for information gathering and option analysis.
- Can backfire if the input provided isn't treated with respect.
- Can be mistaken for consensus.

As I've described it here, the Consult process sounds like a sneaky way to get a Command decision past your team. While it can be used that way, that's not the intent. For a lot of internal teams and small groups, the Consult process is the default.

Counting Votes

How it Works:
A designated voting group votes on one or more options. The winning vote sets the decision.

Pros:

- Clear. Vote results are (usually) unambiguous.
- Time-limited. Voting terminates otherwise lengthy discussions.
- Breaks stalemates. Voting forces a decision when stakeholders can't find consensus.
- Legally validating. Many decisions require explicit votes before they go into effect.

Cons:

- Potentially polarizing. Voting creates "winners" and "losers"; not exactly the happy team conditions you want going into a new initiative.
- Reduces buy-in and commitment to the decision. Just ask citizens of the U.S. East and West Coasts how bought-in they felt about the outcome of the 2016 presidential election.
- Creates delays. For decisions where the rules don't require it, waiting to assemble the group for a formal vote slows down progress.

There are a lot of ways to count votes in meeting and many decisions that require votes in order to go into effect.

That said, because putting a decision to a vote is such a terrible way to go about it if you want to get commitment, most experts recommend you *use voting as a last resort*. If you work with corporate boards, standards committees, or other groups legally required to vote, you'll see that the best of them work very hard to ensure general agreement on the final decision *before* calling the vote. These groups work diligently to achieve consensus up front, then use the vote to formally record the decision. This is an appropriate and useful application of Counting Votes.

The worst use of Counting Votes happens in groups attempting to force majority rule on an unpopular minority. In these situations, Counting Votes puts a quasi-respectable facade on bullying. Because this kind of abuse destroys healthy working relationships, professional facilitators avoid Counting Votes whenever they can.

I've also seen situations where people use voting to dodge direct responsibility. This sounds awful, and it's painful to watch when it happens, but it's also an effective way to keep an organization moving when there are no other strong driving forces. What color should we use for the new logo? No one cares? Put it to a vote! In groups where everyone is taking five steps back, voting forces forward momentum.

I said above that facilitators avoid Counting Votes. Let me modify that. Facilitators often count votes during meetings as a way to gauge consensus. For example, the facilitator might ask for a show of hands in favor of the current option as a way of "getting the temperature" of the group. In this case, counting votes works as a compass pointing the path *toward* consensus, not the actual decision-making mechanism.

Which raises the question: how exactly does a decision by consensus work?

Consensus

How it Works:
A decision is stated, and everyone involved agrees to live with it.

Pros:
- The most inclusive and participatory process.
- Creates greatest shared commitment to the decision.
- Best process for fostering healthy, productive teams.

Cons:

- Time-consuming.
- Can be ambiguous—false consensus is common.
- Process most likely to be sloppily implemented.

Consensus is the process we assume when we say, "Is everybody good with that?" We assume that if anyone has an issue with the decision, they'll speak up. Often they don't, so we get *false consensus*.

Facilitators avoid this problem by defining the consensus process up front, then making the moment of decision explicit. Before the group starts discussing the options, they agree on what a consensus agreement will actually look like.

Consensus can mean:

- Unanimity. Everyone completely backs the decision.
  or
- Everyone can live with and will support the decision.

Of these definitions, smart leaders opt for the latter "Everyone can live with it" definition. In some organizations, this is referred to as "disagree, but commit." In other words, once every team member has had their say and the decision is made, they all get behind it—even if the final choice wasn't a team member's personal favorite.

By contrast, striving for unanimity often results in big delays and weak decisions. Trying to please everyone inevitably leads to compromises. This compromise process can wear out the group, leading them to "agree" on a solution no one particularly likes... just to get it over with.

How to Make the Meta-Decision

To figure this out, ask:

What kind of decision is this?

You're trying to figure out if the decision is above or below your waterline—meaning risky or relatively safe—and if the situation is simple, complicated, or complex.

Who has the authority to make this decision?

Some decisions can be made by a single person, and if they're minor, they should be. Others are complicated enough that they should involve a group. Some decisions can only be made by the board or another governing body.

Who needs to commit to this decision in order for it to succeed?

Decisions lead to action. Some actions can be completed by the person making the decision, but most require cooperation from a group. Make sure you know who's in that group!

Do you have viable options (or can you quickly determine them)?

Before you can discuss the pros and cons of different options, you have to understand the real challenge in front of you and have some options to discuss. Some issues are too complex or too sensitive to work through during the meeting in real time.

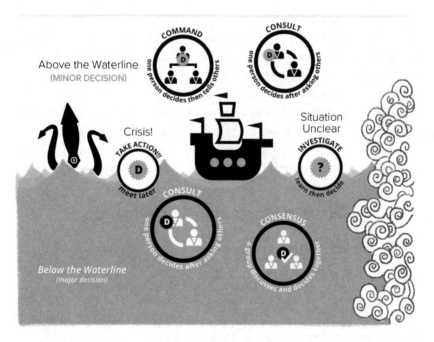

Use the decision-making process that best fits your situation.

The recommended answer to the meta-decision depends on circumstances. You might choose any of these based on the following criteria:

Just Decide and Act
- When the decision is minor and you can execute it yourself.
- When you can delegate the decision to someone who can decide and execute.
- In a crisis, act quickly to stabilize the situation. You can worry about your decision-making process after the fire is out.

Make a Command Decision
- When the decision is minor and you have the authority.
- When you need to act quickly and can minimize the risk of failure.

Consult the Decision Maker
- When the decision is minor, and additional expertise or buy-in is desired.
- When the decision is major or complicated, but the responsibility for execution is clear.
- When the decision is nearly final, but needs additional vetting and/ or buy-in.

Count Votes
- When meeting with the board or another group legally required to do so.
- When you need a tie breaker, deciding between two options with equal and passionate support.

Why isn't Count Votes in the illustration above? Because you don't need a map to know when you're in a board meeting, and for other situations, Counting Votes shouldn't be one of your go-to processes.

Use Consensus
- When the decision is major and requires buy-in from the team to succeed.

You may notice that *Consult* appears twice on the illustration above. That's because the Consult decision-making process works best for most teams most often. "Who's got the decision here?" starts a Consult decision meeting. When you name a specific decision maker in this way, you:

- Create clear accountability for the decision's success. Teams that can't take personal responsibility for their decisions have no way to correct poor decision performance.
- Provide a mechanism for group input. Having the final decision doesn't mean that this person has to think it through alone, or that they're the only one with a valid opinion.
- Save time, as there's no need to go through a big process to build formal consensus.

Additional Resources for Decision Making Meetings

Visit the Decision Making Meetings Resource Center on Lucid Meetings. lucidmeetings.com/meeting-types/decision-making-meetings

Workshops

Answering the Question

We have lots of questions to answer

(and will devote two or more hours to answering them).

Examples

Project, Program and Product Kickoffs

Team Chartering

Design Workshops

Value Stream Mapping

Strategy Workshops

Team Building Workshop

Purpose
- To focus and complete one or more tasks.

Work Outcomes
- Group formation and identity creation.
- Commitment and clarity on execution.
- One or more tangible results. Real work product comes out of Workshops!

Human Outcomes
- A shared memory and experience; possible bonding.
- Insight into other team members' perspectives.
- New knowledge.

Common Challenges
It takes practice and skill to run a Workshop well. Even then, Workshops can suffer when:
- The Workshop focus doesn't feel relevant to some of the attendees.
- There's no plan to incorporate Workshop outcomes into the regular work stream.
- The facilitator lacks adequate information about the situation.
- Previous bad experiences create a hostile environment.
- Workshop planning is rushed, and preparation is incomplete.

What to Expect in Workshops

Expected Participation
Groups are assembled specifically for Workshops and guided by a designated facilitator. These meetings put future work into motion, so the focus may be split equally between the creation of a shared work product (such as a value stream map or charter document) and team formation—since successful team relationships make future work easier. Workshops often incorporate many of the elements you find in other types of meetings. For example, a Workshop may include elements of Sensemaking, Idea Generation, Problem Solving, and Planning all together in one large package.

Because they attempt to achieve so much more than other meetings, Workshops take longer to run and much longer to plan. Most Workshops expect participants to actively engage and collaborate in the creation of a tangible shared result, and a lot of effort goes into planning very structured ways to ensure that engagement.

Typical Duration
Three hours to three days.

Core Structure
1. An opening.
2. An activity (this part is intentionally left very open-ended!).
3. (Breaks are held every 60 to 90 minutes, with additional activities throughout the Workshop....)
4. Finally: Wrap!

Workshops are always custom-designed. Beyond the opening, closing, and some well-timed breaks, Workshops do not follow a strong common structure.

Small kickoffs may follow a simple pattern and be held in the team's regular meeting space, but many Workshops take place in a special location—somewhere offsite, outside, or otherwise distinct from the normal work environment. All these meetings start with introductions and level-setting of some kind: a group exercise, a review of project goals, and perhaps a motivational speech from the leader. Then, the team engages in a series of exercises or activities in pursuit of the work product(s). Since these meetings are long, participants require regular infusions of coffee and cookies. Some Workshops involve cocktails.

Workshops conclude with a review of the work product(s), and often a reflective exercise. That said, these are bespoke meetings that do not adhere to any particular rituals. The people who plan and facilitate the Workshop work intentionally to create opportunities for serendipity: they want the team to discover things about each other and the work to inspire and engage them.

After the Meeting
This is a common failure point for Workshops. Organizations often bring in outside experts to run a Workshop. These specialists work hard to make sure this special event runs well, but it's neither appropriate nor possible for them to dictate how the time spent in the Workshop will result in changes to what happens in the organization afterward.

It's up to the folks who hired the facilitator to make sure the Workshop results get used. Be aware of this potential problem before you start.

Top Tips for Successful Workshops

Up to this point, all of the meeting types have included a set of Top Tips written for the person in charge of designing the meeting. If you're interested in becoming a Workshop facilitator, check out the resources page on the Lucid Meetings website. Here I'm going to focus instead on how to be a successful Workshop *participant*.

Workshops can have a powerful—even transformative—impact on your organization if you keep these tips in mind.

1. Expect to change, and plan accordingly.

Workshops invest a group's focused attention on solving a specific problem or initiating a desired change. If you are bringing in an expert to lead a Workshop, such as a strategic planning or value stream mapping Workshop, then the organization should be prepared to invest in the new strategies and workflow optimizations the Workshop defines.

Outside experts can help your team gain new knowledge and work through the process of figuring out what you need to do next, but they can't make any real changes for you. If your team doesn't know what you're willing to change or doesn't have the resources to make a change, you can't get the best value from your Workshop investment. Cameron Fraser, a certified facilitator from Canada, calls this the "engagement plateau," and it's illustrated below.

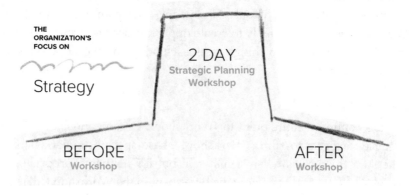

Fraser frequently sees clients get excited about what they could do for the few days they're together, but when he checks in later, nothing has changed. Facilitators everywhere tell the same story, and it makes them sad. They still get paid whether you use that beautiful new plan or not, of course, but they love it so much more when they know they've helped you succeed. Wouldn't that be better for you too?

2. You've got to play to win.

You can outsource the Workshop design and facilitation, but you can't outsource your results.

Many people think that facilitators show up with some flip charts and run the same stock strategic planning Workshop they use with every client. That's true for Training meetings, such as public seminars, which might sometimes be called Workshops. Most real Workshops, though, are designed to achieve a specific set of results with and for the unique people involved.

Workshop facilitators bring a lot of specialized value, but they aren't a one-stop shop for solving your problem. It's their job to design a process that will guide your team through the creation of the results you need. It's your team's job to actually do the work in the Workshop to *create those results*.

When you work with a facilitator, plan to spend several hours with them in Sensemaking and Planning meetings before the Workshop. These pre-Workshop conversations give them the information they need to design a Workshop that will work in your unique environment.

Then, you and your team need to arrive ready to participate with an open mind. Will you be asked to do something that sounds silly to you? Probably! Is the facilitator going to take time to hear from everyone, even those people you think don't have anything to say that's worth hearing? Absolutely. Will the breaks come too soon or too late and always be either too short or too long? I guarantee it. You're intensively working through challenging subjects with a diverse group—there will always be moments that won't thrill you in a Workshop.

After years of reviewing Workshop feedback, I can tell you that whenever there's a moment that makes you cringe, someone else in the room is loving it. Some people love the interaction, some love to sit still and listen, and others just want to draw pictures. If you and your team come ready to participate and roll with those awkward moments, you'll get the result the

Workshop is designed to produce. At some point, we each have to get over ourselves and get into it!

Work That's Fun Still Works

"Yes, well, I suppose it's interesting to learn all these things," my friend said. "I learned them too, earlier in my career. You know, it can be fun and all, and I guess that's important to some people. It just always takes so much longer, you know. Well, you know."

I'd just finished leading a four-hour Workshop and was chatting with the participants afterward. I'd designed the event to be a highly interactive showcase of how you could use a variety of group techniques to achieve results and have fun in the process. Most of the post-event reactions ranged somewhere between pleasantly surprised to inspired. Except for this fellow.

He continued, "I've just found that all this—" he waved his hands dismissively at our sticky notes and markers, "—this is so much extra work, and there's never time for it in my job these days. Maybe there are people who have time to play like this, but I have to get things done."

What a fascinating perspective! I found it especially so since I had shared this perspective myself years ago. I used to think that if we were relaxed and having fun together, surely we must be neglecting the "real" work!

But here's the thing: in this Workshop, we started as a group of 14 strangers. After lunch and before the break for cookies, we planned a project. First, these new acquaintances learned about each other's relevant expertise. Then they divided into groups and brainstormed a list of tasks. We grouped and ranked these tasks, and rated the top 15 according to each one's estimated cost and value. There was debate. There were questions. There were more than a few (mild) disagreements. Finally, the group identified the top three priority tasks and assigned owners.

That whole process took about 45 minutes.

Yes, as the facilitator, I had to spend time beforehand designing a process that would get us that result, but then, that was just my time. I didn't take up the other 13 people's time planning the meeting—they just showed up and followed my lead. Perhaps more importantly, they created and owned the results. I didn't have to worry about any of the project details because they took care of all that, and because they were evaluating their own ideas, they were enthusiastic about signing up for tasks at the end.

Contrary to my friend's belief, we actually got a lot done in an incredibly short time. It just didn't feel like it because *we enjoyed ourselves* along the way.

At Lucid Meetings, we offer Training seminars and lead pre-designed Workshops, but we don't offer custom Workshop facilitation services anymore. You can't hire our team to come in and lead your planning Workshop, for example. Still, I love working with professional facilitators and taking their classes, because I always learn something I can apply to the rest of my business meetings.

Consider this: If you can use highly structured facilitation techniques to lead a random group of people through a project planning session from zero—and arrive at next steps in 45 minutes—what more might you achieve with your established team by using even a bit of light facilitation? When you observe organizations operating at high levels of meeting performance, you'll see techniques developed by Workshop facilitators—icebreakers, dot voting, appreciations, and so on—in regular Team Cadence meetings.

So, yes, this stuff can be fun, but more importantly, it helps teams get work done faster—contrary to most people's expectations and especially when integrated into the flow of everyday work. Remember: work can be enjoyable. Despite what my friend might think, an engaged team can have a good time while getting its work done.

Additional Resources for Workshops

Visit the Workshops Resource Center on Lucid Meetings.
lucidmeetings.com/meeting-types/workshops

CHAPTER 28

The Learn and Influence Meetings

Evaluate, influence, persuade, investigate, inspect, inspire—these meetings are all designed to transfer information and intention from one person or group to another. The people involved can be clearly separated into groups that think of themselves as *us* and the others as *them*. The person who wants something schedules these meetings with the people they want to influence or get something from. **The frequency and manner in which they approach these meetings reveals the organization's values.**

Most people involved in these meetings often have a genuine interest in learning, sharing, and finding ways to come together for mutual benefit. A Training meeting that teaches people how to use your product is designed to influence what those people think and do going forward, and that's okay! That's why the meeting participants showed up; they *want* to be educated and influenced in that way. (Of course, the trainer likely also wants these people to buy more of their product, recommend it to all their friends, and give them a stellar review.)

Because there is this *us and them* dynamic, the Learn and Influence meetings have fewer clear outcomes than other types of meetings. Sticking with the Training example, which is the most predictable type of meeting in this set, the leader will know in advance what they plan to teach, but they can't predict or control whether the attendees learn anything. Introductions don't always lead to a second meeting, and Issue Resolution meetings may not resolve any issues. Contrast that to a Decision Making meeting, where everyone knows that they'll walk out with a decision. Or a Governance Cadence meeting, where the group knows they'll meet their legal requirements by the end of the session. **In the Learn and Influence meetings, the people involved always learn something, but it's not always what they intended at the outset.**

Because each of these meetings involves some form of social evaluation, the basic formats have more to do with etiquette than regulations or work product. Teams that use these meetings often don't use "just the basics." Instead, they develop specialized methods and preferred rituals to increase their odds of success. Where an occasional trainer just shows up and tells people what they know, a professional instructional designer studies training techniques and uses this knowledge to increase their chances of actually teaching something. A career-curious student sitting in informational interviews won't use the same interviewing techniques that a professional journalist or private investigator employs.

To succeed, Learn and Influence meetings need to be approached with the right mindset and skills. Like all meetings, using an appropriate structure helps a lot, but you can't rely on structure as much here. These meetings require you to be more strategic in advance and remain more adaptable in the moment. Salespeople, for example, need to come to Introduction meetings prepared, polished, and confident in their material. Many salespeople develop extensive scripts they use when preparing for meetings with big prospective clients. They must also be prepared to ignore the script and respond professionally to anything the prospect throws their way.

Because success in these meetings depends more on mindset and skills, I'll talk about the *spectrum* of meetings within each type rather than trying to describe a common meeting format. The meetings along the spectrum in any given type are all trying to achieve a similar kind of business outcome, but the way they go about it can feel and look radically different.

Psychologically, people in these meetings struggle to balance *adaptability* and *professionalism*. True learning and influence requires a vulnerability and openness that's hard to balance with the need to impress and control.

LEARN AND INFLUENCE MEETINGS

Qualities to Balance

	A Focus on Adaptability...	A Focus on Professionalism...
Signs You're Getting It Right	• Creates a friendlier tone. • Takes advantage of opportunity in the moment. • Improves listening and learning.	• Improves perceived meeting quality. • Increases control over outcomes. • Demonstrates mastery. • Reduces volatility.
Signs You've Overdone It	• Appears sloppy or unprepared. • Creates confusion. • Fails to achieve concrete outcomes.	• Feels artificial or inauthentic. • Requires far more investment than warranted by the results. • Breaks down easily when faced with unanticipated complications.

One last note before I get into the specific Learn and Influence meeting types:

This is the section of the book most likely to make you say, "Wait a minute. What about...[my specific technique]?"

There is a good chance that if you run any of these Learn and Influence meetings regularly, you've developed expertise that means you know all kinds of specific things that exceed the scope of what I'm discussing in these pages. You may not even think of what you do as "meeting" anymore, because that word is too generic and too small for all the skill you're bringing to your work.

If that "Hey, why aren't you dealing with [my specific technique]?" question comes up for you, then know that you're operating at a high level of meeting performance mastery for this type of meeting. Congratulations! That's what it feels like when you no longer approach every meeting as a generic tool and develop a level of craftsmanship.

Now, look at the other meetings types in the Taxonomy. Consider, what might the impact on your business be if your team had the same mastery for each of these?

CHAPTER 29

Sensemaking

Answering the Questions

What can we learn from each other about this topic?

How can we make sense of this situation?

Examples

Project Discovery Meetings

Incident Investigations

Doctor/Patient Consults

Community Input Sessions

Market Research Panels

Situational Analyses

Informational Interviews

Purpose
- To learn things you can use to inform later action.
- To gain an understanding of the current state of a project, organization, or system.
- To get help figuring something out.

Work Outcomes
- Shared information.
- New data or insights that can translate into action.

Human Outcomes
- Support and a sense of being "in it together."
- A better understanding of the current situation.
- Insight.

Common Challenges
We run Sensemaking meetings precisely because we're unsure about something, which makes these meetings inherently unpredictable. Common challenges include:
- Lack of a useful discussion framework.
- Inadequate skill with the available thinking tools.
- Social anxiety that arises when people don't understand what's going to happen next.
- Uncooperative or antagonistic meeting participants.
- Frustration when the process doesn't seem to be creating any new insights.

What to Expect in Sensemaking Meetings

Expected Participation
People run Sensemaking meetings to figure something out. The *us and them* dynamic arises between the people asking the questions (us) and the people they're asking (them).

These meetings are led by an interviewer, facilitator, or the person who needs help. In some cases, these roles are very distinct: one person is interviewing one or more other people. In other meetings, the roles are fuzzier. Perhaps there's still one person who's asking the questions and directing the process, but that person may also find themselves contributing to the answers along with the rest of their group. Participants include people being interviewed and sometimes a set of observers. Engagement in Sensemaking meetings varies dramatically. It may feel conversational, it may feel very structured, or it may even feel combative. Regardless of how it feels, it always follows a clear question-response structure.

Most trained interviewers work to develop a rapport with those they're interviewing, since people often share more freely with interviewers they perceive as friendly and trustworthy. That said, many Sensemaking meetings have to work without that rapport. This can be fine when everyone involved perceives a mutual benefit. For example, if a doctor asks a patient to describe their symptoms, the patient does so willingly not because they like the doctor but because they expect the doctor will use that information to help them feel better. Similarly, clients will often answer a consultant's probing questions about their business because they want the consultant's help figuring it out.

Other times, though, the goals of the person asking questions and the people being asked are not aligned. This makes for more difficult meetings and lots of drama. Incident investigations may trigger those dynamics.

> Jessup: "You want answers?!"
> Kaffee: "I want the truth!"
> Jessup: "You can't handle the truth!"
>
> —*A Few Good Men*

The Spectrum of Sensemaking Meetings

Some Sensemaking meetings are governed by rules regarding privacy, non-disclosure, and discretion. These formalities may be addressed at the beginning or end of the session. Otherwise, there are no strong shared patterns for a Sensemaking meeting. Instead, people regularly working in these meetings focus on asking better questions and learning a range of specialized sensemaking techniques. Like Idea Generation meetings, Sensemaking meetings delight in serendipity. Unlike Idea Generation meetings, however, the goal is not to invent new solutions, but rather to uncover existing facts and perspectives.

Sensemaking meetings range from Combative/Hostile to Collaborative. Examples across that spectrum include:

Combative/Hostile	Neutral	Collaborative
Purpose: To find out what really happened and whom to hold accountable • Incident investigation • Criminal interrogation	*Purpose: To discover facts and opinions.* • Interview for an article • Project discovery call • Usability study	*Purpose: To get help interpreting a situation.* • Consulting with a group • Situational analysis (SWOT, etc.) • Research analysis

Top Tips for Successful Sensemaking Meetings

Have you heard people talk about how their calendars are full of meetings that don't have agendas and don't seem to come to any useful conclusions? They're describing botched Sensemaking meetings run amok.

It happens all the time. Someone on the team encounters a question they can't answer, or faces a decision they don't feel confident making by themselves, so they schedule a meeting with everyone else to "talk about" the situation. A Sensemaking meeting may be exactly what they need in order to move forward, but *just talking* is neither the most effective nor respectful way to go about it.

When you find yourself in need of others' wisdom to make progress, schedule a Sensemaking meeting using these tips.

1. Do your homework.

At a minimum, write answers to these questions before you schedule the meeting:

- What do you already know?
- What can you find out on your own—quickly?
- What questions do you still need help to answer?

When you take the time to do this work, you may discover that you don't need the meeting after all. You will certainly come with better questions. If you fail to do your homework, you will waste your colleagues' time. They will quickly realize that you didn't try to answer your questions yourself, they'll be frustrated by the interruption, and your reputation for leading pointless meetings will grow.

Personally, I find it offensive when I take my time to give an interview, then discover the interviewer hasn't even reviewed my company's website.

2. Use a sensemaking tool.

Even the simplest Sensemaking meetings benefit from a bit of technique. For example, author Paul Axtell wrote a Sensemaking template called "A Process for Accessing the Wisdom of your Group" that works like this.

A. You tell the group what you know and what you're trying to figure out.
B. You shut up and listen to them as they talk it over.
C. Midway through, you ask a few questions, then you shut up again.
D. At the end, you share the insights you gained from the conversation and thank everyone.

This simple technique works better than having everyone just talk because it forces you, the one with the question, to *listen* for answers—an obvious precursor to learning that many people forget.

When you're trying to piece together a bigger puzzle, use one of the more involved sensemaking techniques. Look for group techniques with the words "mapping," "diagramming," and "analysis" in the description. These words all point toward tools for figuring things out.

3. Provide time for individual reflection.

It takes time to figure things out. We hear a question or see new information, and we often need a bit of quiet space in our own heads where we can put it together. Sam Kaner's landmark book *The Facilitator's Guide to Participatory Decision Making* includes the diagram that follows, calling out this stage in the thinking and labeling it "The Groan Zone." The Groan Zone happens after all the ideas and questions are out there—they have been brought up in the Divergent Zone—and before they converge onto the key points. When you plan and lead your Sensemaking meeting, recognize that the group is likely to enter the Groan Zone at some point, and when this happens, your job is to give everyone space and time to work their way through it.

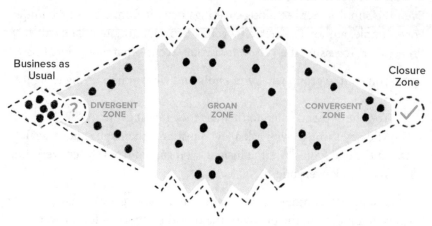

Business as Usual

DIVERGENT ZONE

GROAN ZONE

CONVERGENT ZONE

Closure Zone

Sam Kaner's Diamond of Participatory Decision Making

4. Name your insights and declare your intention.

Sensemaking meetings don't always have tidy outcomes, but that doesn't mean people should leave thinking their time was wasted in a pointless meeting where nothing got done. At the close of a Sensemaking meeting, be sure to articulate the key insights you gained and explain what you intend to do next. Doing so shows respect and appreciation for everyone's time, reinforces that there was a good reason for the meeting because something will happen as a result, and helps you gain clarity in your own mind about what just happened.

By the way: it's okay to say that you're still not sure and have more thinking to do! So if your next step is to do more thinking—fair enough! Regardless of what your next step is, it's always best to let others know if or when they can expect to hear more.

Beyond Elephants:
Embracing the Implications of Distributed Cognition

In Chapter 2 I shared the parable of the elephant in the dark, and I talked about how this illustrates everyone's inability to create a complete picture on their own. That parable originated with religious leaders as a way to help people adopt humility in the face of God's vast unknowableness. This is the realm of metaphysics.

Then I talked about the concept that organizations act as collaborative organisms that feed on communication. The exchange of information between one person-cell and another person-cell is the source of the organization's energy. This is an analogy rooted in biology.

A wise marketing executive once told me, "If you want to get your point across, remember: There are always exactly three things."

So for my third and final illustration, I'll revisit the theme of shared perception through the lens of cognitive science. Let's explore the concept of *distributed cognition*—a concept that clarifies the value of Sensemaking meetings.

Distributed cognition is an approach to cognitive science that views cognition and knowledge as a system of interrelated objects, individuals, and processes, rather than as something each person has all on their own. In short, no one knows all that much by themselves. Instead, they know some things and then rely on their ability to access other people's thinking or use thinking tools to fill out the rest.

The to-do list provides a simple example of distributed cognition, where the awareness of the tasks that need doing is distributed between a person and the list. The list can never know if a task was completed without the person, and there's a high likelihood the person won't remember which tasks to do without the list. Together, though—watch those to-dos get to-done!

Meeting management systems work the same way, encoding the plans for running a meeting and the collected results that come out of the group discussion. When I meet with clients, I always ask them to review the meeting notes for accuracy. When people review and confirm the notes, this increases their awareness and commitment to that result—awesome!—but that's just gravy for me. I need people to review and confirm the notes because I have fully delegated the knowledge about what we agreed to do to the meeting software. I know that there's no way I'll actually remember all those details later, and "the palest ink is better than the best memory," as the proverb says.

But there is a catch. Because we don't realize that we rely so heavily on our ability to draw on the knowledge stored all around us, what we think *we* know might actually be something *our network* knows, not us. We're just not as smart as we think we are.

In their book *The Knowledge Illusion: Why We Never Think Alone*, Steven Sloman and Philip Fernbach write:

We think we know far more than we actually do.

Humans have built hugely complex societies and technologies, but most of us don't even know how a pen or a toilet works.

How have we achieved so much despite understanding so little? Because whilst individuals know very little, the collective or "hive" mind knows a lot.

The key to our intelligence lies in the people and things around us. We're constantly drawing on information and expertise stored outside our heads: in our bodies, our environment, our possessions, and the community with which we interact—and usually we don't even realize we're doing it.

The fundamentally communal nature of intelligence and knowledge explains why we often assume we know more than we really do, why political opinions and false beliefs are so hard to change, and why individually oriented approaches to education and management frequently fail.

Our collaborative minds, on the other hand, enable us to do amazing things.

— Steven Sloman and Philip Fernbach

Sensemaking meetings are a perfect way to intentionally tap into the distributed cognition locked in your network. The Lucid Meetings team maintains a glossary of meeting terms and techniques. We've found more techniques for sensemaking than for any other kind of meeting activity, which makes sense given that these are meetings explicitly designed to facilitate distributed cognition. Distributed cognition means we get the best results when we share the thinking load between the people, the raw information, and our thinking tools.

For example, you may have participated in a SWOT analysis. This exercise asks a team to outline their organization's Strengths, Weaknesses, Opportunities, and Threats. The SWOT diagram holds the knowledge about what kinds of information the group needs to provide and then organizes the contributions from each individual. SWOT is a thinking tool—a kind of sensemaking tool—used to assist a group that needs to gain insight into their organization's place in the competitive landscape.

So hurrah!

Distributed cognition—sharing the task of knowing and figuring things out—provides a way for us to learn and do all kinds of things together that we couldn't possibly accomplish alone, and the tools designed for Sense-making meetings help us maximize that potential.

What else does the concept of distributed cognition tell us that we can use to improve all our meetings? Here are a few implications:

- **There is unique knowledge locked in each individual.** Structuring meetings to increase participation, engagement, and encourage active contributions from everyone makes the group smarter by giving everyone access to that knowledge. The value of the network increases with the number of people actively involved in the network.
- **Improving diversity improves performance.** In this case, I'm referring to diversity of opinion, perspective, and values, and not just ethnic or gender diversity. There is a growing body of evidence suggesting that the more diverse your group, the more successful your outcomes will be. Beyond the fact that group diversity is just morally the right thing to do, it's also extremely logical if you understand that diverse perspectives arise from diverse experiences and access to different kinds of knowledge. As a collaborative organism with distributed cognition, you want all the different knowledge you can get!
- **You do not have to personally master all the special meeting knowledge and techniques to run an effective meeting.** Just as surgeons and pilots use checklists to enhance their own knowledge about how to prepare, meeting designers can distribute meeting skills between the participants and appropriate meeting support systems.

It's worth restating that last point: **You do not have to personally know all the "special meeting stuff" to run excellent meetings.**

I find this especially reassuring when it comes to Sensemaking meetings. The special Sensemaking meeting stuff gets pretty involved. Special techniques include LoNGPESTLE analysis, Ritual Dissent, Future Backward, fish bone diagrams, SWOT, SOAR, Lotus Blossom Technique, and more! It's hard to keep track even of the names of these techniques, each of which involves several useful but non-intuitive steps. Unless you use them all the time, there's realistically no way you'll remember how to do this stuff without a cheat-sheet (like this book).

I've accepted that I do not know all the "special meeting stuff" and I never will. I've been working on effective meetings for over 10 years. I've read nearly 60 books on the topic, designed meetings; been through facilitation training, and Agile meeting training, and UX (User eXperience) training, and parliamentarian training; and published over 40 detailed guides to running specific meetings. I've led meetings, and I've attended them in private companies, schools, agencies, government groups, NGOs, and academia. Even after all that, *every day I find something that I've never seen before* that rocks my world just a little bit.

The problem with being exposed to so much great knowledge is that it's impossible to retain! If I don't use a meeting technique at least once a week, I forget how it works. But that doesn't mean that I start making it up as I go. Instead, I pull out one of the short guides I keep handy and refresh myself on what I need to do. Because I have a solid conceptual grounding, and because I've delegated the task of remembering exactly how I like to run a project kickoff (for example) to my records system, I can run a pretty kick-butt kickoff meeting whenever I need to. This book stores knowledge about meetings that you can access whenever you need it too, which means it's okay to hang onto the big ideas and let the details go. I've got your cognitive back.

When you find yourself facing uncertainty, keep this in mind: **No one actually knows all that much, and what we do learn, we forget.** Sensemaking meetings give us a tool we can use when we want access to that distributed cognition.

Additional Resources for Sensemaking Meetings

Visit the Sensemaking Meetings Resource Center on Lucid Meetings.
lucidmeetings.com/meeting-types/sensemaking-meetings

CHAPTER 30

Introductions

Answering the Questions

How might we work together in the future?

Are we interested in meeting again sometime?

Examples

Job Interviews

First Meeting Between Professionals

Sales Pitches

Sales Demos

First Meeting with a Potential Vendor

Investor Pitches

Purpose

- Learn about each other.
- Decide whether to continue the relationship.

Work Outcomes

- Possible access to new resources (employees, partners, knowledge).
- New sales (or investment).

Human Outcomes

- A new relationship.
- Broadened horizons.
- A possibility for advancement.

Common Challenges

The success of Introductions relies on good timing and making a good impression. These are the "first dates" of the business world, and they have similar challenges.

- The timing factors are difficult to control. A bad sandwich before the Introduction can sink your meeting, and there's no way to control for that kind of thing.
- Social anxiety can make dialogue awkward.
- Mutual trust isn't yet established, increasing the chances that people will misinterpret each other.

What to Expect in Introductions

Expected Participation

Introductions are led by the person who asked for the meeting. The person or people invited to the meeting might also help to lead the discussion, or they may remain largely passive—they get to engage however they want because they're under no obligation to spend any more energy here than they feel is appropriate. Of course, people who accept an invitation to a high-stakes Introduction like a job interview actively participate. People attempt to engage conversationally in most Introduction meetings, but when the social stakes increase or the prospect of mutual benefit is significantly imbalanced, like with sales calls or auditions, the engagement becomes increasingly one-sided.

The Spectrum of Introduction Meetings

There are no strict rules for meetings of this type as a whole, but that doesn't make them ad hoc, informal events. On the contrary: sales teams, company founders, and young professionals spend many long hours working to "hone their pitch." They hope this careful preparation will reduce the influence of luck and the chances of an unhappy surprise. The flow of the conversation will vary depending on the situation. These meetings can go long, get cut short, and quickly veer into tangents. It's up to the person who asked for the meeting to ensure the conversation ends with a clear next step.

Exploratory	Level-Setting	High-Stakes
Purpose: To determine if a relationship is worth establishing. • Meet-and-greet • The "let's have coffee some time" • Meeting with a potential business contact	*Purpose: To determine whether a relationship is worth pursuing for business reasons.* • Initial sales call • Sales qualification call • Recruiter or investor query	*Purpose: To move to the next stage of qualification for a job or award.* • Job interviews • Venture capital pitches • Auditions • The "big one" sales call

Top Tips for Successful Introductions

Consider the Job Interview. That's a meeting with a clear purpose and well-understood outcome. People get together to figure out if they want to enter into a more formal long-term relationship or not. Successful candidates understand this, and they put on their best behavior. Less successful candidates seem to approach the interview as some kind of academic pop-quiz they need to outsmart, or as a bureaucratic nuisance they'll suffer through if they must. Neither approach helps them show off how lovely they might be to have on the team. **Success in Introduction meetings relies mostly on making a good first impression.**

> I've learned that people will forget what you said, people will forget what you did, but people will never forget how you made them feel.
> —Maya Angelou, poet and author

1. Manners matter.

This should go without saying, but since it's the success factor that's most in our control, I'll say it anyway: grooming, polite language, confident handshakes, and proper table manners can all make or break your success in an Introduction.

2. Listen more.

Introductions ask us to make a positive impression, which some people feel means they need to talk about all the ways that they're awesome. Success in Introductions, however, depends more on *how awesome you make the other person feel*. To find out what works for that person, you'll have to listen more than you speak. Richard Moy, a longtime recruiter and talent manager, advises interview candidates in a blog post that "The Secret to a Really Good Interview Is Simply Knowing When to Shut Your Mouth".
   Moy writes:

> When it became clear that certain candidates could've talked about themselves for 25 minutes out of a 30-minute phone screen, I often had to interrupt and politely (I hope) redirect the conversation back to the rest of the questions I wanted to ask. Not only was this uncomfortable, it gave me the impression that candidates were simply trying to 'win' the conversation by selling themselves, which didn't necessarily make me rule them out for the role, but it wasn't a great look.
>
> — Richard Moy

3. Be specific with your appreciations.

The first tip was a reminder about manners, so you already know that you should thank the other person for meeting with you. You can make this thank-you more meaningful and memorable by getting specific. Instead of sending a banal "Thank you, I really appreciated the time" message, list three specific takeaways you got from the conversation. Your takeaway may be a new insight, something specific they said that made you feel nice, or something you're going to follow up on afterwards.
   For example, here's a follow-up email I sent recently to a local facilitator after our first meeting:

Thank you for taking the time to meet me for coffee. Here are my takeaways from our discussion:

- First, I'm inspired by the depth of your practice and your work on creating an international team of co-facilitators. I love the idea of a trained team that can work in tandem to bring both diversity and cohesion to facilitation. As you continue to evolve this group, please keep in touch about any ways we can help.

- I also heard several possible opportunities to collaborate. You could be interested in offering your courses through our online Meeting School, especially the ones you don't have time to market on your own. We could also consider building an agenda template together if there's a process that you're inspired to share that way.

- You may have learning opportunities within your facilitation groups that would be appropriate for me to attend. I would welcome any of these that don't interfere with the group.

And, as promised, here are some links for you....

You can see that this truly requires you to listen actively in the meeting. If you don't listen hard enough to learn anything from the other person, you'll have a really hard time offering sincere appreciations.

4. Close with clarity.

You've met, you've talked, and now what? I've been in many Introduction meetings where the person who asked to meet seems ready to end the conversation with a simple "Okay, that was great. Thanks so much!" which would be fine if we both felt like we never needed to talk to each other again. But I know that's not what people actually want to have happen most of the time. I find this especially frustrating, because I'm busy and I talk to lots of people. If you meet with me and want to do so again, I need you to say so! I'm not a mind-reader, and I'm not going to remember all the implied things we might someday do, especially if you don't seem to care enough to follow-through.

If you felt the Introduction went well and that you'd like to engage with these people again someday, then be sure to say so before ending the meeting: "Okay, that was great. Let's quickly talk about what happens next. I'm going to...."

If you choose to skip this "what's next" discussion in your Introduction meeting, know that the other person will assume this is your polite way of saying that you don't expect to meet again.

INTRODUCTIONS

The All-Important First Impression

Like most of my lady friends who came of age when I did, I have a fondness for movie adaptations of Jane Austen's novel *Pride and Prejudice*. Botched Introductions drive much of the drama in *Pride and Prejudice*. We in the audience know that Lizzie and Darcy are meant to be together, but they spend so much time making bad first impressions (then second, then third) that it seems impossible they could ever recover.

The poet Maya Angelou also once said:

> When someone shows you who they are, believe them the first time.

Most of us don't need this advice when it comes to Introductions. We rely on our first impressions and our needs in the moment, and then decide whether to continue the relationship. To the great satisfaction of romantics everywhere, Lizzie and Darcy ignore this advice. Eventually, despite the disastrous Introductions, these iconic lovers find their way into each other's arms—against all odds.

For those of us who aren't heroes in a romance novel, we need to remember that Introductions are a sale. When we first meet someone, they evaluate us and in turn, we evaluate them. We each then decide: Is this someone I'd like to meet again?

With most of the other meeting types, we can look at ways to logically structure the conversation in pursuit of our goal. We can prepare cogent content and select appropriate engagement techniques. Introductions, however, defy these tactics. Success with Introductions remains firmly in the realm of first impressions—lightning-quick first impressions. Depending on which study you read, it looks like you've got somewhere between two and 15 seconds.

There is *a lot* of fun and frustrating research to read on this topic, especially from experimental and social psychologists. Take a look at the work of Robert Cialdini, Amy Cuddy, Matthew D. Lieberman, and others who have worked to translate what they've learned into digestible advice. A lot of that advice boils down to "relax and be yourself," because people are also very good at detecting inauthenticity. Be authentic, be prepared, and put your best foot forward. That's the best you can do.

Frank Bernieri, a researcher studying interviews and one of the world's foremost authorities on nonverbal communication, says:

> While first impressions are indeed prerational, there are things that you can do before an interview to improve the odds. For example, being well dressed and nicely groomed is in your control. You wouldn't believe the impact of attire on the first impression.
>
> — Frank Bernieri

When we think about job interviews, this advice seems obvious. I'm in a lot of Introduction meetings beyond job interviews, like when I meet potential partners or get a call from a salesperson, and people don't seem to be as concerned about making a positive first impression in these meetings as they should be. I think its because they don't realize the nature of the situation they're in. They don't seem to realize that I'm first and foremost trying to decide if I want to ever talk to them again. They seem to think that our conversation is about some product they're selling, or some way that our businesses might collaborate. While that's true at some level, it's not the biggest factor in the success of our Introduction meeting.

When we enter into a high-stakes Introduction, like a job interview or a pitch in front of investors, we know we need to make a good first impression. We'll put on our nice shoes, strike a power pose before walking into the room, and finally proffer a resume printed on heavy linen paper while firmly returning a strong handshake. We'll find something nice to say about the other person, making sure to point out specifics so they know we're paying attention to them and so we can trigger activity in the reward center of their brain. We'll hope to make them feel good about themselves, and hope they associate that feeling with us.

We know a high-stakes Introduction when it comes our way, but we often fail to recognize that every Introduction, even those exploratory casual ones, includes those 2-15 seconds of *first impression*. Every time you meet with a possible partner or client, they are forming a first impression and deciding if they'd like to meet you again. To succeed, help them realize how much they'll enjoy meeting you again next time.

Additional Resources for Introductions

Visit the Introductions Resource Center on Lucid Meetings.
lucidmeetings.com/meeting-types/introduction-meetings

CHAPTER 31

Issue Resolution

Answering the Question

Given that we do not agree on what to do next,

can we find a mutually satisfactory way to move forward?

Examples

Support Team Escalation

Conflict Resolution

Contract Negotiations and Renewals

Neighborhood Dispute

Purpose
- To reach a new agreement or reconciliation.
- To secure commitment to further the relationship.

Work Outcomes
- An agreement (ideally).
- Clarity on what happens next.

Human Outcomes
- Closure.

Common Challenges
Issue Resolution meetings attempt to resolve a conflict. Conflict is inherently challenging.

What to Expect in an Issue Resolution Meeting

Expected Participation
These meetings are led by a designated negotiator, mediator, or facilitator, or if a neutral party isn't available—by whoever cares most about solving the issue. All parties are expected to engage in the discussion, although how they engage will depend entirely on the current state of their relationship. If the meeting is tense, the engagement should be highly structured to prevent any outright breakdown. If the relationship is sound, the meeting may be conducted in a more conversational style. Obviously, relationship quality plays a central role in the success of an Issue Resolution meeting.

The Spectrum of Issue Resolution Meetings
The format for these meetings is entirely dependent on the situation. Formal negotiations between countries follow a very structured and ritualistic format. Issue Resolution meetings between individual leaders, however, may happen during a round of golf. These meetings are a dance, so while surprises may not be welcome, they are expected.

Issue Resolution meetings range in scale from Interpersonal to International. Examples across that spectrum include:

Interpersonal	Team and Business	International and Large Business
Purpose: To resolve an issue arising from personal disagreements, a values conflict, or an individual's conduct. • Partners conflict resolution • Dispute between neighbors	*Purpose: To resolve a disagreement about what should be done between parties.* • Inter-Department conflicts • Support escalation • Contract dispute	*Purpose: To resolve a dispute between countries, nations and large corporations, usually over access to resources.* • Territory disputes • Treaty negotiations • Trade negotiations

Top Tips for Successful Issue Resolution Meetings

Most organizations work to create systems that prevent the need for Issue Resolution meetings. That's certainly true for my company. We very rarely need to run these meetings. We still have conflict, of course, but we try to address our disagreements in informal conversation before they have a chance to fester. If you, like us, don't get many opportunities to practice your Issue Resolution meeting skills, then **my top tip is to seek help**. Facilitators, mediators, and negotiators are all professionals who have extensive training and practice getting groups through tense situations.

If, despite your best efforts, you find yourself facing the unavoidable necessity of an Issue Resolution meeting, keep these tips in mind.

1. Know the relative costs of failure versus compromise.
Even in the stuffiest of business situations, we all make gut decisions using our instincts. Conflict during Issue Resolution meetings triggers emotions that interfere with our best judgment. Our pride flares, our honor needs defending, and we feel the need to fight for "what's right" as we see it. Fighting to win your point at all costs is fighting, not resolving. When our emotions take hold like this, the Issue Resolution meeting will fail.

To help keep these rash reactions in check, know in advance what failure means in this situation. If you can't find a way to resolve this issue, will you need to shut down your organization? Fire someone? Move out of your home? Will you lose the customer? Will you face a public media backlash?

The cost of failure may be far greater than the pain of a compromise with the other party. Knowing this in advance can help you keep your emotions in check and stay focused on finding resolution.

2. Listen, keep listening, listen some more, and empathize.

You know already that the people involved don't agree and that you're unlikely to get everything you want. To have any chance of reaching agreement, you'll need to start by actively listening to the other side(s) of the story. If instead you begin by trying to explain your point, you'll alienate others and miss the opportunity to uncover common ground.

Active listening requires listening without interruption, then reflecting back (repeating) what you heard. Ask clarifying questions, both to learn more and to demonstrate that you heard what was said.

3. Establish where you already have agreement.

You may all agree on the circumstances that led to the issue. You may all recognize that each party has a justified reason to hold the view that they do. You may all be worried about the same kinds of risks. You may all understand the constraints in play—outside pressures that limit what each party can do to resolve the issue.

Make a list of all the areas where you have a shared understanding. In many cases, the parties may find that they agree on 80% or more of the details, which allows you to focus the rest of the meeting on the small subset of unresolved items. Working through this list can also resolve any issues that arise from simple misunderstandings, as each party describes details that the others may not have realized beforehand.

4. Isolate and address the specific areas of conflict.

The previous tips work to reduce the issue's scope down to a smaller set of specifics which you can then work to resolve. Get these specifics written down so you can look at them together.

Now, you can seek compromises. Is one party willing to concede on some of the specifics in exchange for getting their way on others? Are there opportunities to combine the ideas into a new option that satisfies both parties? Are there other ways to achieve the desired goals that haven't been considered yet? These questions are all much easier to resolve when you're dealing with a documented list of specific this-versus-that issues to compare.

ISSUE RESOLUTION

A Different Kind of Success

I wanted all the stories in this book to provide insight into what *success* looks like for each meeting type. While working on Issue Resolution meetings, I got stuck.

I complained to my partner, "I don't know if I've ever been in a successful Issue Resolution meeting. I don't feel authentic writing about that."

"Are you kidding me?" he said. "You have tons of experience with those. What about all those contract negotiations? And that time that client's technical team accused us of lying to them because they didn't believe we had the features we claimed? Not to mention all those times you had to argue your case with the engineering manager in your last job. Those were all Issue Resolution meetings. Maybe you've just blocked those memories." He winked.

"Yeah, I guess," I said. "I don't really feel any of those were particularly successful meetings, though. I want to talk about meetings that work, and I just don't think I have lots of good examples here."

"Do you still have the same issues today that you had during those meetings, or did they get resolved?" he asked.

"They were resolved. I mean, we got through it. That's not the problem—they just didn't *feel* great," I said.

"Of course not. It's an Issue Resolution—if you're even in a meeting like that, it means you're in a compromised place. We try *never* to get into a situation that requires one of these. When it does happen, you're going to have to let go of something you wanted and face up to some unpleasantness from the other party if you're going to resolve the issue. Usually there aren't any real winners. And if there is a win, it's an ugly win, because it means the other person walks away a loser. **Success in an Issue Resolution is when the issue gets resolved, but that usually doesn't leave anyone feeling great. You need to reset your expectations on this one.**"

This was certainly true with one vital Issue Resolution meeting my partner and I were unfortunate enough to suffer more than a decade ago. I still think about it.

In the early 2000s, the company we worked for provided web development services to other businesses. Through a fabulous combination of skill, luck, and friends in the right places, we landed a contract to build out a brand new website and customer portal for a big company's new product line—a contract worth $100,000. Very cool for a small company! Super exciting, too, because this website was going to be unveiled during an international product launch just two months away. It meant lots of work under extreme deadline pressure, but enough funding to see our company through the next six months. The big company's manager in charge of the new product line signed the contract, and we got to work.

We burned the midnight oil and completed the site a week before the scheduled launch. The big company manager was thrilled! We hadn't been paid yet, because our contract was still working its way through the procurement process and we hadn't yet received a Purchase Order (PO). We weren't worried, though. We'd worked with big companies before; procurement always tells you not to start work until you have a PO, but if you wait that long, it's impossible to hit the deadline. That was literally true in this case—the big launch was now less than a week away, and the PO was still crawling its way through some corporate process we couldn't see. There would have been no way to achieve the goal if we had waited.

You can see where this is going, can't you?

Two days before the anticipated launch, the product line was canceled, and the team we worked with was disbanded. Then the procurement team pulled our contract out of the approval queue and denied our PO; after all, the group that engaged us no longer existed! There we were, having spent two months building this great website, not pursuing other work because we were fully booked, and now we had nothing to show for it—along with a huge gap in expected revenue.

We began a series of Issue Resolution meetings. In this case, we all had a common understanding of what had happened. Gaining a shared understanding of the circumstances that led to the problem—that's a vital first step for any Issue Resolution, and luckily no one disputed the facts in this case. The big company also made clear the constraints that prevented them from just doing the right thing (in our view). "Our hands are tied; we're so sorry. Well, it's just how the process works, you know," they said.

In the end, we managed to recover just half the promised contract price. $50,000 is better than $0, and better than a drawn-out lawsuit, but it left us scrambling to make up the deficit. So, yes, while the issue was technically resolved and the relationship rescued, it sure didn't feel like a success. Both parties walked away feeling less-than-great... and that made it technically a "successful" Issue Resolution. I'll keep my partner's advice in mind about that next time I'm in a similar situation, and set my expectations accordingly.

ISSUE RESOLUTION

Additional Resources for Issue Resolution Meetings

Visit the Issue Resolution Meetings Resource Center on Lucid Meetings.
lucidmeetings.com/meeting-types/issue-resolution-meetings

CHAPTER 32

Community of Practice

Answering the Questions

What can we teach each other that may help us improve our individual practice in this area?

How can we advance this topic together?

Examples

Monthly Safety Committee Meeting

Project Manager's Meetup

Lunch-and-Learn (sometimes called a "Brown Bag," "Town Hall," or whatever your organization uses)

Purpose
- Topic-focused exchange of ideas.
- Organizational and individual capability development.
- Relationship development.

Work Outcomes
- Focused attention in an area that doesn't warrant a dedicated team.
- Organizational capability development: more skilled people.

Human Outcomes
- New knowledge, skills, and attitudes.
- Improved ability to perform the job.
- Recognition.
- A feeling of belonging.
- Larger networks.

Common Challenges
Community of Practice meetings are largely voluntary. Challenges include:
- Too many or too few participants.
- Inconsistent quality and frequency.
- Loss of leadership.
- Confusion about the group's purpose or scope.
- Difficulty creating or maintain momentum.

What to Expect in Community of Practice Meetings

Expected Participation
The people at these meetings volunteer to be there because they're interested in the topic, and in some cases, because participation is rewarded by their employer. An organizer or chair opens the meeting and introduces any presenters. Participants are expected to engage convivially, ask questions and engage in exercises when appropriate, and network with each other in between (and especially after) presentations. These meetings are part social, part content, and part operational, and the style is relaxed.

The Spectrum of Community of Practice Meetings
Most of these meetings begin with mingling and light conversation. Then the organizers will call for the group's attention and begin the prepared

part of the meeting. This could follow a traditional agenda, as they do in a Toastmasters meeting, or it may include a group exercise or a presentation by an invited speaker. Some Communities of Practice work on tangible deliverables, such as recommendations or guidelines for the larger community, but many do not. There's usually time for questions and then more time at the end to resume the casual conversations and networking that began earlier. People in attendance are there to learn about the topic but also to make connections with others and discover opportunities.

Internal Committees	Internal Peer Learning	Community Meetups
Purpose: To put regular focus on developing topic expertise within the organization. • Safety committee meetings • Diversity committee meetings	*Purpose: To share learning with others in the organization.* • Lunch-and-learn • Internal demos	*Purpose: To connect people in the community who share an interest in a topic.* • Small business owners roundtable • Product managers meetup

Top Tips for
Successful Community of Practice Meetings

A Community of Practice meeting brings people together to focus on something they care about outside of their day-to-day job requirements. People participate in a Community of Practice because they find it rewarding intellectually, socially, or even financially. These tips help organizers design Community of Practice meetings that deliver what their community members want.

1. Get clear: what capability will this meeting develop?

Have you ever blocked out time for a Community of Practice meeting, put on your nice outfit, and rushed to arrive in time for networking, only to discover that the meeting wasn't about what you thought it was? I certainly have, and when this happens, I never go back. I don't even try to figure out if my experience was a fluke—that group is dead to me.

Organizers can prevent this disappointing situation by clarifying the specific capability the group helps develop. For example, is your Writer's Community of Practice for people who write mystery novels, comic

COMMUNITY OF PRACTICE

books, or user support manuals? (Or all of these?) Is it primarily for new writers, only published authors, or are fans welcome too? There are so many events out there that it's important to be explicit about the kind of value your meeting will provide—and include this information in any publicity materials about the meeting.

This applies to internal committees as well as external community groups. For example, experts recommend that corporate Safety Committees work to clarify the committee's specific goals for the year. Otherwise, these groups can devolve to just talking about safety once per month, which isn't particularly inspiring or useful to anyone involved.

2. Reward participation.

Some events are rewarding simply because they're interesting. I love my local neuroscience Community of Practice because they talk about fascinating things that I happen to care about, not because they deal with anything directly relevant to my business. That said, because there is no direct benefit to my day-to-day work, this is also the Community of Practice meeting I'm most likely to skip.

Organizations that need sustained participation in internal Communities of Practice, such as a Safety Committee, often compensate employees for the time they spend in these meetings. Participation appears on an employee's record and is factored into decisions about salary and promotion. The organization provides extrinsic rewards for participation and rotates the people on the committee to spread knowledge and refresh the group's energy.

Other Communities of Practice must tap into things that *intrinsically* motivate participation. The networking opportunities available in many Meetups, for example, attract both job-hunters and employers with open positions they need to fill. Speaking at or organizing a Community of Practice meeting is a great way for people to highlight the expertise on their resume and practice public speaking. Many organizers emphasize the importance of posting pictures of the event and personally thanking everyone for their participation, making sure that the event is socially rewarding.

When you design a Community of Practice meeting, consider ways you can reward participants in terms of acknowledgment or access to new resources that will benefit them in their day-to-day activities.

COMMUNITY OF PRACTICE

Community of Practice Meetings Versus Meetings with Your Community of Practice

Just like not every meeting the board attends is an official Board Meeting, the people in a Community of Practice can have other kinds of meetings too. A Community of Practice meeting includes a larger group and focuses on networking and topic-based peer learning through educational presentations and dialogue.

The community organizers may also:

- Meet to plan for upcoming events—that's a Planning meeting.
- Meet once or twice each year specifically to elect leaders and conduct legally required business—that's a Governance Cadence meeting.
- Meet to interview potential speakers—that's an Introduction.
- Gather to train new organizers on how to lead the group or its events—those are Training meetings.

If you are working in a Community of Practice and looking for tips on how to approach your next meeting, please recognize that the meeting you're looking for may be covered in another chapter.

3. Know where you are in your community's lifecycle and plan accordingly.

Communities of Practice emerge when a group identifies a capability they want to develop together. You know that the community exists because it meets. If there are no Community of Practice meetings, there is no established Community of Practice that others can join.

If it's a hot, fresh topic, you can find volunteers to help organize the meeting. People want to speak at your meetings and sponsorship comes easily. But at some point, the topic won't be so fresh—or the people who started with the community will have developed whatever capability it was that they needed to develop, and they'll move on.

The cadence and format for your Community of Practice meetings should take this lifecycle into account. When the group is going hot, you can plan out months of meetings in advance and focus on keeping up with

COMMUNITY OF PRACTICE

the demand. When the group is stable, you can focus on mentoring a new group of leaders who will take over when the current group moves on. When you know that you'll always have new people cycling through as they join the organization, who will then advance beyond what the group offers, you can transition your focus away from the volunteer-driven peer-to-peer mentoring found in a Community of Practice meeting toward a set of organization-supported Training meetings.

The Community of Practice Lifecycle

I remember when the Portland tech community first began gathering at "Lunch 2.0." An event series called "Beer & Blog" followed not long after. At both events, people involved in the world of website and web application development gathered to share food, browse name tags, and figure out who was doing what in this exciting new "Web 2.0" version of the world. We'd all somehow survived the dot-com bubble crash of 2001, not unscathed but mostly intact, and the energy in our industry was picking up. A few years post-crash, and blogs became a real thing that people did. Companies making software that ran "just on the internet" were setting up cool offices downtown, and Lunch 2.0 gave them a chance to show off their foosball tables to everyone.

At first, the crowds were relatively small. You'd show up, and you'd see the same 30+ people you chatted with on Twitter during the rest of the week. (Oh, and Twitter was new and used for having conversations with your community then—it wasn't dominated by outrage and advertising like it is today.) I learned which coding languages people thought were cool. I met someone who became an "online community manager" for a local company—which wasn't a job I realized people could get paid to do. We had heated debates about whether cell phones could ever be useful at work for anyone except traveling salesmen and the people on pager duty.

When these events first started, the tech community in my city wasn't really a community yet. We knew about the old-guard tech companies in town, but we didn't know who the up-and-coming players in the internet game were. The capability we needed to develop was the establishment of our own local network.

It worked—fast. Word got out about these events where you could get a free lunch and hang out with the Web 2.0 tech crowd. Attendance soared. Companies that wanted to host Lunch 2.0 needed to have bigger offices and bigger budgets to deal with the crowds. It became mandatory to RSVP, which you had to do within a day of the list opening up if you wanted to get a spot. If you did make it, some of those same 30 Twitter friends were present, but they were harder to find in the crowds. There were also a lot more people there who weren't actually involved in web development but really wanted to be, and many of the conversations shifted from comparing tech notes to network-building.

To restore some of the focused discussions on technology, and to deal with the demand of a burgeoning community, new groups emerged. The Portland Python User Group held Community of Practice meetings where they talked about the Python coding language. You can bet that was instantly a smaller crowd than a general-purpose Web 2.0 meetup. AgilePDX focused on how development teams could start managing their work using Agile methodologies. The IxDA group, which focused on information design and had been largely dormant, enjoyed a resurgence of interest. Activity exploded around town.

With everything else going on, Lunch 2.0 and Beer & Blog became less compelling. They were still enjoyable meetings. But many of us had established a sense of who was doing what, and now we knew where to go for the conversations specific to our work. After a while, sponsors and organizers lost interest too. The meetings were scheduled further and further apart. Today, both events occur annually during Portland Startup Week. They're billed as "Oldies but Goodies" nostalgia.

Lunch 2.0 was held to develop a specific capability—to grow awareness about cool new companies in town and form a network for internet-based professionals—and it did. Then it petered out to a once-a-year classic. AgilePDX, on the other hand, is still going strong. There's a lot of room to grow one's personal capability with Agile, giving experienced people a reason to stay involved and new practitioners a reason to join on a regular basis. The original organizers have successfully nurtured a new group of leaders who share the effort involved in running these Community of Practice meetings. This group is in a stable phase of its lifecycle.

I've seen other Community of Practice meetings that weren't so successful at matching their planning to their lifecycle phase. I have a relative who served for several years on her company's Safety Committee as the representative for her division. The Safety Committee reviewed new government rules and occasionally shared donuts, but mostly they all enjoyed the small stipend they received for the time spent on the committee. When my relative retired, no one in her division was prepared to take her place on the committee, and no one on the committee worked to develop the now-missing safety awareness capability hole that she left behind her. The committee had mistaken running the meetings as "the point" because that's how they were rewarded. They neglected to nurture a growing safety capability—a true Community of Practice—across the organization.

I work with another organization composed of representatives from many companies. These folks came together to develop a new technical standard, which they did within the first few years. The capability was developed, and the group could have wound down like Lunch 2.0 did, changing the meeting cadence to an occasional check-in so they could keep their work up to date. But they found that they liked regular meetings, so instead of scaling back, they decided to change the name of the group and start work on a new initiative. This community has never enjoyed the same energy as it did in that initial push, but they happily persist and continue to create new capabilities for all to enjoy.

In many ways, the lifecycle stages of a Community of Practice follow the Tuckman Group Development Model. Originally published in 1965, the educational psychologist Bruce Tuckman described how groups go through four stages:

1. **Forming**, where the group first comes together and establishes shared goals.
2. **Storming**, where people's different views about how to proceed often clash.
3. **Norming**, where the group finds a cooperative groove, and...
4. **Performing**, where the group steams along awesomely.

A successful meeting for a group that's just Forming will look very different than when the group reaches Tuckman's fourth level, Performing. When people ask me how to run a successful Community of Practice meeting, I think about this model and all the examples I've experienced myself, and then adjust my recommendations. And occasionally, I point out that Tuckman later added a fifth stage to his model: **Adjourning**. That's a useful stage too.

Additional Resources for Community of Practice Meetings

Visit the Community of Practice Meetings Resource Center on Lucid Meetings.

lucidmeetings.com/meeting-types/community-of-practice-meetings

COMMUNITY OF PRACTICE

CHAPTER 33

Training

Answering the Question

What do I know that you need to learn?

How can we be sure you've learned that successfully?

Examples

Client Training on a New Product

New Employee Onboarding

Safety Training

Seminars

Purpose

- To transfer knowledge and skills.

Work Outcomes

- Knowledge used to improve job performance.
- Certification or credentials.
- Records showing who within the organization has the desired knowledge.

Human Outcomes

- New knowledge, skills, and attitudes
- Improved confidence
- Improved ability to perform the job

Common Challenges

Training meetings are just one form of training and the default choice for people who lack the time or inclination to develop other kinds of training material. This translates to lots of slipshod Training meetings. Common challenges include:

- Trainers who have no experience or guidance on how to effectively train people.
- Training content that's either too easy or too challenging for the learner.
- Boring! Training meetings can be real snoozers. (Technically speaking, you might call this a problem with *engagement*.)
- Training that doesn't lead to any changes in job performance.

What to Expect in Training Meetings

Expected Participation

A trainer leads Training sessions, and participants follow instructions. Participants may be there by choice, or they may be required to attend Training sessions by their employer or an external force (like a certification body). There is no expectation of *collaboration* between the trainer and the participants. These are pure transfers of information from one group to the next.

The Spectrum of Training Meetings

Training session formats vary widely. In its simplest form, the session involves a trainer telling the participants what they need to learn and then answering some questions. Instructional designers and training professionals can make Training sessions far more engaging than that.

One-on-One	Small Group/Seminar	Classroom
Purpose: To train an individual on how to do a specific job. • On-the-job training • Private tutorials	*Purpose: To train a group on a focus topic.* • New-hire orientations • Continuing education seminars • Corporate internal classes	*Purpose: To formally educate a group.* • Certification preparation

Top Tips for Successful Training Meetings

If your job title includes the words Trainer, Instructional Designer, Learning and Development Professional, Teacher, or Professor, you'll know all this material already. This is for the rest of us, who lead Training meetings not because that's part of our job description but because we know some things and have worked here longer than someone else.

Good news for those of us who find ourselves called to train: there's a boatload of helpful information out there for you. Search online for training development frameworks, and you'll get all kinds of step-by-step guidance for putting together your Training meeting. Here are some highlights.

1. Get specific about the learning objectives.

What exactly will the participants in your Training meeting learn? Are you working to improve knowledge, skills, or attitudes? Make a list of the learning objectives. I find that filling in the blanks below helps me clarify what the training needs to accomplish.

Knowledge
- I will teach you about _____ so that you will know _____.
- Example: I will teach you about the *Meeting Taxonomy* so that you will *know how to identify and use different kinds of meetings.*

Skills

- I will show you how to _____ so that you can _____.
- Example: I will show you how to *draft a meeting agenda* so that you can *prepare the agenda for your team meeting.*

Attitudes

- I will share _____ to give you a new perspective on _____.
- Example: I will share *research on how people really feel about meetings* to give you a new perspective on *the value of meetings in your organization.*

2. Know your audience.

Once you've identified the learning objectives, find out more about your audience. What knowledge, skills, and attitudes are they bringing into the meeting? If I am training someone how to craft a meeting agenda, for example, I want to know what kind of experience with agenda-writing they already have. I'd also love to know their attitude toward agendas. Are they intimidated by the task of making an agenda? Are meeting agendas completely new to them? Are they maybe one of those folks who believes they already know everything there is to know? If you are developing a Training meeting for a group, what kind of assumptions can you make about where they're starting from? Training is meant to take people from point A to point B in their learning journey, which doesn't work so well if you've developed all your material for people starting at point C.

3. Ask for commitment to learning.

The advice you'll find online about how to develop better Training meetings is all geared toward the trainer. Tools for trainers, models, learning systems, professional associations—it goes on and on. But Training meetings aren't primarily for the trainer. They're for the *learner,* and unfortunately, there's nothing you as a trainer can do that can make someone else learn.

Have you ever attended a Training meeting where the trainer simply read to you for 30+ minutes? Or one in which the Power Point slides never seemed to end? On the Spectrum of Engagement, this forces the leaner to be passive. They can try to be attentive and take notes, but realistically, they'll have a hard time staying focused.

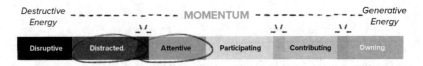

Trainers can change how they deliver content to make it more interesting, but that still doesn't guarantee learners will be engaged. When I visited Zingerman's (see Chapter 12), they shared the Training Compact they use. The Training Compact acts as a special set of ground rules specifically for Training sessions, creating an agreement that the trainer and the learner are equally responsible for the success of the Training meeting:

> This compact recognizes the important truth that, although we can require our staff to attend training, we cannot make them learn what they need to know. They need to take responsibility for their own learning—by asking questions, making sure they understand what is expected and practicing, practicing, practicing.
> —Maggie Bayless, Managing Partner of Zingtrain

Taking notes is attentive. Responding to a quiz when prompted is participating. Asking questions, probing, digging deeper—that's contributing to the group and owning your own learning. Finally, teaching what you know is ownership. It is possible to design Training meetings where everyone there is asked to engage across this full spectrum.

4. Evaluate and improve.
Training meetings can and should produce specific measurable outcomes. The Kirkpatrick Four-Level Training Evaluation Model says you should evaluate the:

1. **Reaction**: Did the learners find the meeting enjoyable and/or valuable?
2. **Learning**: Did they learn the content?
3. **Behavior**: Did their behavior change as a result? Maybe one week, two weeks, or three months later?

4. **Results**: Did the Training meeting have a positive impact on the organization's bottom line? (This is a very explicit look at the NPI factor discussed in Part 1.)

Those of us thrust into more informal Training meetings don't have any systems to support this kind of evaluation, but that shouldn't keep us from seeking informal feedback and using it to refine our approach.

Training as Leadership Development

Training isn't the point of a Training meeting. *Learning is the point.* The training is simply the means to that end. That doesn't mean, however, that the learning has to be one-sided.

> *Docendo discimus.* (Latin for "By teaching, we learn.")
> —Seneca the Younger, Roman Philosopher

In my interview with Elph at Zingerman's, he said that all supervisors and managers across the company were required to teach at least one class. The Zingerman's community of businesses offers more than 70 internal classes, and each individual business has its own set of Training meetings specific to the jobs within that business. There's a lot of opportunity to teach. Zingerman's has this requirement for a variety of reasons.

First, there's no better way to learn than by teaching. What Seneca pointed out over 2,000 years ago has been backed by research in recent years and dubbed "the protégé effect." I know the protégé effect to be real from my own experience both leading Training meetings and writing educational content. As I work to outline the information I plan to teach, I discover gaps and flaws in my own understanding, and I'm driven to learn more. I want to find more useful models, better examples, and I want to know that I can answer the questions people are likely to ask during the session. If I can't fully explain something, that means I myself do not fully understand it.

Several studies on Reciprocal Peer Teaching—which is a fancy way of saying that students take turns teaching each other—have shown it as an effective way to improve learning outcomes in medical school classes on gross anatomy. What's more:

By assuming the responsibility of teaching their peers, students not only improve their understanding of course content, but also develop communication skills, teamwork, leadership, confidence and respect for peers that are vital to developing professionalism early in their medical careers.

—Krych, March, Bryan, Peake, Pawlina, and Carmichael (2005)

That's just the sort of thing we all want in our organizations, right?

This benefit—developing leadership capacity at every level of the organization—is the primary reason the people at Zingerman's cited for requiring their managers to teach.

If leaders at Zingerman's need to be ready to step onto the dish line to help when the dishwasher's feeling a bit overwhelmed, then my anarchist orientation clearly dictates that, conversely, dishwashers also ought to be prepared to step up and help lead if and when a manager starts to slide off course. We are, after all, all in this together: knowing what position we've each agreed to play is important, but at the end of the day, it's all one team. Regardless of title, we all need to lead. So, let me say it again. *The commitment to being effective leaders has to be part of what we expect from every single person in the organization, regardless of seniority, job title, or anything else.*

—Ari Weinzweig, *Zingerman's Guide to Good Leading, Part 2: A Lapsed Anarchist's Approach to Being a Better Leader*

Or as the historian C.L.R. James wrote: "Every cook can govern."

The second reason organizations like Zingerman's, Lucid Meetings and many others ask employees to lead training is that it makes our products better. For example, when I prepare to lead a software Training meeting, I take a fiercely critical look at every feature I'm going to share. I ask myself, "Is this clear? Will people remember how to use this after the Training meeting is over, or is there something getting in the way that will make it harder than it needs to be? How quickly can we improve this? Get out of the way! We've got code to write!"

This same dynamic occurs when I train internal staff. Are the processes and systems my company has set up working well? Am I trying to train someone how to complete a task that, now that I look at, has too many steps and is too prone to failure? People who are responsible for both managing and training the people they manage can more easily see when systems need to be improved.

The third reason to have new managers lead your Training meetings is that this approach often works better. Social psychologists theorize that this is because people may feel more comfortable learning from near peers, rather than from stuffy authorities. Maybe that's the case. I prefer the theory that says peers are better trainers because they can still remember what it was like to learn that information themselves. They have a better sense of where the learner is starting from. They know their audience because not so long ago, they were in those shoes.

The Gordon Training Institute developed a model called the Four Stages of Competence that illustrates this point.

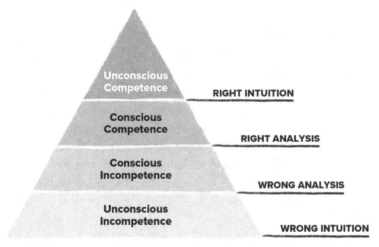

Hierarchy of Competence

1. **Unconscious incompetence**: The individual does not understand or know how to do something and does not necessarily recognize the deficit. They may deny the usefulness of the skill. The individual must recognize their own incompetence, and the value of the new skill, before moving on to the next stage. The length of time an individual spends in this stage depends on the strength of the stimulus to learn.

2. **Conscious incompetence**: Though the individual does not understand or know how to do something, they recognize the deficit, as

well as the value of a new skill in addressing the deficit. The making of mistakes can be integral to the learning process at this stage.

3. **Conscious competence**: The individual understands or knows how to do something. However, demonstrating the skill or knowledge requires concentration. It may be broken down into steps, and there is heavy conscious involvement in executing the new skill.

4. **Unconscious competence**: The individual has had so much practice with a skill that it has become "second nature" and can be performed easily. As a result, the skill can be performed while executing another task. The individual may be able to teach it to others, depending upon how and when it was learned.

—Gordon Training Institute

New managers and recently hired employees may have just entered Level 3: Conscious Competence, which means they know how to do the job but they still have to think about it. The people they're training are still at Level 2: Conscious Incompetence. Level 2 people know there's something here to learn, but they don't yet have a handle on the topic.

This model helps us understand why *sometimes the people with the most expertise on a topic can make the worst trainers.* They've developed to the point where they no longer have to think about or even pay much attention to the mechanics that are still a mystery to the people just starting out, so they forget to mention all those vital steps they breeze through on autopilot.

(Quick note: Before all of the Learning and Development professionals start sending me nasty letters about how I've undervalued their expertise and I'm leading people astray, please know that *I'm not advocating that organizations turn all their training over to junior supervisors.* I have two sisters-in-law who work as Instructional Designers for large corporations, and I think the work they do is incredibly valuable. I also know that they focus on the design and management of the organization's overall training program; they aren't experts in the content, nor do they always lead the Training meetings themselves. Instead, they work with the people who know the job and help them lead better Training meetings.)

Additional Resources for Training Meetings

Visit the Training Meetings Resource Center on Lucid Meetings.
lucidmeetings.com/meeting-types/training-meetings

CHAPTER 34

Broadcast

Answering the Questions

What do we know that we feel should be shared with our larger group?

With the outside world?

Examples

Marketing Webinar

Press Conference

Team Announcement

All-Hands Announcement

Purpose
- To share information that inspires (or prevents) action.

Work Outcomes
- Knowledge distribution.
- Improved or repaired reputation.
- New sales leads.
- Improved group cohesion.

Human Outcomes
- Awareness of what's available from other organizations.
- Awareness of what's happening in your organization.
- Feeling of "being in the know" and part of the group.

Common Challenges
Broadcast meetings suffer from poorly aligned motives. People leading Broadcast meetings are often trying to push a message without consideration for how this serves the people listening. Challenges that arise include:
- The meeting feels like a "bait and switch" when people are lured in by one message but then hear another.
- The perception (or suspicion) that the meeting leader is inauthentic.
- Frustration and anger when important messages are delivered badly.

What to Expect in a Broadcast meeting

Expected Participation
Broadcast meetings are led by the meeting organizer. This person officially starts the meeting and then either runs the presentation or introduces the presenters. People invited to the meeting may have an opportunity to ask questions, but for the most part, they are expected to listen attentively. While Broadcast meetings include presentations in the same way a Community of Practice meeting does, they do not provide an opportunity for participants to engage in casual conversation and networking. These are not collaborative events.

The Spectrum of Broadcast Meetings
Broadcast meetings are like shows: they start and end on time. They begin with brief introductions, which are followed by the presentation.

Questions may be answered periodically or held until the last few minutes. Because these meetings include announcements or information intended to inform later action, participants often receive follow-up communication: a copy of the slides, a special offer or invitation, or, in the case of an All-Hands meeting, a follow-up meeting with a manager to talk about how the big announcement affects their team specifically. The people leading a Broadcast meeting do not expect and do not welcome surprises. The people participating often don't know what to expect.

To Your Team	To Your Organization	To External Audiences
Purpose: To share a big announcement with the team. • A strategic update • Personnel announcements (hires, fires)	Purpose: To inform employees and encourage cultural cohesion. • All-Hands meetings	Purpose: To generate leads and manage public reputation. • Webinars • Press conferences

Top Tips for Successful Broadcast Meetings

Broadcast meetings are "push" meetings. One or more people are pushing a message out to another group of people. This makes the typical engagement profile for a Broadcast meeting pretty weak.

Any time you're holding a meeting where you aren't asking the attendees to do anything specific except pay attention, you'll need to figure out how to be worth watching.

1. Hone your message.

How can you make what you're sharing more compelling, more entertaining, or more necessary for the people attending? Give yourself time to have others review your presentation in advance. If you're using slides, use pictures. People like to look at pictures.

BROADCASTS

2. Practice, then practice again.

People who run marketing webinars know to practice. At Lucid Meetings, we try to run through every webinar at least twice before the event. This helps us check the timing, refine the content, and get confident with how we'll use whatever broadcasting technology is necessary.

We're aware that because the audience doesn't have anything specific they have to do during a Broadcast meeting, they're not our collaborators during the event. They're spectators, and they will be evaluating our performance. That means that even in an internal All-Hands meeting, we need to bring out our public speaking skills.

Practice your presentation in advance so you can work out any rough spots and increase your confidence during the live meeting.

3. Know your audience.

If you read chapter 34 on Training meetings, you'll see that these tips sound familiar. Training meetings are the other type of meetings that easily devolve to pure "push" meetings, and many of the tips apply to both types. With Training meetings, trainers need to know their audience so they can design training that matches the learners' current understanding of the topic.

With Broadcast meetings, however, leaders need to understand their audience so they can avoid pissing them off. There's a risk with any Broadcast meeting that the people attending will find your presentation misleading, pandering, or insincere. A botched Broadcast meeting that fails to speak to the audience in a way that they find credible and authentic has powerful negative ripples. See the stories that follow for examples.

4. Try to find ways to give people a job.

Leaders can make Broadcast meetings more entertaining and slightly more engaging by giving the audience things to do. In webinars, it's common to open up the chat and post a few polls so the audience has something to click on. In All-Hands meetings, employees may be asked to give a presentation or be called up for special recognition. In webinars, Training, and All-Hands meetings, I've seen meeting leaders hand out sheets of paper with partially complete notes. These papers look like boring MadLibs sheets. The audience is then expected to fill in the blanks as they listen along.

For example, the paper might include these lines:

In Q3, we beat our revenue plan by _____%. The Q4 pipeline looks good.

Right now, we're forecasting $_____ in sales for the quarter.

Is it cheesy? Yes! But it works. As an audience member, I'd fill those blanks in if I cared about my company's financial performance.

The challenge leaders face in all Broadcast meetings is that *you can't make people pay attention or play along*. These engagement techniques are worth trying, but ultimately, you'll want to focus more on making the show worth watching.

The Ugly, the Meh, and the Good Broadcast

"I can't believe this [bleep]! Who do they think they're fooling?! Those [bleepers]!"

The lady sitting two rows ahead of me was clearly upset. I was riding with six other people in a shuttle heading for the Seattle airport. We'd been happily chatting about the food carts and craft brewing we'd visit when we got to Portland, when our new friend in the front started to swear.

"My bosses are the most awful, hideous, hateful people, and look what they just did! Can you believe this?" she demanded, then passed her phone back to us. She had an email showing a group of smiling people holding big yellow cards that read "Thanks!" and, "You're Great!" They weren't models or anything, but I wouldn't have called them hideous. Her reaction seemed a bit extreme.

She explained, "I'm traveling, so apparently I missed the Employee Appreciation Day meeting. Now they're sending out this email to everyone who wasn't there. Employee Appreciation! Ha! Like I'm going to buy that. There are thousands of us, and no one says anything nice all year. There's nothing specific here about me or my work—and they think this is going to make me feel appreciated? They sent the same stupid yellow card to every single person. They're crazy. The whole place is a sinking ship, and we're all just rats trying to escape. And now they 'appreciate' me! What an insult!" She was so angry that she was vibrating.

"That doesn't sound good," said the friendly chap in the third row. "Where do you work? Maybe you should quit. Go into business for yourself instead."

"I work for the Department of Energy, and with this new administration, we've got this whole new leadership group that spends all their time talking in stupid meetings making stupid decisions that pad their fat backsides and make our lives miserable," she explained.

"Oh. Got it." The fellow in the third row paused, and we all knew why. I don't normally name names when providing the worst-case examples, but it's no secret that the changes made by the Trump administration across U.S. government operations have created unrest, particularly inside the agencies.

"Well, I used to work for a terrible company too," the friendly third-row gent continued. "Then I quit and went into business with my wife. Now we're professional window washers. We aren't rich or anything, of course, but people are always happy to see us. And every March we travel around the world. I'm really looking forward to beer in Portland, and the music. There's a great music scene in Portland, right?"

The mood was beginning to recover!

The angry lady slumped. "I have two and a half more years until I can retire. If I can just hold on...."

The leadership group at the U.S. Department of Energy had run a disastrous Broadcast meeting. These leaders have a problem: employee engagement and morale is at a record low. So, they decided to run a Broadcast meeting to try to solve their problem. They decided they should tell employees how much they appreciate them and that would improve morale! The leaders identified their problem as employee retention and engagement scores, a big nebulous measure of performance. The unhappy employees, however, are not concerned with how to improve engagement scores. This Broadcast was made by the leaders in an attempt to solve their own problem, but it didn't acknowledge or address the needs of the group receiving the Broadcast in any way.

This was an extreme example of an ugly Broadcast meeting. There are lots of ugly Broadcast meetings. Any time a leader feels like they have to communicate with a group, but they don't actually want to, you'll get an ugly Broadcast meeting. Often the leader doesn't particularly respect the group they're addressing, so the message is sharp and curt, and questions are unwelcome.

In my own career, I've worked under two CEOs who seemed not to like people very much. They held All-Hands meetings every four months or so, mostly because the other people in the leadership team forced them to. In these meetings, the full staff saw slides about the current state of the business and a few notes about big projects. The presentation details were always vague, and there was plenty of uncomfortable foot shuffling in the audience. In one particularly memorable Broadcast meeting, the staff had lined up against the perimeter of the room and was literally pressing up against the walls. The CEO and his VPs, all trying to maintain smiles that never touched their eyes, were left standing in a wide, empty circle that everyone else clearly needed to escape.

That's the Ugly.

Let's move on to the Meh. Webinars are Broadcast meetings put on by organizations as a marketing activity. They are neither inherently good nor bad. Some can be quite interesting. Others are mildly engaging. Many are dull. The challenge with webinars is the same as it is for all Broadcast meetings. The stated purpose of the webinar—to teach people about a new idea or share a case study, for example—is not the organization's true purpose for holding the webinar. The organization's purpose is to get people to sign up for the webinar so they can sell things to them.

Any time you have a meeting where the meeting leader's purpose for holding it and the attendees' purpose for showing up don't match, you increase the risk that you'll create a brazenly inauthentic experience that rubs people the wrong way and backfires. Luckily for all the marketers out there, most people understand that webinars, press conferences, and meetings of this ilk are designed to sell, so they aren't offended when they're asked to buy. They *are* judging, though. Everyone's a critic, and with marketing Broadcast meetings, they know you're putting on a show.

This brings me to the Good.

Many organizations hold regularly-scheduled All-Hands meetings where they share the current state of the business, discuss their vision, and highlight key accomplishments. These organizations know that to perform well, employees need to have current information about the business context. Employees need to understand the organization's strategy so that they can see how their work supports it. They need to understand the challenges so they can help overcome them.

In very small organizations, these All-Hands meetings are indistinguishable from Team Cadence meetings. Lucid Meetings, for example, doesn't have any internal Broadcast meetings because we're not big enough to need them. As organizations get larger, though, the Broadcast meeting becomes the only practical way to make sure everyone gets access to the same information at once.

SoundCloud, an internet music service, grew from tiny startup to 300+

employees across multiple time zones in just a few years. At first, they ran their All-Hands meetings like Lucid Meetings does: everyone was invited, and anyone could share any topic they felt everyone should hear. As the company grew, they found that this became disjointed, chaotic, and awkward. The topics lacked coherence, and people started opting out. David Noël, SoundCloud's VP of Community, talked about this in an interview with First Round Capital. Noël said, "We would have an All-Hands where we opened the floor for questions, and no one would ask anything. I thought, 'Whoa, this is brutal.' One of our values is to be open—this was the opposite. And I wanted to take responsibility for that. I thought, 'How do I make this a forum where we can really live that value of openness, where asking challenging questions is encouraged?'"

Instead of canceling the meetings, they became more focused. Now, every All-Hands at SoundCloud is planned months in advance. Noël explained: "Before the beginning of each quarter, we know exactly how many All Hands [meetings] we'll have—these days, at over 300 employees, it's usually about 6 to 8 times a quarter."

Each meeting has a theme. In one meeting they may focus on technology. In another, it's reports from the board. It's business finances in the next. Presentations are prepared and rehearsed in advance, and everything is timed. A group supporting the meeting technology shows up an hour early to make sure everything's working properly so that people in each of the office locations can tune in—this is quite literally a Broadcast.

SoundCloud's Broadcast meetings include time for questions, but not a lot. Free-form discussion just doesn't work well when you have several hundred people who want to talk. They still want to encourage dialogue on the All-Hands topics, though, so they've also set up a system of Open House meetings to complement the All-Hands meetings. These Open House meetings are voluntary, open forums dedicated to discussion around a specific topic. This is smart—SoundCloud has paired a Broadcast meeting with a Community of Practice meeting so that the information gets shared (Broadcast) and there's room for dialogue (Community of Practice).

SoundCloud works hard to run good Broadcast meetings where the needs of the leadership group—to support an informed and cohesive corporate culture—are aligned with the needs of the employees—to feel that they are a valued part of the group and understand how their work aligns with the company's strategy. SoundCloud also recognizes that these are fundamentally "push" events rather than collaborative meetings, so they put in the work required to improve the production value of the Broadcast. Finally, they schedule lots of collaborative meetings afterwards with smaller groups.

That doesn't mean it's all roses and happy melodies for them, though. In 2017, a SoundCloud employee contacted the press about the company's financial troubles using information he heard in an All-Hands meeting. For months, the company took a public beating as they battled the rumors and fallout this kicked up. Am I sharing the story of the leaked financials to imply that SoundCloud should stop sharing financials with employees during their All Hands? Absolutely not—I'm sharing it because it's a useful reminder that meetings are complex. Even the best of us make mistakes, and it's possible to do everything "right" and still have things go wrong.

In SoundCloud's example, however, the fact that they're working to do so much right—that these meetings are well-planned, recorded, and well attended—meant that when this problem with the press came up, they were prepared to deal with it.

Additional Resources for Broadcast Meetings

Visit the Broadcast Meetings Resource Center on Lucid Meetings.
lucidmeetings.com/meeting-types/broadcast-meetings

BROADCASTS

CHAPTER 35

From Meetings to Meeting Flows

Designing an Organization's Communication Architecture

> "Perhaps the CEO's most important operational responsibility is designing and implementing the communication architecture for her company. The architecture might include the organizational design, meetings, processes, email, yammer and even one-on-one meetings with managers and employees. Absent a well-designed communication architecture, information and ideas will stagnate and your company will degenerate into a bad place to work."
>
> -Ben Horowitz, partner of Andreessen Horowitz and author of *The Hard Thing About Hard Things*

Now that you've become familiar with the different types of meeting tools in your toolbox, you can use these to build the foundation of your organization's communication architecture. The rest—the email, the reporting systems, the documentation—will be reviewed and discussed in these meetings. All your other communications provide input for the decisions you'll make when you talk together, which makes it vital to know when you'll get that opportunity to talk.

Using Meeting Flow Modeling to Streamline Business Processes

A Meeting Flow Model shows the meetings and sequence you anticipate will be held as part of normal business operations. A Meeting Flow Model can be simple, listing the different type of meetings that a group holds. Combine this with a standard structure for each of these meetings, and you've got a basic communication architecture that anyone on the team can use.

How will we figure out what content we might produce? Well, looks like we have this Idea Generation meeting in our model. When will we see the timeline and budget? We should get a preview in the Planning meeting. Even a simple Meeting Flow Model helps answer loads of tricky questions.

Meeting Flow Model for Scoping a Project

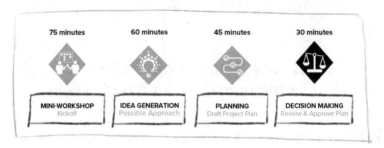

Meeting Flow Model for Client Projects
A simplified example for a 6 week project

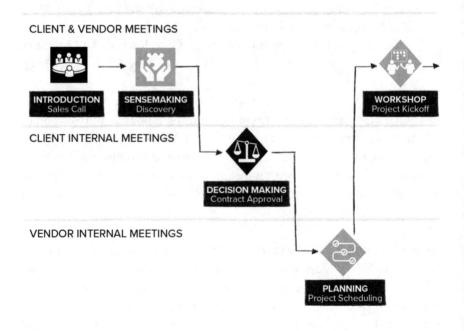

For processes that involve different groups of people, the Meeting Flow Model can be expanded with swim lanes for each group, as it is for the Meeting Flow Model for Client Projects.

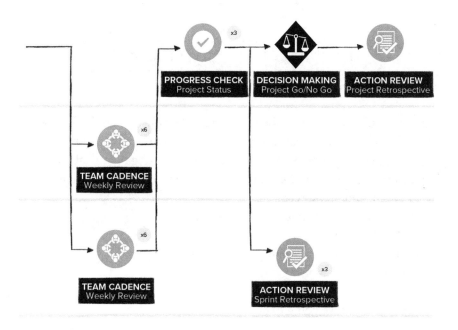

I find Meeting Flow Models especially useful during moments of crisis and confusion. For example, below is a Meeting Flow Model for an incident response. This shows how a team can take a moment of panic—"Holy cow! Everything's on fire, and we have no idea what to do!"—and break it into smaller problems that can be solved one at a time.

An Example
Incident Response Meeting Flow Model

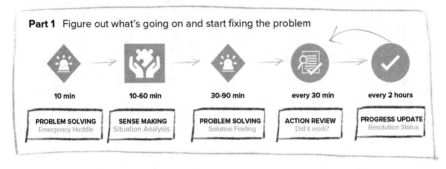

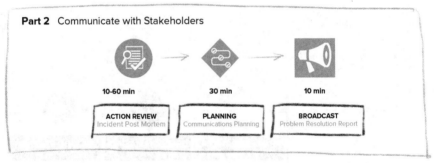

Your Meeting Flow Model for an Incident Response might look different than this, of course. Whatever it is, it will show the team when they will talk about what's going on and, because each meeting type deals with different kinds of information and produces different results, what they'll need to talk about and when.

Here's how the example above works.

- The first **Problem Solving** meeting covers:
  - What's going on?
  - What are our options?
  - What are we going to do next?

That 10-minute **Problem Solving** meeting is used to initiate immediate triage steps and identify areas for others to start researching more deeply.

- The **Sensemaking** meeting focuses those investigations. In it, investigators compare findings and figure out what the options for addressing the problem might be.
- The second **Problem Solving** meeting starts with this deeper understanding of the issue and evaluates which of the solution options to pursue.
- Then the solution implementation team works together, running **Action Reviews** every 30 minutes to share what's working and what's not, and checking in with the rest of the organization for quick **Progress Checks** every two hours until the problem stabilizes.
- During any incident, there may be some communication out to stakeholders, acknowledging that there's a problem and that you're working on it. Talk about an anxious time for frontline staff! With a Meeting Flow Model like this one, at least they don't have to guess what to say or wonder if anyone will help out; they can tell customers that a team is working on the problem and will provide a report on what happened as soon as they can.
- To make sure that this report is accurate and informed, the incident response team runs an **Action Review** meeting to clarify what they learned.
- This provides the information the communications group needs in a **Planning meeting** where they'll work out their response. If the incident is big enough, the public communication response might even include a **Broadcast** meeting for the press.

When you have a Meeting Flow Model for a business process, you create a shared language about how you'll work together. You've established what it means to structure an effective meeting. You know the different types of meetings that work in your business. Now, with a few key processes outlined in Meeting Flow Models, you've set expectations about how these meetings will work in sequence to accomplish a goal. The Meeting Flow Model for a process is a form of working agreement, giving everyone a shared foundation to build upon.

As you may remember from Part 1, people feel that a meeting is high quality when the clear expectations they formed in advance of the meeting are then met. The same holds true for our interactions with our team members, our vendors, our clients, and our leaders. When we all have a shared expectation about how we'll engage with each other, and then we meet that expectation, work gets a whole lot more enjoyable. Drama declines, productivity increases, and we get an opportunity to create more meaningful work together.

Tool: Meeting Flow Models

The Meeting Flow Models we just saw have varying levels of detail because they model different kinds of processes. Despite the variations, all examples create a common understanding and shared language for the people involved.

What It Is

A Meeting Flow Model is a form of process documentation that highlights the main meetings used to achieve a business result.

How It Works

A Meeting Flow Model works by describing the specific meeting tools designed for each situation. Like all process documentation, these models reduce ambiguity and create a common language for getting work done that, when applied properly, speeds execution.

Meeting Flow Models are composed of one or more reference documents. Each model includes:

- The Meeting Flow Model's name (e.g., Webinar Production or Leadership Team Cadence).
- A description of what teams can achieve using this flow.
- A list of the meetings in the flow.
- An indication of how these meetings work together, including the meeting sequence, cadence, and other timing considerations. This is most often documented in a diagram.
- Guidance for running each of the meetings in the model.

The Meeting Flow Models we design at Lucid Meetings also clarify each meeting's meeting type, and when we're getting deluxe, we'll show other details that are most helpful in that situation.

For example, you can show how the meetings in one process relate to meetings in adjacent teams and processes, the criteria (or "gates") for moving from one meeting to the next, and the conditions that signal it's time to break out of a meeting feedback loop.

Getting Started with Meeting Flow Modeling

You can start by modeling any common business process. That said, it's often most useful to start with your team's core meeting cadence for two reasons.

First, you should already know this flow. What a help this is! The advice to "write what you know" works for authors and meeting flow modelers alike.

Second and more importantly, this flow describes the core of how your team interacts and who you are as a group. In Part 3, I talked about the importance of seizing cultural ownership in your meetings, and this ownership starts with the meetings your team holds on a regular basis.

The process of documenting your team's basic meeting flow model will reveal opportunities. You may spot ways to work more efficiently, or holes in your communication that contribute to persistent execution problems. You'll also see ways to improve the way these meetings create and sustain the team culture.

Everyone on your team can collaborate on refining the model, turning this into an opportunity to experiment, refine core practices, and strengthen working relationships.

Pacific Bold Achieves
Level 3 Meeting Performance Maturity

Bert is running late. He hurries in the door and dashes up the stairs to the conference room as quickly as he can given, his stiff shoes and his desire to appear dignified in front of all the Pacific Bold eyes tracking his progress.

Then he slows and frowns. He's easily 10 minutes late, yet the lights are off in the main conference room and the door is closed. Haven't they even started? Bert arrived expecting to swallow goblets of grief for his late arrival, so the dark room is a relief but also a surprise. The Pacific Bold leadership team has become quite professional about their meetings—no one drifts in late anymore without a good reason.

As Bert gets closer, though, he hears voices inside. He peers through a window set high in the door. The chairs pushed around the room's perimeter look empty in the dim light, but he definitely hears talking. Not just one person talking, either—several people talking all at once. Confused, he cautiously cracks open the door and peers inside.

"Hello?" Bert ventures, followed by, "Why on earth are you all lying on the floor?! What's happened now?"

"There you are, Bert!" Charla calls from her spot across the room. "It's an experiment. Want to join us?"

Craig, Charla, Angie, and Nelson are all lying on their backs in the dimly lit room, gazing at the ceiling. They had all been talking at once, but now they're grinning up at Bert. Bert freezes halfway through the door and considers retreating farther.

"No! I mean, um, why?" Bert stammers. "What exactly is it that you all are doing there? Are you sure the floor is clean?"

"It was Craig's idea," Charla says as the team members begin picking themselves up from the floor. "Something he picked up in Brazil when we did that work for the cattle farmers. Angie, help me up." She and Angie brush themselves off. "You know, I think it's clean, but it sure is cold. Next time bring blankets, Craig."

"Next time?" Bert asks. Standing halfway out the open door, he's still ready to flee.

"Yeah, maybe not," Craig replies. "It's an interesting idea, but I get the sense we'd need to practice a lot more to make it work. It's not really practical here. I might try it with my family sometime, though."

Reassured that he wouldn't be asked to crawl around in his new slacks, Bert comes in and closes the door. "So what's this experiment about?"

"When I was in the Mato Grosso, I met a man from a local Xavante village, and I wanted to learn more about him and his people," Craig explains. "I learned that they had this totally different way of finding consensus. We've been doing all this work to improve our meetings and still make sure everyone gets a voice in decisions. The Xavante achieve exactly that—but in a totally unique way.

"The Xavante meet every night in the center of the village and sit in a circle. Then after a while, one person stands up and introduces a topic they want the group to decide on. So far, not so different from any meeting, right? But then, while this guy is still standing there and talking, the others all start talking too. The first guy sits down and starts talking with the others—they're all in this circle talking at the same time—and pretty soon they lie down to look up while the talk continues. Everyone who has anything to say about the topic just says it, everyone all at once, so that it's even a little hard to tell who said what. They know they've reached a decision when all the voices are saying the same thing.

"It struck me as a really cool way for everyone to have a say, and like it could be especially useful for involving our introverts in certain kinds of meetings. I know they have good ideas, but they don't like standing out sometimes. This way, no one really stands out! So we were just seeing what it might feel like while we waited for you. I didn't think you'd be 10 minutes late, Bert." Craig smiles—the reprimand is truly gentle.

Angie pulls out chairs. "It was pretty awkward," she says. "I have to think the Xavante have a lot more practice making decisions this way."

"And warmer floors!" adds Charla. She and Nelson lift the table back into the center of the room, and Craig pulls out a chair for Bert. Everyone takes a seat.

"I'm facilitating today," Nelson says, "and I think we can consider that our icebreaker. Angie, are you our note taker?" Angie nods.

"Okay, sweet." Nelson and Angie both pull out their laptops. "Let me connect to the projector, and we'll get started with the scoreboard review. Bert, what can you tell us about top line revenue?"

Bert smiles, relieved to be in familiar territory and pleased with the good news he has to share. "It's looking really good. Last month came in just ahead of forecast, and this month it looks like you're going to beat forecast again by at least 5%. The new work you're doing for the grower's associations is really paying off."

===================================== PB =====================================

When we first met Pacific Bold, they were in financial trouble and desperately trying to avoid laying off employees. Productivity was stagnant, and while they had a healthy client base, they weren't making enough profit to sustain the company. They discovered that they were wasting an incredible amount of non-billable time in meetings, so they put their focus on fixing their bad meetings problem.

Eighteen months later, they're happily beating their revenue targets each month. How did this happen? Am I suggesting that by fixing their meetings, Pacific Bold's world transformed into a magically productive wonderland full of rainbows and profits?

Yes and no. I am suggesting that fixing their meetings improved their operations and made it possible for them to execute more effectively. Bad meetings inhibited their success, undermining employee morale and draining profitability. Better meetings created clarity, engaged employees, and spurred positive forward momentum.

Pacific Bold successfully broke the bad meetings doom loop. They matured from Level 1 on the Meeting Performance Maturity scale to Level 3. At Level 3, they now know what an effective meeting looks like in their company and hold each other accountable to those standards. They understand and use meeting roles. Who could have guessed that Nelson would turn out to be a natural facilitator? He and a handful of others sought professional facilitation training, skills they now use both for their internal meetings and when meeting with clients.

More importantly, the Pacific Bold leadership team took a hard look at their internal processes to figure out exactly which meetings they really need to run and which ones they don't. In the year since they met with the Lucid Meetings consultants, Pacific Bold leaders identified the different types of meetings that drive their business and figured out how to run each one successfully.

Along the way, they learned what I learned long ago: **A problem with bad meetings is never really a meeting problem.** Bad meetings are a symptom of bigger, harder, and more important issues. In Pacific Bold's case, they needed to get a grip on how to run their business. They needed to clarify roles, map out how to deliver their services profitably, and identify and track more meaningful business metrics. They needed to update their vision.

Bad meetings aren't the real problem, but better meetings are always part of the solution. Now when the Pacific Bold leadership team meets each week, they look at a scoreboard that focuses them on key business metrics. Every meeting generates ripples. Changing this one weekly leadership team meeting to include a scoreboard review meant changes for everyone else in the company, since now every group is accountable for improving performance and reporting numbers. It wasn't so much the meeting itself that made the difference—it was actually all the work required to make that meeting a success.

Let's take a look at the Meeting Flow Model adopted by the Pacific Bold leadership team. It's not very complicated. There aren't any if-then branches, and it doesn't try to deal with every possible thing they may ever need to discuss. This model outlines a simple, predictable pattern they use to manage the business.

The Pacific Bold Leadership Team's Meeting Flow Model

A leadership team's job is to lead the organization. This group makes decisions, monitors performance, and ensures that the rest of organization has what it needs to keep going. The leadership team uses a connected series of meetings to ensure they're all leading in the same direction, to coordinate their actions, and to make sure they keep focus on what's important.

...In theory, at least. Not every leadership team knows how to use their meetings wisely. Those that do use a set of distinct meetings scheduled at regular intervals, each of which helps them address a specific part of their job.

Pacific Bold didn't invent this model—they didn't have to. Once they learned to pay attention to how meetings can drive work, they realized that the business books they were reading all seemed to talk about a similar set of meetings leadership teams needed to run. They simply formalized and adapted these recommendations into a Meeting Flow Model that keeps them connected and lets the whole company know what to expect from their leaders.

These are the meetings in their flow.

A Leadership Team's Meeting Flow Model

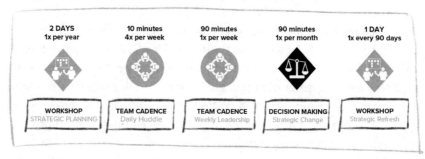

- The Strategic Planning Workshop at the beginning of the year sets the overall strategy and key goals.
- Day-to-day operations are kept in sync with a short Daily Huddle Team Cadence meeting each morning.
- A longer Weekly Leadership Team Cadence meeting gives the team time to review progress toward the strategic goals and collaborate on solutions to any tactical issues they've run into.
- Once per month, the team reserves time to work through an important decision in the Strategic Change Decision Making meeting. They don't know in advance which big decisions they'll need to make in any given month, but they can be certain something will come up. It always does.
- Every 90 days (or so) they spend one day offsite in a shorter Strategic Refresh Workshop. This helps them all keep the overall goals clear in their mind and make adjustments to the strategic plan based on what they've learned that quarter.

Here's how the schedule for these meetings works out.

Week 1:

Days 1-2: All day Annual Strategic Planning (16 hours)
The team set the strategy, annual priorities, and target metrics for the first quarter.

Day 3: The First Daily Huddle (10 minutes)
Huddles take 10 minutes. The Huddle is a short meeting with verbal reports, so no one needed any extra prep time.

Weeks 2-13:

Monday mornings: Weekly Leadership meeting (90 minutes)
Before this meeting, everyone needed to update their metrics, open action items, and get ready to discuss any issues they were facing. Each person spent up to 20 minutes prepping for this meeting.

In the first week, there wasn't much to report. As the weeks went by, though, it got easier to see which parts of the plan weren't working out as planned. Some issues were straightforward, so the team knocked those out in the weekly meeting. Others were harder, so they were put on the list for the monthly strategic meeting.

Tuesday through Friday: Huddle (10 minutes)
Huddles were held every day except Monday, when the team already spent 90 minutes together. After a few weeks of this regular check-in, everyone began to notice patterns. First, they discovered that the different functional groups weren't working at the same pace, creating constant delays. Then they learned that some teams were crushing it and others always seemed to be struggling. No big emergencies, but they got a feel for the pulse and a sense for where they needed to make adjustments in how the organization operates.

Weeks 4 and 9:

Thursday afternoon: Monthly Decision Making Meeting (90 minutes)
In one of the Monday meetings, the team brought up a problem or an opportunity that couldn't be resolved in 30 minutes. So in the Weekly Leadership meeting, the group assigned one or two people to conduct more research and make recommendations. The leaders researching the challenge dug into the details and sent a report

to everyone, outlining the facts. They also worked with their teams and colleagues to find at least three viable options to decide between. Depending on the challenge, this could have taken hours or days—time spent making sure the team makes the best possible decision they can.

Not everyone on the leadership team needed to attend the Monthly Strategic meeting. If one month's challenge came from the design department, and the finance lead doesn't really have any skin in that game, they may have bowed out. Those who did participate made sure they read the reports in advance and came prepared, each spending up to an hour getting ready for the meeting.

At the end of the Monthly Strategic meeting, the team had a decision and a set of new action items to add to the list they reviewed during the next Weekly Leadership meeting.

Week 14:

Monday afternoon and Tuesday morning: Quarterly Strategic Refresh (8 hours)

By week 14, it's been 90 days since the team set the strategic plan. With the Daily Huddles, they've learned the day-to-day rhythm of how work flows through the organization. The Weekly Leadership meetings have shown where the original plan worked well, and where it did not. The whole team has remained deeply involved in the small, important work of execution. Finally, during the Monthly Strategic meetings, they learned how to critically examine big issues and refine specific strategies.

After 90 days, it was time to pull back and look at the big picture again. Given everything the team learned about each other, the organization, and the work at hand, what needed adjustment? What should the targets for the coming quarter be? Which big challenges do they still need to dig into? The team dedicated a Monday afternoon and Tuesday morning to refining the plan, and enjoyed a nice dinner in between.

After the Quarterly Strategic Refresh, one person made sure that the new targets were all set up so they could start monitoring them in the following Monday's Leadership meeting.

This meeting flow model is an appropriate starting point for many organizations. Start at the beginning, work through to the end, and repeat.

A 10% Time Investment that Drives the Organization

I did the math, and here's a surprise. While the plan above looks and sounds like a ton of time spent in meetings, it represents just 10% of a full-time employee's available time.

Actually, just under 10%; 4.9% spent in Cadence meetings (26.5 hours) and 5% in Catalyst meetings (27 hours) over the course of 13 weeks and 2 days (536 hours), a nice equal balance between strategy and operations.

In reality, some people will spend more time than this. Anyone researching an issue for the monthly Strategic Decision Making meeting needs to spend considerable time there. Everyone needs to add another hour or two over the course of the quarter to prepare for weekly meetings by updating their metrics and action items.

The quarterly meeting requires yet another hour or two of prep from everyone involved. Annual Planning also takes more time—but far less in years two and three than it did before teams put this cadence in place, because in future years they build and refine instead of starting from scratch.

This is an incredibly efficient approach to managing a business.

Personally, I've worked in environments without this structure, where we spent way more time talking about our progress, lack of progress, and strategic challenges—and rarely ever deciding on ways to solve our problems. We just kept talking about them and pointing fingers and bemoaning how impossible it all was because we didn't know what else to do.

This was Pacific Bold's problem too. They used to spend all kinds of time talking. Now they meet with purpose and get things done. How very different things are for Pacific Bold! They no longer wonder whether they should have a meeting or what a meeting might accomplish. They're providing the services they've always provided, but oh so much more effectively. By using the taxonomy, establishing a few key Meeting Model Flows, and getting specific about how they'll structure the meetings they need to run for their business, they've improved productivity, increased morale, and cut out a bunch of unnecessary drama. Most importantly for Craig and Charla, they didn't need to lay people off to get there.

You just knew there'd be a happy ending, didn't you?

Meetings in a Complex Adaptive System

Throughout this book, I talked a lot about *getting it right*—holding the right meeting with the right structure at the right time. The right question will spark the right ideas that lead to the right decision.

But of course, there is no such thing as "right" when you're working in a complex situation. For most of us, especially when it comes to the meetings that have the biggest impact on our organizations, the situation is deeply complex. Cause and effect aren't clear; there are just too many moving parts and personalities in play for anyone to hope that they can figure out a perfectly correct solution. Instead, we can make our best attempts and learn from them as we go.

Organizations are complex-adaptive systems. Stimulus, response, and effect involve multiple people both inside and outside the organization, working across a vast sea of information. It's messy, it changes quickly, and much of what happens feels unpredictable.

It's all of this.

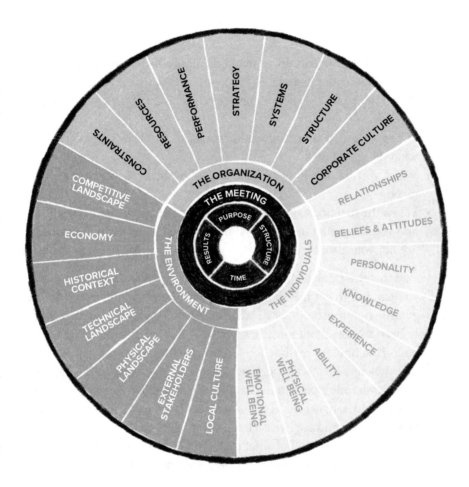

This creates important implications for meetings:

1. There is no one true right way.

Instead, we get best attempts, and we get to keep learning.

2. Meetings provide feedback loops.

They either reinforce the existing flow—keeping your organization steady-going and potentially stagnant in a bad meetings doom loop—or they prod the organization toward a new shape. This makes meetings a powerful center of sensemaking, learning, and adapting when they're used well, and a heavy anchor when they're allowed to drag along untended.

While there is no ultimate "right way," I hope you now understand why there are clear "wrong ways," such as:

- When your team tries to solve a difficult problem in the middle of the weekly team meeting.
- When the board is asked to make a big decision at the end of a long meeting.
- When the group is brainstorming solutions, but they don't agree on what the problem is.
- When you assume someone else will follow up on tasks after a meeting.
- When the meetings and the projects and the people all just feel *blah*, and you think that meeting dysfunction (and your company culture) are not your problems to fix.

I hope that this book has given you a new perspective on meetings—one that you can use to get meetings more right more often and to power the next phase of your growth as a leader. I hope too that, although this has clearly been a book about meetings, you can now see that meetings aren't *the point*. This book is really about running better businesses. It's about solving problems. It's about working with people in a respectful way that brings out everyone's potential. It's a book about how we work together to increase profits, drive change, make discoveries, teach and learn, overcome challenges, and save lives. The meetings are the means: a way for us to shape and experience all of what really matters as it comes into being.

The meetings aren't the point, but they are where the action is.

Acknowledgments

This book would not have been possible without the help and guidance of so very many people. My deepest gratitude and appreciation go out to all of you.

My husband and partner, John Keith, for reading every page, challenging my ideas, steering me straight, keeping me healthy, bolstering me up when I lost my way, and making the time it took to write this behemoth possible. For saying yes whenever reasonably practical.

Thank you to our parents John, Suzanne, Toni, Vickie, Jeff, and John again, who all provided encouragement, resources, babysitting, and, on occasion, much needed bottles of wine.

Thank you to the many facilitators and coaches who have shared their wisdom and their stories with the Lucid Meetings Community—most especially to Diana Larsen and Beatrice Briggs for their mentorship and friendship, and to Michael Wilkinson, for first opening my eyes to the wonders of facilitation.

Thank you, Christoph Haug, who looked past my lack of academic credentials and invited me to participate alongside the researchers at the Gothenburg Meeting Science Symposium. I nearly didn't go but am so glad I did, because I learned much that shaped this book. Special thanks to John Kello and Wilbert Van Vree for their generous collaboration in the months following the symposium.

Huge hugs and a shout-out to the reformed anarchists and makers of deliciousness at Zingerman's community of businesses. Thank you so much for opening the doors of your meeting rooms to outsiders, for answering all my persistent questions about meetings, business, leadership development, and publishing, and for allowing me to retell those stories here. Also for the mustard tasting.

Thank you to Jim Gillen, Bob Smith, and Jenny Tubbs for answering my many questions about how to go from idea to a physical book, which was quite the learning curve for my all-digital all-the-time crew. Thanks to my editor Chris for helping me make better sense and for politely tempering those times when the language in this business book became a touch unsafe for work. Thank you, Katie, for your awesome illustrations, which make a book about meetings so much more fun. Thank you, Janet, for saving the day. John's right. You are the win.

Rowan, Collin, and Maggie: I love you all. You've kept me grounded and inspired me to finish this work so we can go play more. Now let's go play!

Notes

A note on sources.
The content in this book was inspired by the work of hundreds of others who have touched on the topics of meetings, organizations, business, and how all these relate. You'll find a handful of sources mentioned in the notes that follow. A selected bibliography and and an easy-to-click version of these notes can be found online here:
https://www.lucidmeetings.com/book/wtai-sources

In several cases, I've provided links to the WikiPedia articles for conceptual frameworks such as Metcalfe's Law or the Tuckman Group Development Model, which I know is a big faux pas for any "serious" writing. For these high-level concepts, however, I've found WikiPedia does an excellent job of summing up the key ideas and providing links to further reading for those who want to go deeper, so I will continue to recommend WikiPedia as a useful place to start.

Chapter 1
4 **50% to 80% of the time they spend in meetings is a big fat waste of time** These statistics are outdated, out of context, and hugely popular. For one very fancy infographic that draws lots of traffic for Atlassian, see: www.atlassian.com/time-wasting-at-work-infographic

Chapter 2
11 **between 55 and 65 million meetings and 84% of people rate meetings as effective** Lucid Meetings conducted a meta-study of available research concerning the number, cost, and perceived effectiveness of meetings in 2015. This study includes links to many others, so if you feel a need to justify any effort you plan to spend on improving meetings with numbers, make sure to review this one. https://blog.lucidmeetings.com/blog/fresh-look-number-effectiveness-cost-meetings-in-us

15 **displace millions of jobs** Quartz published a nice summary of the dooms-day-to-utopia scale estimates for how many people will be displaced by technology. Estimates in 2017 ranged from 5% to 47% of U.S. jobs will be replaced by AI and robots in the coming 10 to 20 years. That's quite a range! It's also not clear how many people this represents, since people often complete many more tasks than the specific tasks the robots will be taking on. Predicting the future remains a dicey business. https://qz.com/1032663/predictions-for-what-robots-will-do-to-the-us-workforce-ranked-from-certain-doom-to-potential-utopia/

17 **The coaches at Leadership Strategies** I took the 4-day Effective Facilitator training from Michael Wilkinson in Atlanta in 2014, where I first heard the Hand, Head, and Heart breakdown of meeting outcomes.

24 **Metcalfe's Law States** You can read about Metcalfe's law on WikiPedia here: https://en.wikipedia.org/wiki/Metcalfe%27s_law and see another perspective on its application to organizational communications here: https://blog.imaginellc.com/why-metcalfes-law-can-destroy-your-business-growth

Chapter 3

34 **A Lesson from History and Politics** Adolf Hitler is a universally recognizable dictator, but he's by no means the first nor last to restrict freedom of assembly as a way of controlling a conquered population. I first came to appreciate this by reading Wilbert Van Vree's book *Meetings, Manners, and Civilization: The Development of Modern Meeting Behaviour*, which traces the history of meetings in the Western world. Civilizations that subdue the population using centralized control of violence, which you see in relatively primitive warrior states and modern dictatorships alike, also restrict the people's ability to have a say in meetings. I noticed the specific details about the Reichstag Decree both on Wikipedia and in series of graduate student presentations posted online, so decided to include the story here.

36 **Agile methodologies** Agile started as a manifesto for software developers who wanted an alternative to the heavy, time-consuming approach to developing and shipping software that most teams used at the time. (See http://agilemanifesto.org/) Instead of big requirements documents up front and elaborate project plans, Agile leaders advocated breaking the work into smaller chunks and continuously iterating toward completion. This approach decreased the documentation requirements but also meant teams needed a lot more meetings. Agile has since become popular across all business divisions.

Chapter 6

63 **Creating a Mental Model** In his book *Peak: Secrets from the New Science of Expertise*, Anders Ericsson discussed his research into what it takes to develop true mastery. He studied chess masters, musician, athletes—all kinds of people who have become truly exceptional. While he

confirmed the necessity of many hours of practice, he also found that practice itself was not enough. The practice must be deliberate in pursuit of a new goal and the practice must then help the budding expert improve their understanding, or mental model, of the task. This knowledge helps us understand why, despite the countless hours of practice many people have, they're often still really bad at leading meetings.

67 **research findings from cognitive science** There's an enormous body of research on this topic. Inattention blindness, rapid task-switching, decision fatigue—this is a huge topic that defies end notes. Please see the online resources listing for a host of relevant links.

67 **comes from a team of investment bankers** RFS Finance, "The Power of Silence in Meetings" http://www.karma-tube.org/videos.php?id=7515&utm_content=53430018

67 **favorable conditions necessary for critical thinking in the brain** "Mindful multitasking: Meditation first can calm stress, aid concentration." http://www.washington.edu/news/2012/06/13/mindful-multitasking-meditation-first-can-calm-stress-aid-concentration/

67 **hormone readings from saliva swabs** See Amy Cuddy's research on power posing before high-stakes social evaluations and the subsequent impact on stress hormones as measured by saliva samples.

68 **One indigenous community** This example is widely distributed through the facilitation community, but I was unable to track down the source. http://english.iifac.org/beatrice-briggs/coffee-break-march-2014/

68 **Quaker meetings** https://forum.kunsido.net/t/what-to-expect-in-a-quaker-meeting-for-worship/350/4, the note about meetings in feudal Europe come from *Meetings, Manners, and Civilization.*

83 **only 50% of the meetings that had agendas** Niederman, F., & Volkema, R. J. (1999) *The effects of facilitator characteristics on meeting preparation, set up and implementation.* Small Group Research, 30, 330-360, dos:10.1177/104649649903000304

Chapter 7

87 **only 70% of internal email messages** "Email Overload: Research and Statistics" https://blog.sanebox.com/2016/02/18/email-overload-research-statistics-sanebox/

89 **Temporal Courtesy** *Meeting Preparation and Design Characteristics* Odermatt, König, Kleinmann (2015) doi:10.1017/CBO9781107589735.004

91 **up to 27 second to regain full focus** "Up To 27 Seconds Of Inattention After Talking To Your Car Or Smartphone" https://unews.utah.edu/up-to-27-seconds-of-inattention-after-talking-to-your-car-or-smart-phone/

92 **People who lead meetings tend to rate their own meetings** We've found this to be true in the meeting ratings we collect through the Lucid Meetings platform and have seen it echoed in many other studies. For example, In the conclusion of *Perceived Meeting Effectiveness: The Role of*

Design Characteristics, Leach, D.J., Rogelberg, S.G., Warr, P.B. et al. J Bus Psychol (2009) 24: 65. https://doi.org/10.1007/s10869-009-9092-6 stated, "More senior managers viewed their meetings more favorably than others. This positive bias could create blind spots in these leaders' ability to identify problems and make positive improvements."

Chapter 8

104 the more people present in a meeting The studies cited earlier on perceived meeting quality found this relationship between group size and participation; namely that the larger the group is, the less likely people are to participate. The decision-making studies get very specific in this regard. Sheila Margolis has a nice summary of those findings here: "What is the optimal group size for decision-making?" https://sheilamargolis. com/2011/01/24/what-is-the-optimal-group-size-for-decision-making/

Chapter 9

108 net-positive movement "It's the leading edge of sustainability, but we've not cracked it" https://www.theguardian.com/sustainable-business/2015/jan/22/net-positive-leading-edge-sustainability by Oliver Balch for *The Guardian*, Jan 22, 2015

110 employee engagement and retention Allen, J.A., Rogelberg, S.G. (2013). *Manager-Led Group Meetings A Context for Promoting Employee Engagement.* Group & Organization Management. 38. 543-569. 10.1177/1059601113503040.

110 overall job satisfaction Rogelberg, S. G., Allen, J. A., Shanock, L. , Scott, C. and Shuffler, M. (2010), *Employee satisfaction with meetings: A contemporary facet of job satisfaction.* Human Resource Management, 49: 149-172. doi:10.1002/hrm.20339

117 up to 25 minutes "Brain, Interrupted" https://www.nytimes. com/2013/05/05/opinion/sunday/a-focus-on-distraction.html

118 a 10-point decline in their IQ This study is fun to cite because it has such a sensationalist title. I've also read studies showing a decline in IQ associated with alcohol, emotional distress, new parenthood, lack of sleep, and poverty. Raising the question: under what circumstances might we establish a stable IQ? Because that sounds like every other day to me. "Infomania' worse than marijuana" http://news.bbc.co.uk/2/hi/uk_news/4471607.stm

118 task-switching on productivity This group collected studies on the changes in people's ability to concentrate and the impact ever-increasing information volume has on people's mental health and performance. Information Overload Research Group http://iorgforum.org/

119 faster, but at a price Gloria Mark, Daniela Gudith, and Ulrich Klocke. 2008. *The cost of interrupted work: more speed and stress. In Proceedings of the SIGCHI Conference on Human Factors in Computing Systems (CHI '08).* ACM, New York, NY, USA, 107-110. doi:10.1145/1357054.1357072

119 **research into creativity** "How Constraints Force Your Brain To Be More Creative" https://www.fastcompany.com/3067925/how-constraints-force-your-brain-to-be-more-creative

120 **The Flow** I had long heard people talk about getting into the flow, but hadn't previously seen the research behind this idea. Beyond the basic criteria, I discovered that Csíkszentmihályi and his colleagues provide a series of leadership training modules designed for organizations that want to maximize flow in the workplace. Start with the TED talk "Flow, the secret to happiness" https://www.ted.com/talks/mihaly_csikszentmihalyi_on_flow and "Flow" (*WikiPedia*) https://en.wikipedia.org/wiki/Flow_(psychology) to learn more.

122 **when people are deeply engaged** There's a lot of research into employee motivation and several competing theories. Most studies agree, however, that intrinsic motivators (like a chance to contribute to a meaningful larger goal and fun at work) are more effective than extrinsic motivators like money. For a nice summary of the current thinking on this topic, read Daniel Pink's book *Drive*.

Part 3

139 **post expectations on the wall** Boeing has a "Code of Cooperation" for teams—or they did at one point, at least. The last time I visited Intel, I saw several questions designed to encourage better meetings on the wall outside of conference rooms. You can read more about the origin of Intel's rules here: https://maxineattong.wordpress.com/2011/10/06/intel-knows-meetings/

Chapter 11

143 **People Capability Maturity Model® (P-CMM®) Version 2.0** The model is available as a hardback book or as a free PDF download here: http://cmmiinstitute.com/resources/people-capability-maturity-model-p-cmm

159 **what's focal is causal** This is one of many psychological principles described in Robert Cialdini's books *Influence* and *Pre-suasion*. I highly recommend these books for all experience designers, meeting designers included, because they provide useful insights into underlying triggers of human behavior.

Chapter 13

174 **swifts from a chimney** My editor felt that comparing ASTM's productivity to bats swarming from a cave wasn't the right metaphor. Swifts flying from a chimney look similar, with an added bonus murmuration. This cool phenomenon can be seen on YouTube here. https://www.youtube.com/watch?v=gHgEAIK8P18

Chapter 14

176 **Man in the Yellow Hat** from the children's book series *Curious George* by H.A. and Margret Rey

182 **Robert later wrote** From the brief biography of Henry M Robert on the U.S. Army's online archive http://www.usace.army.mil/About/History/Historical-Vignettes/General-History/038-Church-Meetings/

184 **as one witness related** I learned this story in a conversation with a government employee involved with the event. You can listen to audio recordings of these meetings here: https://soundcloud.com/your-alberta/ministerial-panel-on-child-intervention-archive-january-24-am?in=your-alberta/sets/ministerial-panel-on-child

185 **RSF Social Finance** This story was shared by Birju Pandya in a video with the Greater Good Society http://www.karmatube.org/videos.php?id=7515

Part 4

199 **structure that works well for Action Review** This is the Adaptive Action structure from the Human Systems Dynamics Institute. Read more about it here: http://wiki.hsdinstitute.org/adaptive_action

Chapter 18

224 **start all action items with a verb** This best practice shows up frequently in facilitation books and in the personal productivity advice blogs. Fans of David Allen's book *Getting Things Done* know the difference between project verbs and task verbs, for example. This blog post nicely summarizes this advice and includes useful examples: https://www.productiveflourishing.com/7-ways-to-write-better-action-items/

224 **they've publicly committed and which they've written themselves** Cialdini, R. B. (2009). *Influence: Science and Practice*

Chapter 19

232 **well-architected communication infrastructure** "A good place to work" https://a16z.com/2012/08/18/a-good-place-to-work/

233 **ask these questions of their managers** "One on One" https://a16z.com/2012/08/30/one-on-one/

Chapter 20

240 **Wildland Fire Leadership council** There are several detailed structures for Action Reviews on their website here: https://www.fire-leadership.gov/toolbox/after_action_review/format.html

241 **Retired General Tom's story** The HBR article about OPFOR: https://hbr.org/2005/07/learning-in-the-thick-of-it

243 **Bob Sutton** The quote in this article was about Action Reviews. Bob Sutton is more famous for his book *The No Assholes Rule*, which is also chock-full of lovely advice. https://hbr.org/2007/06/learning-from-success-and-fail

Chapter 21

247 40,000 Special Districts This *Last Week Tonight with John Oliver* segment provides a quick overview of Special Districts and includes footage of some awesome SD board meetings: https://www.youtube.com/watch?v=3saU5racsGE

249 Jeff Bonforte, CEO of Xobni "The Secret to Making Board Meetings Suck Less" http://firstround.com/review/The-Secret-to-Making-Board-Meetings-Suck-Less/

253 under stress Here's a short stressful read "The Impact of Stress" https://psychcentral.com/lib/the-impact-of-stress/

Chapter 23

264 avoided the series of violent revolts Prior to the Reformation, the areas that would later become the Netherlands already had a system of citizen governance with their Water Boards and city governments. These citizens then moved into church governance and helped shape policy. By contrast, much of the rest of Europe was still dominated by monarchies, landed nobility, and the bishops. Wilbert van Vree *Meetings, Manners, and Civilization*, chapter 5

265 share an embarrassing story This study found that people became more creative when they were less concerned about appearing impressive. The study groups started by either telling each other their accomplishments, or instead, the embarrassing story. The group that shared their accomplishments, supposedly establishing a reputation they now had to protect, restrained themselves to safe and respectable ideas. I would love to see research build on this idea of moving past ego in a less humiliating fashion, as I can see how this could go quite badly in the wrong group. "Research: For Better Brainstorming, Tell an Embarrassing Story" by Leigh Thompson https://hbr.org/2017/10/research-for-better-brainstorming-tell-an-embarrassing-story

265 if the word is PIGS This warmup technique and many others can be found in Michael Michalko's book *Thinkertoys*.

Chapter 24

273 plans being worthless Eisenhower wasn't the first to express this idea. The Quote Investigator digs into the modern origins of this important reminder. https://quoteinvestigator.com/2017/11/18/planning/

275 No battle plan survives Yet another example from the military. It would be lovely to have more examples from gardening clubs or artist retreats, but the historical records just aren't as rich in the non-violent disciplines. This look at Helmuth von Moltke the Elder provides a bit of insight into a pivotal point in history, where everything seemed to be changing in the world, and an opportunity to reflect on any modern parallels you might see there. https://blog.seannewmanmaroni.com/

no-battle-plan-survives-first-contact-with-the-enemy-966df69b24b9

275 **No business plan survives** Hurrah! An example from business. Steve Blank's book *The Four Stages of the Epiphany* and his blog are great resources for entrepreneurs. https://steveblank.com/2010/04/08/no-plan-survives-first-contact-with-customers-%E2%80%93-business-plans-versus-business-models/

Chapter 25

283 **psychological safety** Dr. Amy Edmondson's TEDx talk provides a compelling introduction to her research https://www.youtube.com/watch?v=LhoLuui9gX8

284 **Who is on a team matters less** The People Analytics team at Google investigated what made for the most successful teams across their vast empire. Their findings echo prior research in the field, with the added weight of a large sample size. The findings are also more sensational, because it's Google and because they had expected different results. I bet Dr. Edmondson could have saved them some time. "The five keys to a successful Google team" https://rework.withgoogle.com/blog/five-keys-to-a-successful-google-team/

285 **Hand Model of the Brain** I first learned this from my yoga instructor Jim Gillen and his wife, Lynea, who do wonderful work bringing yoga into the classroom as a way to connect and focus young children. "Dr. Daniel Siegel's Hand Model of the Brain" https://www.youtube.com/watch?v=gm9CIJ74Oxw

Chapter 26

290 **financial results correlated at a 95% confidence level** from "The Decision-Driven Organization" https://hbr.org/2010/06/the-decision-driven-organization

291 **development of civilization** This is *Meetings, Manners, and Civilization* again. See my interview with the author here: https://blog.lucidmeetings.com/blog/battle-axes-to-boardrooms-wilbert-van-vree

Chapter 29

313 **You can't handle the truth!** From *A Few Good Men* by Aaron Sorkin https://genius.com/Aaron-sorkin-a-few-good-men-you-cant-handle-the-truth-annotated

317 **the palest ink** Origins for this proverb diligently traced here: https://ask.metafilter.com/247533/Is-this-really-an-ancient-Chinese-proverb

319 **Improving diversity improves performance** The team at Cloverpop, an online decision-making platform, confirmed this recently using data from their platform. https://www.forbes.com/sites/eriklarson/2017/09/21/new-research-diversity-inclusion-better-decision-making-at-work/#2134309c4cbf

Chapter 30

324 The Secret to a Really Good Interview Article here https://
www.themuse.com/advice/the-secret-to-a-really-good-in-
terview-is-simply-knowing-when-to-shut-your-mouth

326 between two and 15 seconds David Jensen reviewed relevant research on first impressions in this article for Science Mag
"Tooling Up: First Impressions—Are Interview Results Pre-
ordained?" http://www.sciencemag.org/careers/2004/08/
tooling-first-impressions-are-interview-results-preordained

326 Take a look at the work of Amy Cuddy's work on power posing is documented in her book *Presence: Bringing Your Boldest Self
to Your Biggest Challenges,* Bernier's work on handshakes (*The Influence of Handshakes on First Impression Accuracy*) and more can be
found on Research Gate, Robert Cialdini talks about the influence of using heavier paper for resumes in *Pre-Suasion: A Revolution-
ary Way to Influence and Persuade,* and Matthew Lieberman explains
reward systems in *Why Our Brains Are Wired to Connect,* 2013.

Chapter 32

342 Tuckman Group Development Model Get a quick overview from Wiki-
Pedia; then if you're hungry for more, dive into the original material and all
the derivative, rebuttal, and other work Tuckman inspired from there.
https://en.wikipedia.org/wiki/
Tuckman%27s_stages_of_group_development

Chapter 33

348 The Training Compact This article originally written for Gour-
met Retailer includes the Zingerman's training compact http://
www.zingtrain.com/content/essential-guide-staff-training

348 Kirkpatrick Four-Level Training Evaluation Model This model
was outlined in the book *Evaluating Training Programs: The Four
Levels,* 1996. You can find a nice summary of the levels on Mind-
Tools https://www.mindtools.com/pages/article/kirkpatrick.htm

349 the protégé effect Annie Murphy Paul summarizes the
research into this effect here: https://www.psychologyto-
day.com/blog/how-be-brilliant/201206/the-prot-g-effect

349 medical school classes on gross anatomy Krych, A. J., March, C. N.,
Bryan, R. E., Peake, B. J., Pawlina, W. and Carmichael, S. W. (2005),
*Reciprocal peer teaching: Students teaching students in the gross anat-
omy laboratory.* Clin. Anat., 18: 296-301. doi:10.1002/ca.20090

350 Every cook can govern. I'm grateful to Ari Weinzweig for sharing the
work of C.L.R. James, which I would never have found on my own.
Online excerpts from the archives can be found here: https://www.

marxists.org/archive/james-clr/works/1956/06/every-cook.htm

351 **Social psychologists theorize** Olle Ten Cate & Steven Durn-
ing (2009) *Dimensions and psychology of peer teaching in medical education,*Medical Teacher, 29:6, 546-552, doi:10.1080/01421590701583816

351 **Four Stages of Competence** The Gordon Training Institute has shifted this
model a bit in the past 30 years to focus on skills rather than competence.
See their update here: http://www.gordontraining.com/free-workplace-ar-
ticles/learning-a-new-skill-is-easier-said-than-done/ I originally learned
and prefer the earlier version, which you see described on WikiPedia
https://en.wikipedia.org/wiki/Four_stages_of_competence. In addition to
this four-stage model, Paul Dyer from Avid 4 Adventure suggest a fifth level
is in order. Once a person achieves Unconscious Competence, they can rest
there and become stagnant, or they might stay curious, deliberately pushing themselves back to Conscious Incompetence by asking new questions.
This approach to continual learning sounds very like true mastery to me.

Chapter 34

360 **SoundCloud, an internet music service** First Round review pub-
lishes many in-depth interviews with founders and leaders in the tech
startup world about how they run their businesses. Many of the details
about SoundCloud's All-Hands meeting came from one of these articles. http://firstround.com/review/how-soundcloud-keeps-communica-
tion-flowing-across-4-offices-in-4-time-zones/ First Round also shares
articles about one-on-ones, board meetings, sales meetings, and more.
A search for "meeting" on their blog will turn up tons of useful stories.

Chapter 35

371 **The Xavante achieve exactly that** GRAHAM, L. (1993), *a public sphere in
Amazonia? the depersonalized collaborative construction of discourse in Xavante.* American Ethnologist, 20: 717-741. doi:10.1525/ae.1993.20.4.02a00030

Index

Note: information found in notes is indicated by an n following the page number

job satisfaction and, 110
Meeting Performance Maturity Scale
    benchmarking, 108, 164–165
organizational goal clarity for, 122–123
at Pacific Bold, 114–116, 117, 118, 129
productivity costs and, 116–123
stakeholder satisfaction benchmarks
    for, 169–170
systems approach to, 107
time blocking improving, 123–124
Newport, Cal, 123
next steps. *See* follow-up plans
Noël, David, 361
note-taking. *See also* records of meetings
    in Broadcast meetings, 357–358
    engagement and, 91, 97, 101, 102, 103,
        105, 106
    knowledge conveyed via, 317, 320
    Meeting Performance Maturity Model
        requiring, 138–139, 144, 148, 155, 162
    meeting structure including, 76
    optional meetings possible with good,
        127, 138–139
    perverse psychology of meetings in
        relation to, 30
    technology used for, 103, 105, 317
    in Training Sessions, 348
    visibility of and access to, 53, 61, 105,
        106
NPI. *See* Net Positive Impact

obligations, meetings as usefully imposed,
    31–32
One-on-One meetings
    appreciation of take-aways from,
        expressing, 230, 231
    cadence or frequency of, 228
    challenges of, 227, 230, 234
    in communication infrastructure, 232,
        233, 234
    consistency and fairness of, 228–229
    desired outcomes of, 227, 230
    differentiation as, 48
    engagement in, 100
    examples of, 226
    expectations for, 227–228
    follow-up to, 228, 230, 233

meeting structure of, 228, 230
opportunities and value offered by,
    229–234
participation in, 227
preparation for, 228
purpose of, 227
questions answered by, 200, 226, 233
resources for, 235
tips for successful, 228–230
Opposing Forces (OPFOR) unit, 241–243
optional meetings, 127, 138–139, 222
organizations
    as collaborative organisms, 28, 316–317
    as complex adaptive systems, 378–380
    culture of. *See* culture, organizational
    employees of. *See* employees; teams
    goals of, 122–123. *See also* desired
        outcomes
    leadership or management of. *See*
        leadership
    macrostructures of, 77
    meetings at. *See* meetings
    microstructures of, 77–78
    Pacific Bold as. *See* Pacific Bold
outcomes, desired. *See* desired outcomes

Pacific Bold
    cancellation of meetings at, 29, 30,
        32–33, 38, 39–40, 57, 117
    differentiation of meetings at, 40–41,
        192
    facilitators at, 372–373
    governing rituals and rules at, 114–116,
        139–140
    growth of company and meeting time
        at, 8, 9, 24, 26–27
    market position of, 7–8
    Meeting Flow Models at, 373–377
    meeting guidelines at, 139–140, 192
    Meeting Performance Maturity Model
        at, 138–140, 149, 166, 192, 369–373
    meeting structure at, 74
    meeting-job performance ties at, 37, 128
    Net Positive Impact of meetings at, 114–
        116, 117, 118, 129
    note-taking at meetings of, 138–139
    optional meetings at, 138–139
    organizational culture at, 8–9, 115

About the Author

J. Elise Keith is one of the founders of Second Rise, LLC, a company specializing in services that help organizations scale effective meeting practices. Second Rise is the team behind the Lucid Meetings online meeting management platform, named by Gartner as a 2017 "Cool Vendor" in Unified Communications. Prior to starting Second Rise, Elise worked in many software companies and pancake houses, because that's what you do with a degree in theater and mouths to feed.

Elise lives in Portland, OR with her husband and business partner, John, three children, and a rotating cast of extras. In her free time, she enjoys cooking, action movies, travel, and listening to people tells stories about their meetings.